THE WAJDA TRILOGY

MODERN
FILM
SCRIPTS

ASHES AND DIAMONDS
KANAL
A GENERATION

three films by

Andrzej Wajda

Simon and Schuster, New York

SBN: 671-21081-5

Library of Congress Catalog Number: 72-90595

Manufactured in Great Britain by Villiers Publications Ltd,
London NW5

CONTENTS

A NOTE ON THIS EDITION

This edition of the three screenplays which make up the *Wajda Trilogy* has been prepared and translated from the Polish by Boleslaw Sulik. The description of action is based on the original Polish scenarios and release scripts, augmented with material obtained from shot-by-shot analyses of the final versions of the films. The dialogue has been directly translated from the original Polish. Although technical description has been cut to the minimum to make for easier reading, each change of shot is indicated by paragraphing for readers who wish to make a closer analysis of the films. The screenplays are printed in chronological order.

We should like to thank Contemporary Films Ltd of London, for providing prints of *A Generation, Kanal* and *Ashes and Diamonds*.

INTRODUCTION

by Boleslaw Sulik

There are firm links between the themes of Andrzej Wajda's first three films — *Generation, Kanal* and *Ashes and Diamonds* — and his own background and early experiences. The tragic generation of Poles portrayed in this so-called trilogy (the term applied to it more widely outside Poland, than inside it) is Wajda's own. He had shared the emotional commitments of his heroes, while at the same time remaining more of a close observer than a direct participant in the actual action. As he has said himself: "I was thirteen when war broke out, so I couldn't take any part in the fighting of 1939. Then the occupation, and again only a minimal chance of taking part. To be sure, I became a soldier of the Home Army, but in a quite unimportant sector, and the German reprisals never touched me. It appears to me, in this connection, that my post-war films — especially the first three, or even four, because I would include *Lotna* here — are a kind òf recompense for the fact that, while others have led magnificent, interesting and eventful lives, these hard and rugged experiences have somehow by-passed me."

As he has modestly mentioned in passing, Wajda joined the Resistance at sixteen, in the provincial town of Radom, in central Poland. There was enough going on there for him to see "the sections who were carrying out sentences of death. I have myself brushed against certain Resistance events. I was close to them. I was also close to the men who gave their life, who were killed fighting in the Resistance . . ." The early influence of the parental home, the pre-war memories, have all helped to direct his sensibilities to the patriotic cause. His father was a professional soldier, a commissioned officer; his mother was a teacher.

7

No doubt it was the later, vivid recollections of the occupation and the Resistance fighters which fed Wajda's sceptical responses to the ponderous and stilted cinematic representations of heroism current in the early 'fifties: ". . . young people, a song on their lips, knowing exactly what they were doing, were giving their lives for their country . . . If young people are not cheated, they only become heroic when life demands it of them . . ."

Wajda's interest in the visual arts awakened and developed at that time. Already under the occupation in Radom he used to assist artists re-decorating the local churches. After the war he progressed, logically, to the Cracow Academy of Fine Arts. But he found the solitude of the painter's work rather trying, and, in the end, disillusioning . . . "It apeared to me that some element of staging, an element of community, of some group of people working towards something, was missing." Searching for it, he found himself in 1950 in the newly created School of Cinematography in Lodz.

In 1954 Andrzej Wajda directed his first feature, *Pokolenie* (A Generation), projected as a graduation work both for him and his young cameraman, Jerzy Lipman. It was, indeed, very much a group venture, a joint enterprise by several young artists, all with Resistance connections back in the occupation days, all with rich memories of that time, but quite inexperienced as film makers. Apart from Wajda himself and Lipman, other people closely associated with it were Bohdan Czeszko, whose own war experiences were gained in the left-wing underground and who wrote the screenplay from his own novel (first published in 1951) and several young actors, of whom only Tadeusz Lomnicki and Tadeusz Janczar had ever appeared in front of the camera, and only Janczar in a leading part (in Aleksander Ford's *Five from the Barska Street*, on which Wajda himself had served his apprenticeship as an assistant director). Lomnicki, now one of Poland's most distinguished stage and screen actors, was at the time very much in the formative period, full of undirected ambition, and by all accounts his impact on the film was considerable. One mentions those influences not to diminish in any way Wajda's own contribution, which was undoubtedly decisive, but to underline the fact that this was an enterprise which was both exploratory and idealistic.

Nineteen fifty-four was an auspicious time to embark on a career in cinema. In Moscow, Stalin had just died and, although Kruschev had yet to make his revelations about the dead dictator, the first rumblings of change were already making themselves heard. The old, Stalinist canons were still in force, but the Party was rapidly losing confidence in its own authority to enforce them. The bureaucratic art, directed from behind a desk, was ready to retreat, and among creative people there was a dawning awareness of new opportunities.

Wajda's *A Generation* carries the signs of this transitory period. Outwardly it conforms to the requirements of "socialist realism", the exclusive "artistic method" of the time : it presents a positive hero of working-class descent, and it idealises his social environment and his own experience. The plot, a story of a boy's growth to maturity through contacts with revolutionary resistance groups, showing the development of political awareness and a gradual assumption of responsibility for his own and others' actions, has been the socialist-realist favourite ever since Maxim Gorky. And the total effect of the film is properly optimistic and uplifting. But this is far from the official, textbook optimism, incompatible with any exploration of genuine human conflicts, transforming drama into a schematic, didactic lecture. The feelings idealised in *A Generation* are truly personal recollections, and the intended result is therefore lyricism, not propaganda.

The social, revolutionary theme, although stated most attractively, is really of secondary importance here. Its development owes a lot to Tadeusz Lomnicki's remarkably controlled and sensitive performance as Stach, the working class hero. Restrained and technically simple, avoiding excessive stress on class characteristics, relying on a frank, open manner rather than any marked stylisation of speech or gesture, it is a performance of great strength and depth — whether in Stach's early thirst for new experience, or at the end, when through his grief he achieves an emotional maturity — which can only come from a total commitment to a part.

But with the knowledge of Wajda's later work, one imagines that for him the character of Stach must also have been meaningful in a different way. His principal concern was not social, in the strictest sense. His aim was to define a condition of pure idealism, of innocent political faith — a necessary point of departure (no

9

doubt not consciously planned) to his later preoccupation with the fate of a "betrayed generation". This is achieved not through any intellectual definition of patriotism, or a valid political philosophy, but through an idealised portrayal of Stach's human relationships. They are simple, even naïve, but gain conviction from an extraordinary sense of intimacy. There is a feeling, certainly familiar to all who ever took part in any conspiracy, of a participation in a close, cosily exclusive world, a shared mystery. The hero's growing love for Dorota, a girl who happens to be his political superior in the organisation he joins, is determinedly wholesome. There is no portrayal of passion, and by current standards their mutual attraction may seem curiously unsexual. But there is genuine warmth in some of their scenes together, the texture of the images is marvellously sensual and the love imparts joy to the process of Stach's political and personal self-discovery.

The qualities of *A Generation* are manifest, and yet elusive. One has a feeling of seeing easily through this film, and yet one is never quite certain of how its achievements are accomplished. Wajda's technique was at that stage relatively unsophisticated, and the cinematic influences easily picked out, but, as usual with him, not in themselves very illuminating. In this case the main "foreign" influence is of Italian neo-realism. It shows in the general structure of the film and the visual treatment of Warsaw backgrounds — as in the opening shot of the film, a slow and very long track through the fields and the shacks on the outskirts of the city, setting the scene for action, introducing the main character and describing, with some aid from the commentary, his background. As Wajda himself confirms, these were conscious influences, an expression of his and his young colleagues enthusiasm for the work of Italian neo-realists. But Wajda's own intentions and involvement in the theme, the effort to crystallize and express poetically certain personal memories, are foreign to the naturalistic aesthetic of neo-realism. Indeed, one feels throughout his first film that Wajda was already moving sharply away from neo-realism, without having ever fully absorbed it.

The director's later method is present in embryo in *A Generation;* the cinematic richness of images, the strong emotional contrasts (not clashing as violently here as in later films, though apparently the two most drastically brutal scenes were cut out against Wajda's wishes), the liking for long takes and a moving camera, but all employed in a simple, straightforward way. The dialogue scenes are handled with an almost naïve simplicity : mostly in close two-shots, with the camera favouring the actor speaking the lines.

There is a typical dialogue sequence early in the film, when Stach gets his first instruction in Marxism from an old socialist, Sekula. It is all the more worthy of attention, because it is one of the scenes that prejudices some viewers against the film, especially in Poland, where they were at the time saturated with crude political propaganda. It starts with a conventional two-shot favouring Sekula, as the old worker begins his elementary, naïvely-phrased exposition of the theory of surplus value. The camera moves in on the words, "There once was a wise, bearded man, by name of Karl Marx" — perhaps not the happiest choice of words to emphasise by the track in, since in Poland they are bound to raise a laugh from any audience — isolating Sekula in a close-up. Then we get a series of close-ups of the two men, cutting from one to the other, with a gradually increasing emphasis on the boy, who is listening greedily, with a radiantly expectant expression. The climax of this little sequence comes after Sekula's statement that the workers fight for their rights, and Stach asks him, with a joyfully knowing smile : "And do you . . . fight?" The scene is beautifully played by both actors; there is a feeling of an easy flow of communication, and the boy's eagerness for knowledge, and his fresh enthusiasm are expressively conveyed. It is the boy's first direct contact with somebody from the Resistance and an implied opportunity to join it. Stach's excitement because he realises this, not the dialogue, forms the scene's real content. The crude Marxist propaganda, seen and deplored by some people, is not really there.

A Generation seems most successful when the handling is simple, unaffected, direct. But these are not the qualities one associates with Wajda's later work. Indeed, Wajda's art has developed from elements which in the first film play only a subsidiary part, and are not always well integrated in it. One thinks of the scene when Dorota, seen for the first time, distributes leaflets in the night school attended by Stach. She is seen either in long shot, thronged by a multitude and rising above it, or from a low angle and towering across the screen. The scene is composed as a tableau, "the spirit

11

of revolution", a treatment out of key with the rest of the film.

In this attempt to refer the viewer to a ready, pre-digested fund of emotion, Wajda's electicism can be seen at its worst. But there are other instances, when scenes inspired by traditional imagery seem most apt. One thinks immediately of the justly-celebrated last little sequence of *A Generation,* coming after Dorota's arrest, with Stach afflicted by the most profoundly painful experience of his young life, but obliged to take immediate command of the newly formed detachment of the underground army. Stach's meditative and somewhat statuesque attitude in this scene is taken from a folk-art representation of a "suffering Christ". Similar figures can be seen in little road-side chapels in some parts of the Polish country-side. This is not to say that all audiences in Poland can instantly recognise the likeness. But their instinctive associations would include a sense of dignity, of human suffering shown in that image, of a certain ceremonial reverence towards it. Something of the same feeling no doubt communicates itself also to viewers outside Poland, even if it is not anchored in a familiar idiom. And the director's handling of the whole little sequence develops one's response further in the same direction : the curious short figure and face of the youth who approaches Stach, looking a bit like a primitive wood carving, the ritualistic exchange of the peculiar password, the empty meadow behind and the strange appearance there, apparently from nowhere, of a group of followers, approaching their new leader with signs of trust and respect. And Stach, the hero, turns his face away and weeps for his own youth, already over.

Thus ends the story of Stach, tracing the story of the film's positive hero. It successfully combines an expression of an accept-ably optimistic social and political position with true lyricism, an idealisation of personal experience, of remembered attitudes. And the first is dependent on the second. The final scene sums it up. In it, Stach is presented to us as almost a sort of political saint, meeting the responsibilities of political action and leadership with a moving gesture of self-denial. After the loss of his girl, the sacrifice of his private hopes, Stach's idealism moves into a different dimension.

In a political film, a celebration of simple virtues, courage, strength of character, loyalty, disinterested devotion to a cause, implies a certain limitation of intellectual scope. This is true about *A Generation,* at least as far as Stach's character is concerned. The successful presentation of his development is achieved at the cost of leaving out all the complexities. He is, in fact, a successfully simplified figure. All his problems, trials, challenges, seem to come from outside. He develops by rising to meet them, by growing out of one environment and into another, out of one attitude into another, socially more responsible. But it never seems to involve dealing with some inner and contradictory forces within himself. In this sense Stach, although he is set up for us as an embodiment of wholesome attitudes, is not himself a morally aware person. Characteristically the need for killing Germans, a desire for revenge, does not pose a moral problem for him; the problem is not faced seriously in *A Generation* at all. The revenge killing of a German officer is condemned by Dorota in a scene at the brickworks as an act of anarchy, against the organisation rules, rather than on any moral grounds.

There is another character in *A Generation*, Janek, subsidiary to Stach and played by an actor, Tadeusz Janczar, without Lomnicki's range and expressive force, but complementing the hero in an important way. He is a nervous, vacillating youth, full of contradictions, totally involved in conflicts of a moral nature. Basically drawn as a simple contrast to Stach, a weak boy, lacking his friend's resolution to commit himself irrevocably to a cause, Janek is given considerable weight in the film. Obviously this character meant a lot to Wajda. Partly, perhaps, because here was a chance to extend the range of comment and include some harsher truths: Janek's excitement after killing has undertones of hysteria in it, which is a reaction no less "true" than the joyous sense of participation in an exclusive brotherhood, conveyed in other scenes by Stach. More significantly, in Janek's hesitations and attempts to come to terms with various contradictory motives, and his final, tragic and absurdly heroic death, the director saw an image of the Pole as a victim of his country's history, forced to abandon a private, uncommitted position and destroyed by his patriotic obligations. Janek's death in the ghetto became one of the film's grandest moments. As presented on the screen (in Czeszko's novel, Janek's death appears in a different context, simply as a tragic incident in the normal course of duty) it is an irrational gesture, supposedly made to atone for his failure to help a Jewish friend, but really quite suicidal and private. Janek dies as a martyr to a cause which

13

makes little sense in terms either of practical politics, or conventional morality. Yet his death is not shown as meaningless, but as fatalistic, inevitable. The best one can say is that he gives himself to an idea of Poland which is an abstract, an absolute, and demands exclusive, religious obedience. It is a very different kind of self-denial from the one Stach communicates in his final scene. But then, Stach's idea of Poland must have been different from Janek's.

On closer inspection it seems clear that not only are Stach and Janek opposites, but the director's interest and commitment to their attitudes is basically contradictory. In *A Generation* this conflict is not immediately apparent, because the impressive and attractive figure of Stach and the course of his growth dominate the film so much. But after *A Generation* Wajda was to leave behind for good Stach's political simplicity and monolithic strength. He was to concern himself, almost exclusively, with articulating the conflicts embodied in the character and the story of Janek. And he was to employ, increasingly, the kind of symbolic, evocative imagery he used to describe his death.

A Generation came out early in 1955. It was respectfully received by the critics, though without excessive enthusiasm. It enjoyed a fair success with the Polish public, with above average box-office returns.

No one, however, could perceive at the time that it was going to prove a key film in a sudden artistic explosion in the Polish cinema. But then, in those days, few people concerned themselves with the artistic future of Poland. Political events were dominating the public interest to such an extent, that the conventional, "official" view of the Polish reality was under constant revision and new attempts to express it in art were bound to be judged primarily on how far they had managed to keep pace with this process, or, more correctly, how far they had advanced the cause of freedom. In such a dynamic political situation the main battleground was bound to be in journalism, and not surprisingly, the journalistic virtues of topicality, immediacy, clearness, plus an unambiguous, but passionate political commitment were assuming an overriding importance in the arts. Cinema, because of a considerable time span between the birth of a project and the exhibition of the film in its final shape, was at an obvious disadvantage.

14

A Generation was strikingly different in tone and feeling from the earlier films, but its poetic and human qualities might have seemed at the time obstructed, or flawed, by the presence of certain political conventions, which were soon to become obsolete. The most irritating one to the Poles was the presentation of antagonisms between the left-wing underground and members of the Home Army. The division is shown as strictly following the front-line of class antagonism; in Berg's shop, where Stach gets his first "decent" job, the owners and the foreman all have Home Army connections, while the genuine workers are at least emotionally committed to the communists; in the few scenes focused on the "Nationalist" conspirators, they are drawn as heavy caricatures, and when they go after Stach to recover a lost gun, they suffer a comic defeat at the hands of Stach's working-class neighbours. But as the political "thaw" spread dramatically, removing some of the false historical horizons and revealing publicly a number of truths which most people had always acknowledged privately, one of the first important operations in this field became the rehabilitation of the Home Army rank and file, if not its leadership. It was a purifying act of great significance. Quite apart from its political role — and one should remember that its traditionally pro-Western orientation and adherence to the parliamentary system of government could find a political expression only at the very top of its structure, mainly in Warsaw's isolated headquarters of "the Underground State" — the Home Army exerted a considerable influence on Polish life. It sucked in most of the cream of the new, rising generation, the best, the most courageous, the most idealistic, which also usually means, at that age, the most imaginative and talented individuals. They had died in their thousands, which in Poland, with its history of periodic sacrifice and a vigorous romantic tradition, could only add weight to the emotional legacy left by them. There was no greater moral damage done in the Stalinist years than the persecution of former Home Army members, whatever its political logic.

We can guess that Andrzej Wajda himself, an ex-combatant of the Home Army, came to feel some sense of guilt at the treatment of the "Nationalist" underground in *A Generation*, although at the time it must have seemed an absolutely unavoidable concession to official dogma. Certainly the choice of subject and its treatment in his next film would be consistent with some personal need for

15

expiation. *Kanal* was based on a longish short story by J. S. Stawinski, adapted for the screen by the author, another former A.K. member. It was directed by Wajda in 1956 — the days of heady, almost anarchistic freedom.

The fact that all the leading characters in the film are members of the Home Army may seem incidental. *Kanal* does not touch on questions of ideology or political loyalty. It pictures defeat, painted in oppressively heavy, fatalistic colours. This was, no doubt, the prevalent Polish feeling about the last war, and especially about the destruction of their capital. But the leftist underground, communist inspired and directed, won in the end a resounding political victory. Its Poland lay in the hopeful future, not in the ruins of the past. It is only for those, whose patriotism was inspired by traditional sentiments, that the defeat became all-embracing and final. It meant the end of the kind of Poland they were committed to.

In this sense *Kanal* represents a major switch of interest (though not necessarily, of course, of political conviction) on Wajda's part. In terms of *A Generation* it is a switch from Stach to Janek, from optimistic involvement, controlled by hope, to a fatalistic, self-destroying one. But the director's attitude to this second position remains ambiguous. There is some attempt to present it as a tragedy, with the representative heroic group meeting the inevitable judgement of history. However, this confrontation lacks true nobility, perhaps both because the "fate" is really of human, and questionable origin, and the nature of the compulsion which leads the Poles to defy it is never made clear.

The ambiguity which exists in *Kanal* is not an expression of some unresolved conflict in Wajda himself, but a direct consequence of certain weaknesses inherent in the film. The director was largely concerned here with the sheer size and intensity of the catastrophe, and not content with what could be achieved by direct description, he was searching for a suitably grand parallel, something that would make images transcend the limitations of subject matter. He found it, or thought he had, in Dante's *Inferno*. The descent into the Warsaw sewers, filled with defeated, retreating insurgents, is likened to Dante's descent into hell. The reference is made explicit through the character of the composer, who, parted from his family, joins the detachment, loses his reason as the pressure builds up, and wanders through the sewers playing an ocarina and quoting appro-

16

priate verses from the *Divine Comedy.* It must be said that the parallel doesn't work. In a film which is not really about individual emotions the composer looks like a stray, incongruous figure out of some expressionist drama. The reference to Dante which he presses home with such immoderate insistence, is of literary inspiration, and yet it doesn't transcend certain purely physical, visual associations. Dante's characters in hell all carried a burden of individual guilt, while Wajda in *Kanal,* though he may hint at the tragic bankruptcy of the traditional outlook, could not have meant to attach any individual blame to his heroes. Again, the tortured humans in the *Inferno* are all given a truly heroic stature; the insurgents in this film, for all their outstanding bravery, do not reach any commanding stature as individuals, and appear dwarfed by an overwhelming sense of fate. Thus the grand parallel, far from clarifying the author's attitudes, only manages to confuse them, if it is taken seriously.

An unsuccessful, undisciplined work often provides more persuasive evidence of an author's talent than an unqualified success. *Kanal,* now seen as a linking film between the more definite achievements of *A Generation* and *Ashes and Diamonds,* shows a marked growth in Wajda's command of the medium. The monumental outdoor scenes, before entering the sewers and coming out of them, often involving battle action and complex crowd movements, are conceived and executed on a level of technical sophistication never approached in *A Generation.* Take the very first shot of *Kanal,* devised, most ambitiously, to introduce all the characters, give some indication of the tone and stature of the drama, set the scene and start the action itself, all in one continuous, uninterrupted camera movement. This single, virtuoso take encloses over four minutes of screen time, and must have been impossibly hard to achieve with tracks laid over a long stretch of difficult terrain and the changing action staged on it. There are other, equally brilliant and technically complex scenes: the milling, panicky, disorientated crowd; the terrifying moment when Madry, the second-in-command, comes out of the sewer into the blinding light of day and finds himself surrounded by the Germans. Or the bold change of pace when the men enter the sewers, when the seconds become painfully drawn out and time loses its normal measure. These are the moments where supposedly realistic scenes are seized on by an obviously powerful imagination, condensed and transformed into images of visionary intensity.

Wajda's next film, *Ashes and Diamonds,* premiered in October 1958, was and still is regarded in Poland as the true fulfilment of his early promise. The director here achieves that confrontation he seemed to be feeling towards in his previous two films. If, in the consciousness of witnessing a violent end of one epoch and a dawn of another, *A Generation* can be accepted as an expression of political hope, and *Kanal* as a look at the catastrophe and the horror left behind from the point of view of traditional involvements, *Ashes and Diamonds* brings the two positions face to face in a dramatic and irreconcilable opposition. It is a film about the morality of being a Pole in our and Wajda's own time.

Other Polish films, then and in the succeeding years, have presented the same conflict. But *Ashes and Diamonds* is still unique in tackling it in such an absolutely central, exclusive way. And it produced a statement which Poles of Wajda's generation recognise almost universally as valid in terms of their own experience, and which can yet aspire to a wider, historical synthesis.

The film was based on a novel of the same title by Jerzy Andrzejewski, one of the leading contemporary Polish writers. The novel was originally published in 1948, at a time when there was still in existence a fairly widespread network of subversive underground organisations and even some guerilla activity in large forests. The Home Army had been officially dissolved back in 1945, but many of its younger members — in some cases complete detachments — had unquestioningly accepted directives from the new underground political centres, like the right-wing WIN (Freedom and Independence). The official pre-war doctrine of "two enemies", well-grounded in traditional attitudes and the Polish historical experience, based on an equal suspicion and fear of Nazi Germany and the Soviet Union, has retained a hold on the political imagination of many young Poles.

Andrzejewski's novel, a very effective piece of narrative with competent delineation of character and motive, was clearly designed as a reasoned plea to these people to stop fighting and save themselves physically and morally by joining a new life. It made a considerable impact at the time, but with the onset of Stalinist terror and the general petering-out of underground activities, its political conclusions lost much of their point.

When Wajda chose this novel, ten years after it had been written, as the basis for his third film, the political situation and the country's general mood were, of course, quite different. Practically the whole nation had been involved — for many, sometimes contradictory reasons — in the ferment of the "Polish October" of 1956, and thus the change in Party leadership, its declaration of new policies, including a promise of a different, less subservient relationship to the Soviet Union, assumed a tremendous emotional meaning. Some regarded it at the time as an effective substitute for a genuinely Polish revolution.

By the beginning of 1958, when Wajda started work on *Ashes and Diamonds,* things were settling down again, inevitably bringing new political disappointments and frustration, but also leaving a fairly large if undefined space for individual freedom. The recent radical changes had renourished the Polish sense of history, and opened new perspectives on the whole "Polish drama". It seemed an apt time to re-state it in terms of contemporary experience and Andrzej Wajda was the artist with the right background, imaginative equipment, emotional attitudes and ability for the job.

Wajda collaborated with Andrzejewski on the screen-play of *Ashes and Diamonds.* They reshaped the novel considerably, evolving out of it a completely new structure, both simpler and more arbitrary. The realistic narrative in the novel is carried over a considerable span of time and several characters are given equal weight in it. The film is given a time unity, all the essential events having been compressed into twenty-four hours, starting on the morning of 8th May, 1945, the date of the German surrender, and the first day of official peace; several of the leading characters have been completely eliminated and certain of their dramatic functions transferred to one of those retained, Maciek, who has been expanded in this way into a central, dominating figure. Thus, having lost some of the novel's scope — at least in terms of realistic motivation — the film has gained a hero.

The changes may sound like a conventional simplifying operation, of the kind continuously practised in Hollywood. In fact in this case their significance is different. They move the screenplay away from realism and from the specific nature of political problems

19

discussed in the novel, making of it a draft for a symbolic drama not exactly timeless, perhaps, but certainly intended to burst the bounds of time and place : the drama of conflicting political attitudes and worthy individuals destroyed by their inability to resolve this conflict within the terms of the code they live by. The intention was to intensify and universalise the drama, to crystallise attitudes in poetic, not realistic terms. Therefore the arbitrariness of the time framework and all the confrontations that constantly take place within it, which could have seemed irritatingly artificial in a descriptive film, appear quite appropriate and natural here, as does the violence of the emotional contrasts.

Maciek and Andrzej, two strangers in a provincial town, Home Army survivors, veterans of the Warsaw Rising and anti-German resistance, are there on orders to assassinate Szczuka, a visiting communist leader. They find themselves eventually in a local hotel, where official, but increasingly riotous celebrations of the end of the war and birth of the new Poland go on late into the night, with Szczuka as a reluctant guest of honour. In the end the fun draws in most of the people around, of whatever political hue. The idealists on both sides, the heroic characters, used to acting out their beliefs, come face to face, tragically; and so do the opportunists, the camp followers, coming together, harmlessly, to celebrate their own survival with a ritualistic booze-up.

This central design, made up of grand and abitrary dramatic confrontations, is amplified with various minor subplots, full of equally premeditated, violent, head-on collisions : Szczuka's long lost seventeen-year-old son turns up the same night in the local prison, with other captured Nationalist guerila fighters; Szczuka's sister-in-law, the queen of local society, prepares to flee to the West and harbours the Nationalist leader who has ordered Szczuka's assassination; a maid in the hotel where Maciek is staying has been engaged to one of the two men he has killed that very day, and when he walks with Krystyna into a bombed-out church they come upon their bodies. The violence of all these cross-references, the cross-grained density of the whole structure, leaves little room for delineation of character, or development of any non-public, non-political themes. Everything has to be stated in more or less symbolic terms.

This includes the relationship of Maciek and Krystyna. The

sudden transition from a casual encounter to a deep and tender feeling is handled attractively and seems plausible. For the bedroom scenes the camera style changes: soft close-ups and slow movement over the nude bodies convey a generalised feeling of tenderness and intimacy. But one cannot claim that the actual promise of a different life, which leads Maciek to try and abandon his commitments to the anti-communist underground, has really been formulated here, or in any of the subsequent scenes. Wajda simply refers the viewers to their private values and knowledge of love at its best and most beautiful.

In the context of this film it seems enough. Love is just as much a symbolic device here as everything else. It is there as a foil, to illuminate the forces of history — the real protagonists of this drama. These forces are dramatised in the structure of the film, in all those moral confrontations; but their compelling power is expressed throughout in direct images, which borrow richly from the tradition of Polish literature, art and popular culture. In fact, while giving dramatic shape to his audience's shared political dilemma, Wajda was using the key of national culture to unlock their responses, one by one. He does it in various ways: sometimes by direct reference, sometimes by attempting to tap the emotional significance of certain symbols and incorporating it in his own inventions. A clear example of the first use is an opening shot of the film's second sequence, immediately after the first, abortive killings. This curiously composed image, with a furrowed field filling most of the screen, and a peasant, a plough and a horse at the very top of it, refers to a painting by Chelmonski, an early impressionist, known and loved for his Polish landscapes. It stands, one supposes, for Poland as an almost mystic entity of land and people, wider than any particular conflict; and it serves to introduce Szczuka's encounter with the peasant activists — the only point, incidentally, where the film pays rather formal homage to the declared ideals of the new Poland.

One can quote other instances: a white horse, a past symbol of victory, which enters the frame, from nowhere, as the lovers part; or the final image, with Maciek writhing in agony on the symbolic rubbish heap, while a cloud of black crows whirls above him — a reference to an old saying about "ravens and crows picking us to pieces", which served as a title for Stefan Zeromski's book of

21

short stories. In other sequences, especially when the action keeps to the hotel, indirect evocations of various national myths and images are woven into a really potent mixture. There is, for instance, the scene where a girl singer sings *The Red Poppies of Monte Cassino* — a sentimental song of the Polish Second Corps, which took the Cassino Monastery in May, 1944, after suffering heavy losses, while in the adjoining room Maciek and Andrzej reminisce about fallen comrades over blazing glasses of vodka. *The Red Poppies* song is one of several intentional anachronisms in the film. The battle of Cassino took place barely a year earlier, and very soon assumed legendary dimensions, joining other Polish Pyrrhic, politically futile victories and gallant defeats. The song, in fact, reached Poland later, after the war. Maciek's gesture in putting a match to the vodka glasses refers to the religious custom of commemorating the dead with candle lamps, flickering on countless graves on Halloween night. The juxtaposition is obviously ironic, yet the scene is loaded with nostalgia. Wajda, in spite of himself, still finds the sentiments he is trying to move away from violently attractive.

The contradiction runs through the whole film and proves dramatically most fruitful. There is constant tension between the attractions of the traditionally patriotic attitudes, the compelling power and beauty of the images that refer to them, and the bitter realisation of their present uselessness. In a sense, the plot, some of the dialogue and characterisation run counter to the romantic content of the visuals. This duality comes close to being resolved only in a great symbolic scene near the end. The film builds up to it gradually. Maciek's killing of Szczuka, full of unashamedly theatrical pathos, is conceived in directly symbolic terms: the dying communist falls into his killer's arms and in that very moment a cascade of fireworks, celebrating peace and the dawn of a new era, shoots up from behind a dark horizon.

The following scenes, describing the dying moments of the night, are quite realistic at first: Maciek prepares to leave the hotel and the town; in the restaurant the party has ended and a waiter is preparing to clear up the mess; the orchestra is about to leave the platform. But the merry guests, by now including both the local reactionaries and the "progressives", want to go on. One of the "reactionaries", Kotowicz, a tall, middle-aged figure, glowing with the impeccably-assured style of a traditional Polish gentleman, takes charge. He stops the orchestra and persuades it to have a go at a polonaise. As he arranges the dance, Krystyna opens the window and the diffuse light of dawn falls on her. Maciek enters and the two of them make their farewells in a hauntingly beautiful, Rembrandt-like composition, with a single streak of light piercing the shadows of the low room. Maciek leaves and Kotowicz prepares to lead the polonaise : he stands in a long shot, his back to the camera, arms outstretched, the morning light flooding the room behind him. He is thus seen as a black, cross-shaped silhouette, out-lined against the brighter background; shimmers of refracted light shoot off his hands and head : a mystic, messianic figure. The intensely mysterious, and religious quality of this image unhinges any connection the polonaise scene might have had with common-place reality. The remaining few minutes tell of Maciek's inevitable progress to a stupid, unnecessary death. His horrible agony is then intercut back to the polonaise.

Understandably, some critics have seized on Maciek's death as a key symbol and a convenient starting point for any explanations or criticism of the film. But in fact it is the polonaise scenes which have the greater density of feeling.

The polonaise is the central symbol in this climactic sequence. It refers, probably quite deliberately, to a final scene in *The Wedding*, a symbolic verse drama written at the beginning of this century by S. Wyspianski, which ends with a spell-bound dance of all the characters, inside a charmed chalk-circle. This final scene is com-monly taken to express the political impotence of the intelligentsia, their inability to break out of the circle of self-indulgent romantic and sentimental ideas, and to give a sense of direction and true leadership to the peasant masses.

Wajda has taken great care to make his reference to *The Wedding* most striking. As in Wyspianski's drama, the sequence takes place in the dying hours of the night, with the dawn bringing in a new era. The visionary character of the scenes leading to the polonaise, the spell that suddenly takes charge of the dancers, point the analogies in a pretty direct way. In *The Wedding*, however, Wyspi-anski was being aggressively political, using his powerful imagina-tion to attack chosen targets. Wajda's way of tapping ready-made responses makes his references much more generalised and sweeping. In *Ashes and Diamonds* his symbols, references and metaphors appear to be largely instinctive, controlled mainly by Wajda's feeling for their emotional truth.

The importance of the polonaise is that, in it an extremely powerful evocation of familiar symbolic imagery has, in a sense, been turned against itself. Wajda plainly feels that sensitivity to such images, which he shares with his Polish audience, is a compulsion at best inhibiting and at worst destructive. The strength of Maciek's response to them leads him to kill Szczuka — the finest, most genuine of the new men — and in the end to his own useless and wasteful death. The others, less true to themselves, not heroic, accept existence in an artificial world of romantic affectations, of visions and rituals which open up only on the past.

Both in motive and form the film represents a somewhat decadent form of romanticism. But this very corruption of the original, inherited romantic impulse, formed a bond between Wajda and his proper, Polish audience. It corresponds closely to cultural attitudes prevalent among the Polish intelligentsia. And decadence can be a natural, inevitable, honest response to the passing of a great and dynamic tradition.

Anyway, in Wajda's case romanticism is a great deal more than an inherited manner. Most of his films — and none more forcefully than *Ashes and Diamonds* — are in varying degrees animated by a true heroic impulse, desperately frustrated: a nostalgia for heroic action, made absurd by its context, its nobility corrupted by the modern Polish experience. The frustrated heroic sense can be turned against itself, but never extinguished. It gives the Wajda work its scale, feeds and intensifies inherent tensions.

In *Ashes and Diamonds* this ever-present nostalgia for heroic action found an additional, direct channel in the performance of Zbigniew Cybulski. This remarkable actor's temperamental make-up seemed to mirror Wajda's own in this respect, but in a purer, more naïve form. Cybulski, who died in a tragic accident in 1966, was one of those actors who equate their professional with their private life and trail one through the other. Restless and gushingly emotional, often impatient of other people and quarrelsome, but constantly searching for company and pathologically afraid of loneliness, a sensualist full of idealistic notions, a heavy drinker in constant pursuit of women, yet apt to fall in love in an almost schoolboy fashion, he seemed possessed by a curious sense of mission —

rather like Brando, or James Dean. Intensely patriotic and very conscious of belonging to a particularly tragic generation of Poles, Cybulski felt an obligation to make his own feelings, experiences and attitudes appear as representative and significant. Like Wajda, he grew up during the war and became marked for life by the intense fear and elation of the fight against the German occupants. In fact, he used to carry around a curious collection of props, which obviously symbolised for him those early, formative experiences: an old, worn-out rucksack, a battered German mess-cup, a tin spoon to match, a prayer book of equal age — an assortment of things which, having outlived their former use (though the sack served its owner till the end, and the cup would occasionally, at some intimate ceremonies, be filled with vodka) became religious relics in some mysteriously private ritual. Cybulski used to tell confusing stories about their origin, intent, perhaps, on hiding more than he was prepared to reveal.

With his compulsive theatricality, his nostalgia for heroic action, his rather absurd sense of mission, Cybulski needed the context of art to become, momentarily, a fully coherent character. No wonder that he seized on the chance offered him by Wajda, and dragged into *Ashes and Diamonds* his own personal attitudes, his mannerisms, his private rituals and ritualistic props. He identified with Maciek totally. If Wajda succeeded in *Ashes and Diamonds* in articulating the popular feeling, the emotional contradictions of his time, his debt to Cybulski is incalculable.

CREDITS:

Director	Andrzej Wajda
Screenplay	Bohdan Czeszko, adapted from his own novel of the same title
Artistic supervision	Aleksander Ford
Assistants to the director	Konrad Nalecki, Kazimierz Kutz
Photography	Jerzy Lipman
Camera	Stefan Matyjaszkiewicz
Assisted by	Czeslaw Grabowski
Art direction	Roman Mann
Scenography	Jerzy Skrzepisanski, Jozef Galewski
Costumes	Jerzy Szeski
Music	Andrzej Markowski
Played by	Warsaw Philharmonic Orchestra, conducted by the composer
Sound	Jozef Koprowicz
Assisted by	Zygmunt Nowak, Jozef Tomporek
Editing	Czeslaw Raniszewski
Assisted by	Hanna Rubinska
Make-up	Zdzislaw Papierz
Assisted by	Stefan Szczepanski
Script girl	Maria Pietrzak
Floor manager	Roman Kowalski
Assisted by	Zygmunt Rybarski, Romuald Hajnberg
Lighting	Jozef Ciecwirek
Production manager	Ignacy Taub
Shot in	Wroclaw Feature Films Studio, 1954

CAST:

Stach	Tadeusz Lomnicki
Dorota	Urszula Modrzynska
Janek	Tadeusz Janczar
Sekula	Janusz Paluszkiewicz
Jacek	Ryszard Kotas
Mundek	Roman Polanski
Grzesio	Ludwik Benoit
Kostek	Zbigniew Cybulski

A GENERATION

A thunderous drum roll opens the film, soon breaking into gentler, rather lyrical music. Credits appear over an open, semi-industrial landscape. There is a large factory building in the background, with a vast stretch of waste land in front of it. The roofs of other buildings are visible in the foreground. A flock of wheeling doves turns low over the buildings. Other factory buildings gradually become visible, then a line of pylons, a church spire and a number of high chimneys. Boys are playing football on a small stretch of open ground between two of the buildings in the foreground. A horse-drawn cart passes them. Behind them a woman is hanging out a line of washing. A lorry moves along a road through the waste ground. A dove appears in the foreground. We see more children playing and women moving around; there is a line of shacks in the background. A cycle-taxi moves past, with two people seated in front and a man pedalling hard behind them. Several people are gathered in a group around a knife-grinder. It is a desperately poor environment, but one which is teeming with life. The sad tones of an ocarina become audible. A woman is standing with a small child. Seated on the ground, enveloped in a voluminous coat with a large hat pulled low over his eyes, is an old man playing an ocarina. In the distance a woman is gathering something among the grass.

STACH reminiscing over: *I was born here in the shanties, on the outskirts of Warsaw. I grew up in poverty. I made my first friends here, had my first lessons. I had a tough time, when I was a kid, because I didn't know my friends from my enemies. I had too much confidence in myself — in my legs and fists.*

We come upon a group of three teenage boys, huddled together on the ground. One of the boys is throwing a knife into the ground, trying to make it stick upright. One of the other boys, laughing, tries to grab the knife from the thrower.

STACH over: *My ma tried to keep a pretty firm hold over me, trying to push me off to work. But I treated it like typical woman's*

27

*nagging. I preferred playing knives with my mates instead. I had a
system. I was really good at throwing off the cap.*

STACH, the boy in the centre, wearing a crumpled cloth cap,
with an open, rather plebeian face, takes the knife and, resting
the point of the blade against his cap, throws it with the flick
of his finger. It somersaults before sticking into the ground.
STACH repeats the trick quickly several times.

STACH over : *But Kostek was even better. He could make the knife
do anything.*

KOSTEK, the dark-haired boy, flashing a brilliant smile, now
takes the knife and shows off his prowess. He throws the knife
from various angles and positions, making it stand up again
and again. But in the end he fails and the two other boys,
laughing, make a grab for the knife. A train whistle sounds off.
They stop and look up at once.

STACH over : *This wasn't our only occupation. In 1942 supplies for
the German army were being transported east by train. I used to
throw the coal down from the trucks — a patriotic thief.*

A freight train, pulled by a steam engine, moves slowly along the embankment, approaching a bridge. The three boys appear in the foreground. They run towards the embankment, as if meaning to intercept the train. The engine moves on to the bridge while the boys sprint towards the tracks. They reach the embankment and disappear from sight in its shadow. The train rattles past.

VOICE off : *Zyzio!*

The third boy, ZYZIO, seen from a high angle, jumps and clings to a rail fixed to one of the trucks of the train.

STACH runs along the embankment beside the train, close to where ZYZIO is clinging to a truck. He angles his run as he prepares for the final leap. Finally he jumps and clutches a rail at the corner of another truck.

A close view of STACH clinging to the moving train; grinning, he swings himself over to the truck in front of him.

KOSTEK sprints along beside the train. He grabs hold of a rail and swings his body over on to the truck.

ZYZIO scrambles over large lumps of coal on top of his truck. He stops over one particularly large lump and tries to push it over the side of the truck.

The face of a German guard appears in a small look-out aperture in the guard's van. He peers intently, then pushes a rifle through and takes aim.

ZYZIO has got his shoulder behind the large lump of coal and is straining to push it over the side. Suddenly a shot rings out and ZYZIO collapses spreadeagled on top of the coal.

The German guard at the look-out window takes aim once again and fires.

ZYZIO's body lies motionless on top of the swaying truck-load of coal.

STACH's face suddenly comes into view over the side of the truck. He looks out, tensely.

ZYZIO's face : a trickle of blood is running down his cheek.

STACH ducks suddenly, hiding his head behind the end of the truck, as another shot rings out and a spurt of coal splinters is kicked up close to where his head has been.

A general view of the truck, with ZYZIO's dead body in the background.

STACH raises his head cautiously to have another look, and

29

ducks quickly again as another shot rings out.

KOSTEK lets go of the truck he is clinging to and jumps down. He lands on the ballast of the next track. Two more shots are heard.

STACH looks about anxiously.

STACH shouting : *Kostek!*

KOSTEK, receding into the distance, scrambles to his feet and runs across the other railway track. He disappears behind the embankment just as another shot rings out.

STACH shouting off : *Kostek, let's get Zyzio!*

STACH jumps off the train and lands by the side of the track and falls to his knees; he remains crouching as the wheels of the trucks rattle past. The train moves away and STACH raises his head and looks wildly around him.

STACH shouting : *Kostek! Kostek!*

He scrambles to his feet, runs across the tracks and disappears down the other side of the embankment.

STACH is seated on the ground, looking very wretched. He gets up and moves away, towards a distant brick structure.

STACH enters a dark archway, which leads to an old and partly-

ruined brick kiln.

Inside a brick-lined tunnel: STACH enters, crouches down, and starts looking around anxiously.

STACH calling anxiously: *Kostek! Kostek!*

A man is lounging in the shadows: he sits up at the sound of STACH's voice. He is middle-aged, with a long, lean face.

GRZESIO: *What's that?*

A close shot of STACH's startled face.

GRZESIO off: *Pinching me jacket?*

GRZESIO leans against the brickwork of the tunnel, wagging an admonishing finger. He grimaces as if in distaste, then looks up at STACH again and yawns loudly.

GRZESIO: *What time is it?*

There is no reply.

GRZESIO grimacing horribly: *Got no watch, eh . . . ?*

He searches in his long jacket, finds a crumpled cigarette and sticks it in his mouth. He looks sideways at STACH, suspiciously.

GRZESIO: *Weren't there three of you prowling round the brickworks?*

STACH leans out of the shadows. He strikes a match and holds it out.

STACH's arm appears in front of GRZESIO's face as he accepts the light and draws on his cigarette. The little flame illuminates STACH's hand and GRZESIO notices drops of blood on it. He whistles in surprise.

GRZESIO: *Wait! Wait a sec!*

STACH: *What?*

GRZESIO: *Doing the trains?*

He laughs loudly.

GRZESIO picks up a bottle and holds it out in front of his face, so that it distorts and obscures his features.

GRZESIO: *There!*

STACH accepts the bottle eagerly, putting it to his lips and taking a long draught. Suddenly, the bottle is knocked flying from his hand. There is a sound of breaking glass as it crashes to the ground.

GRZESIO, crouching in the foreground, grins wickedly. STACH, standing over him and looking down, growls under his breath.

STACH: *What?*

31

GRZESIO rises, coughing and spluttering, and moves away into the tunnel. He beckons to STACH, who is at first reluctant to follow.

GRZESIO : *Come on, get moving. Don't be afraid. I used to thieve, too, at your age.*

Persuaded, STACH follows him.

Dissolve to a low-ceilinged, smoke-filled bar room, lit by a single bulb. A number of men, mostly workers, sit around tables, drinking. GRZESIO and STACH enter through a side door and walk up to the bar counter. A couple of customers look up and greet the older man.

VOICES : *Hey, Grzesio, hey . . .*

GRZESIO addresses the BARMAID behind the counter, a woman no longer in her first bloom of youth.

GRZESIO : *Two large ones, your highness!*

GRZESIO and STACH at the counter. GRZESIO, towering over his young companion, looks down on him; STACH seems dazed and numb.

GRZESIO : *That'll buck you up in a jiffy. I got a wound too, back in 'thirty nine, at Modlin. Got a scar to prove it!*

He starts to pull his shirt out of his trousers, baring his belly.

BARMAID off : *Mr. Grzesio.*

A close view of the BARMAID, jokingly admonishing GRZESIO.

BARMAID : *Not your obscenities again?*

At the bar, GRZESIO is still holding his shirt up, clearly for the benefit of the BARMAID rather than STACH. He succeeds in attracting some interest, and a couple of men move closer to him. One brushes against STACH's wounded arm, and the boy doubles up with pain.

WORKER I : *You having a bath, or what? A beer, please!*

A close shot of a man, SEKULA, drinking beer at a table. He looks up.

GRZESIO off : *Watch it! Don't squeeze the lad, he's wounded.*

SEKULA, a worker in his mid-thirties, with a strong and decent face, rises from his seat.

GRZESIO, quite possessive in his attitude to STACH, pushes the WORKER away. SEKULA comes up to the counter at the other side. The BARMAID appears fleetingly in the foreground.

WORKER : *Then what are you making him drink for?*

32

SEKULA takes the glass from STACH's hand.

SEKULA ironically: *Vodka's antiseptic, isn't it?*

GRZESIO peers round towards him.

GRZESIO: *Ah, comrade Sekula! Taking his Saturday pale ale!*

SEKULA: *Who's this kid, Grzesio?*

GRZESIO shrugs his shoulders. Suddenly he is no longer interested in STACH, who is now looking quite ill. SEKULA watches him anxiously.

SEKULA: *He should have it seen to.*

STACH looks utterly exhausted.

SEKULA off: *He's going to faint!*

AUNTIE off: *Time, gentlemen!*

An older woman, the probable owner of the place, known as AUNTIE WALERCIA, is cleaning up the tables, collecting glasses. In the background men at the bar are drinking up hurriedly. The mood has changed suddenly. Undertones of panic can be felt.

AUNTIE: *Curfew! We're closing.*

In the background, the BARMAID is pushing STACH away from the counter.

BARMAID: *Go home, lad!*

AUNTIE seen in a close shot, looking anxiously towards the bar. An old wall clock is behind and above her. Its dial is in the form of a comic negro's face, the eyes of which move in time to the ticking of the clock. As she speaks, AUNTIE turns away and takes a key from the side of the clock.

AUNTIE: *Take him away! There'll be trouble.*

She inserts the key into a hole in the dial to wind the clock up. SEKULA, STACH and the WORKER come out of the bar into the street.

SEKULA: *What's your name?*

STACH: *Stach, Stanislaw Mazur.*

SEKULAR: *Who got you?*

STACH: *The blacks.*[1]

SEKULA and the WORKER are walking behind STACH, obscured for most of the time by his head.

SEKULA: *One day you're really going to get it, my boy. It'll be in*

---

[1] The German railway police, because of their uniforms, were known as "the blacks".

your guts, and you won't know what's hit you!

WORKER : *The foreman's supposed to be looking for apprentices. What about ...*

They disappear one by one.

The dim interior of an obviously poor working-class home : a middle-aged woman, her face set rigid in anxiety, sits still in the foreground. A door opens at the rear of the room and STACH appears. His MOTHER rises and runs towards him. She notices his wound at once and without a word turns to the kitchen stove, takes a jug of hot water off the fire, soaks a cloth in it and applies it to the boy's shoulder. He winces and groans with pain.

STACH : *Mum! Mum! ... What ... a night!*

At last STACH gets himself under control and starts talking coherently.

STACH : *Did Zyzio Koscielniak come back?*

Instead of answering, his MOTHER slaps his face. Suddenly the wail of an air-raid siren is heard. The MOTHER walks over to a small lamp and dims it. The roar of aeroplane engines intensifies, as the woman comes back. They both sit down.

STACH's face is now close to the face of his MOTHER.

STACH : *Has Kostek been here?*

The MOTHER sighs deeply and tears well up in her eyes.

STACH : *He didn't care enough to ask? ... Why do you cry? I'm alive. The arm'll get well. I'll get some work. Mum, for Christ's sake! It'll all work out, you'll see!*

MOTHER sobbing bitterly : *It'll all work out ... sure. In my grave ...*

She turns suddenly to look STACH straight in the face. The sound of aeroplanes fades away.

Looking down a street, with a row of tall houses on one side, and a very high wooden fence on the other, with a sign, "BERG BROTHERS, mechanical joiners", painted over a double gate. STACH, is walking jauntily along the pavement; he stops at the gate and pushes it open. But he backs out almost immediately, as a big dog comes out of the doorway, straining at a leash. An old man appears behind the dog, holding the leash.

A closer view of the old man at the gate : he is wearing a

leather hat with long ear-flaps and a thick sheepskin coat. He looks at STACH warily.

OLD KRONE : *Apprentice?*

STACH : *Yes.*

OLD KRONE : *Go on then.*

He turns and points through the doorway.

Inside the gate is the yard of a woodwork contractor. STACH walks smartly across towards the workshop. He stops near a young man working at an outside bench. The man, JASIO KRONE, dark-haired and wearing a peaked cap, looks up from his bench.

STACH : *Good morning!*

JASIO : *Good morning. Apprentice?*

STACH nods his head.

JASIO derisively : *Don't nod your block. Answer when you're spoken to.*

STACH : *Yes.*

JASIO : *Really? Serves you right. Sit there and wait for the boss.*

STACH turns and walks across the yard, filled with benches, piles of wooden planks and paint pots. He sits himself on one of the benches, legs swinging, still obviously in a pretty good mood.

A general view of the yard, with STACH smiling in the foreground : the main door opens, to let in a group of workers. They remove their hats as they enter, exchanging greetings and jokes.

VOICES : *Good morning! Good morning!*

ZIARNO : *Hey, Gubrecki. Had a rough night?*

GUBRECKI : *Yes, smuggling tobacco, for fear of God.*

GUBRECKI, a stout man with a bad-tempered expression, also in a peaked cap, is talking to the small and arrogant-looking ZIARNO.

ZIARNO : *Can you wangle me a quarter of a pound?*

GUBRECKI : *I only work wholesale.*

ZIARNO notices STACH, who is grinning foolishly.

ZIARNO : *Take your arse off that bench. It's not the bog.*

STACH muttering : *Take a running jump!*

But he climbs off the bench lazily. ZIARNO comes up to him and fixes him threateningly, but after a second turns and withdraws. SEKULA appears in the background. STACH sits down on the bench again. JASIO greets the passing SEKULA.

JASIO : *Good morning, Sekula.*

SEKULA : *Hey! Well, Jasio, here's the new apprentice to replace you.*

JASIO, hearing this, puts his tools down at once.

JASIO : *About time! I qualified almost a month ago.*

The smiling SEKULA walks up to STACH to shake hands. More workers come in behind them. SEKULA admonishes STACH good-humouredly.

SEKULA : *Eh, Stach! You don't sit on a bench! That's not the proper place.*

STACH gets up at once. In the yard the new arrivals exchange greetings.

VOICES : *Good morning! Good morning!*

SEKULA : *Let's go.*

A stout, middle-aged man with heavily ringed eyes, one of the BERG brothers, walks by. He glances at SEKULA and STACH.

BERG II : *You want me?*

SEKULA and STACH follow him towards a glass-panelled door. Inside the office. BERG II hangs his hat up on a stand. Obviously in a good mood, he is humming a tune to himself.

SEKULA and STACH enter the office and stop, waiting. BERG II looks at them at last.

SEKULA : *Here's the lad, guvnor. Will he do?*

BERG II is taking his coat off, looking at the boy.

BERG II : *How do I know? Come here!*

STACH steps forward, taking his cap off. BERG looks at him taxingly.

BERG II : *Looks a bit too keen. You're not light-fingered, are you?*

STACH slightly offended : *Who, me?*

BERG II : *Who else, me? Are you healthy?*

STACH raises his arm, flexing his muscles.

BERG II : *Are your papers in order?*

STACH : *Yes.*

He takes some documents from an inside pocket and hands them to BERG, who starts looking through them.

BERG II : *You'll bless me one day. But you must try, try hard!*

He folds the papers up and pats STACH patronisingly on the

36

shoulder. The other brother BERG I, comes in, dressed in a suit, white shirt and a tie. He exchanges greetings with his brother.

BERG I : *Good morning Rysio.*[1]

BERG II : *Good morning Waldzio.*[2]

The ritual completed, BERG I turns to SEKULA.

BERG I : *Mr. Sekula, please ask Mr. Ziarno to come here.*

SEKULA leaves the office. BERG II moves after him.

BERG II shouting through the open door : *Jacek!*

A young workman comes to the door. The buzzing of machinery can be heard.

BERG II : *Show him how to make stretchers. Get down to it, lad. Work!*

STACH goes out with JACEK. ZIARNO passes them by in the doorway, BERG II closing the door after he has entered.

BERG I, taller and cooler, more businesslike in his manner than his brother, nods curtly to him to leave the room.

Reluctantly, BERG II moves towards the door, opens it and slowly closes it behind him, while the two men wait silently. After he has left, ZIARNO walks to the door and makes sure that it is properly closed. He then turns to face BERG I.

In the corner of the office BERG I opens a drawer and takes out a thick wad of paper money. He locks up the drawer and turns. ZIARNO reaches out for the money, but BERG I pulls the wad back with a wry smile.

BERG I : *Where's the receipt?*

ZIARNO silently gives BERG I a slip of paper. BERG I hands over the money and examines the receipt.

BERG I : *Signed with a code name. How can I be certain that the money really goes to the cause?*

ZIARNO, half turning away, is counting the money.

ZIARNO casually : *You can ask the major, when you see him.*

BERG I : *What about all that arsenal you've set up in the shop?*

He comes closer to ZIARNO and gazes at him sharply. The sound of the circular saws is audible again.

BERG I : *Get all that bloody junk out of here!*

ZIARNO : *I've already conveyed your wishes to headquarters.*

---

[1] A diminutive of Ryszard.
[2] A diminutive of Waldemar.

BERG I : *I want some peace. Cash for the organisation, yes — you're welcome to it. But take away those guns! I don't want to hang because of you!*

The door opens and BERG II pushes his head in.

BERG II : *Waldzio, Lieutenant Hirschweg is here.*

He disappears and closes the door.

A part of the main work area : STACH and JASIO pick up a large wooden framework, which is in fact the top of a bunk. They carry it across the room.

Three Germans — two officers in uniform and a civilian in a Tyrolean hat — are walking leisurely across the yard, accompanied by BERG I. They come closer, inspecting the bunk frames. They are talking in German.

BERG I : *Das ist das . . .*

He points at the frames. The Germans start to exchange remarks.

OFFICER I : *Not bad at all. What do you think, Lieutenant?*

The other two peer inside the frames. The civilian seems sceptical.

CIVILIAN : *They don't seem very comfortable.*

STACH comes into view, carrying another bunk. From the other side BERG II approaches.

BERG I : *We only use the best materials.*

BERG II climbs with some effort on to one of the bunks and starts bouncing up and down, turning his clown's face towards the Germans.

BERG I : *Here you are . . .*

BERG II in broken German : *Prima! Prima! Fein!*

The German are highly amused by his antics. They laugh, and BERG I joins in, somewhat artificially. STACH is looking on, astonished and disdainful. The Germans, still laughing, walk away. The smile disappears from BERG I's face and he glares at STACH.

BERG I : *Get back to work!*

BERG II, now sad-faced, rises heavily and slides down from the bunk.

ZIARNO is standing over a number of steaming glue-pots.

ZIARNO : *Glue, blast you!*

BERG II's face appears suddenly at a window. He pushes it up.

BERG II shouting : *Hey, boy!*

STACH runs into shot. He dashes through the swing doors, but BERG's voice stops him.

BERG II off : *Hey!*

STACH runs back.

A close-up of BERG II, leaning out of the window and yelling.

BERG II : *Hurry up!*

In the foreground shavings are flying off a planing machine. STACH seems to stumble into it.

STACH falls on his back under the machine, which showers wood shavings on him.

ZIARNO appears at the swing doors.

ZIARNO yelling : *Glue! Damn you!*

STACH at the stove, trying to lift several glue-pots at once. One falls and spills over.

VOICE off : *Boy!*

STACH turns his back on the spilled glue and runs away out of sight.

BERG II, at the window, hands STACH a mess tin and keys to

the store-room.

BERG II : *Get some more glue from the store-room.*

The hectic pace drops for a while, as STACH enters an empty store-room. He has to climb over some boxes to get to a large can containing the glue. Stepping down he knocks over a round box, and the contents spill out. STACH stops and begins to stuff all the trash back in. One of the final items is a piece of rug, and as STACH picks it up, an automatic pistol falls out of it. He stares at it, fascinated. ZIARNO's voice reaches him from the outside.

ZIARNO off : *Glue, kid, or I'll kick it up your arse!*

STACH wraps the gun up in the rug again, and replaces it at the bottom of the box.

ZIARNO runs into the store-room.

ZIARNO shouting : *Glue, damn you!*

SEKULA appears and approaches ZIARNO. Clearly, there is no love lost between them.

SEKULA : *What glue? We knock off in a moment. Can't you lay off the boy for a sec?*

He picks up a pot of glue and hands it disdainfully to ZIARNO.

SEKULA : *There! For your overtime.*

ZIARNO turns and leaves just as the bell sounds for the end of the shift.

The machines cut out, but the bustle and noise increase as the workers run around, hastily packing their work away. SEKULA, ZIARNO and STACH push behind a crowd towards a row of taps in the foreground. One man stays behind, calmly reading a newspaper.

VOICES : *That's it! Knocking off time!*

SEKULA : *Easy, men, easy, this isn't a tram queue.*

ZIARNO : *Let a man wash, you filthy bums.*

He elbows his way in.

A general view of the workshop : in the foreground JASIO is tying his sack up. In the centre STACH is clearing up wood shavings. The two BERG brothers walk by; the fat one addresses STACH.

BERG II almost mechanically : *You must try, lad! Try hard!*

He walks off with his brother. In the background workers are leaving, shouting their good-byes.

VOICES : *Good night! Good night!*

OLD KRONE, staggering slightly, approaches with his dogs. STACH is still cleaning up, seemingly in no hurry to leave. OLD KRONE speaks sententiously, commenting on BERG's admonishments.

OLD KRONE : *Work and pray, and you'll grow a hump!*

JASIO, sitting with arms folded, looking down at STACH with a superior smile.

JASIO shouting : *Leave him alone, dad!*

STACH, who is moving slowly towards JASIO, gathering shavings, looks up.

JASIO : *They really did let you have it today, didn't they?*

STACH puffs his cheeks out, looking on.

JASIO : *I'd been catching it . . . yes . . . for four years. No one helped me.*

OLD KRONE and his dog come closer. JASIO gets busy with his sack, still grinning down at STACH.

JASIO : *Don't look at me like a whipped pup. I'm not going to help you. Sort it out yourself.*

41

He ties a rope round the neck of the sack.

JASIO : *Remember: don't trust anyone. Keep out of trouble, just look after number one.*

He dusts his sack with a quick flick of the hand and looks down at STACH again.

JASIO : *That's what I've been doing and look — I'm a craftsman now.*

He gets up, swings the sack onto his shoulders and goes out, with a final look at STACH.

JASIO giggling : *And I was a poor devil, just like you! Get on with it, get on!*

STACH watches him go, then reaches out and takes a mug from the bench beside him. He takes some water from it in his mouth and blows his cheeks out, spitting out the liquid in a fine spray to settle the dust. Fade out.

Fade in on the workshop : STACH is in the foreground, planing the edge of a door, to make it fit tightly. SEKULA walks over casually and inspects his work.

SEKULA : *Well, not bad for a beginner.*

He tries to close the door, and both of them disappear for a moment behind it.

SEKULA : *A bit too much off the bottom, Stach. Make it strong, so that it'll last. Well, all right. Let's finish the beading. Right . . . it'll fit! Smoke?*

He takes out a packet of cigarettes. STACH takes one and follows SEKULA across the workshop, towards a glowing brazier. STACH crouches in front of the brazier, a cigarette between his lips. He rubs his hands together vigorously. SEKULA is visible in the background working at a bench.

STACH : *Berg's building a new shop. He's buying machines. Business's good. It must cost tons of money, doesn't it, Mr. Sekula?*

SEKULA : *That's right.*

STACH raises a burning piece of paper to the cigarette and draws on it.

STACH : *Where does he get it from? From the Germans, or what? Mr. Sekula, from the Germans?*

SEKULA walks across and stops behind the crouching STACH, so that only the legs of the older man are in view.

SEKULA: *When they give, you'd better not be there to get it. It's from us!*

STACH looks up and laughs.

STACH: *From us? We've got nothing to give.*

SEKULA crouches down beside him.

SEKULA: *We've been giving for ages, Stach. But not for much longer.*

He raises a burning taper from the brazier, lights his own cigarette, and blows the taper out.

SEKULA continuing: *It's a simple count. How much time did it take you to fit those doors?*

STACH: *Two hours.*

SEKULA: *And what is your weekly pay?*

STACH: *Thirty-six zlotys.*

SEKULA: *In other words, you take home six zlotys a day?*

STACH: *Yes.*

SEKULA: *And Berg charges twelve zlotys to fit a door. It takes you two hours to do the job, so in one hour you earn your day's wages.*

SEKULA rises and walks out of frame, leaving STACH astonished and calculating hard.

STACH: *I see . . . So he takes twelve for one fitting . . . twelve divided by two is six . . . and I take six a day . . .*

SEKULA off: *So in fact you do eight hours' work for the price of one.*

STACH: *I see . . .*

SEKULA smoking a cigarette. STACH enters the shot and stops near him. He is obviously greatly intrigued by SEKULA's arguments.

SEKULA: *Let's go on. Supposing you adjust doors all the time. You do four a day. Berg gets forty-eight zlotys for it, and pays you six. So he's making forty-two zlotys out of your work, day after day . . . Out of you, out of me . . . all of us. Day after day, day after day . . .*

He draws reflectively on his cigarette.

SEKULA: *There once was a wise, bearded man, by name of Karl Marx.*

STACH is listening with shining eyes, perceiving the importance of the lecture.

SEKULA off: *He wrote once that the workers were only given barely enough . . . just enough to recoup their strength.*

Close shot of SEKULA, very serious.

SEKULA : *Nowadays we don't even get that. We have to fiddle to survive.*

Close shot of STACH, very attentive.

STACH : *Can't we, the workers, do anything?*

Cut to a close shot of SEKULA.

SEKULA : *If you only knew, mate, how much blood has been spilt because of this simple arithmetic — among other things. The workers fight for their rights. They always have done.*

A close-up of STACH, all excited attention.

STACH : *And now?*

SEKULA off : *Now, too!*

STACH smiling knowingly : *Mr. Sekula, you say that the workers keep on fighting. And you?*

A fleeting close-up of SEKULA, returning the smile.

SEKULA : *What do you mean?*

STACH smiles radiantly.

STACH : *And do you ... fight?*

Back on smiling SEKULA. Camera tracks back as SEKULA reaches out and playfully tags STACH's ear. They are both laughing.

SEKULA : *You ...*

STACH : *What ... ?*

SEKULA : *Listen — we've established we're both workers, so don't you "mister" me, use my name. The "misters" have gone, along the Zaleszczyki road.*[1]

The continuous sound of sawing stops suddenly and a bell rings in the background. It startles STACH out of his knowing grin.

STACH : *Hell. I must run!*

SEKULA : *Where to?*

---

[1] In pre-war years Zaleszczyki was a town in the southernmost part of Poland, on what was then the Rumanian frontier. During the 1939 September campaign the Polish Government and other members of the ruling elite crossed over there, with their families, into the then neutral Rumania. The entire exchange with Sekula does not appear in the original screen-play. Instead, there is a reference to the difficulty Stach finds in absorbing terms like "dialectics", or in remembering names like Hegel. Leaving Berg, Sekula regrets that he won't have time to expound the basic concepts of Marx to Stach.

STACH : *To school. Berg says I've got to attend, says it's compulsory, so I go there, but not much.*
SEKULA : *Skipping classes?*
STACH : *Well . . . ?*
SEKULA : *Don't do it, Stach. Learn!*

He turns and walks away.

STACH calling after him : *It can't be a proper school if the Germans allow it!*

SEKULA is back at work, bending over a plank of wood.

SEKULA : *That is the way it is; but don't you neglect it!*

STACH appears in the background, still grinning. He makes a rather contemptuous sound. SEKULA admonishes him good-humouredly.

SEKULA : *Well, well, well. Don't be so smug. Learn wherever you can.*

Using the window for a doorway, STACH, still laughing, jumps out. Fade out.

Fade in to a classroom, camera looking down the aisle between rows of seated students. A PRIEST in a cassock is facing the class, walking in from the background. Behind him a large crucifix over the blackboard provides the only decoration in a bare room. As the PRIEST talks, STACH is seen entering stealthily in the background.

PRIEST : *In these sad times, our Catholic faith, the refuge and mainstay of us all, ought to shine in our souls with special power.*

A reverse angle. The PRIEST walking down the aisle has his back to us. STACH slips quietly into a seat at the front of the class.

PRIEST : *. . . Because one knows not the day, or the hour, when only It — the Faith — will remain of the things that belong to us . . .*

STACH opens his coat, looking rather ill-at-ease. The PRIEST continues on his way down the classroom, glancing from one side to the other.

PRIEST : *I would like to get to know you.*

A paper dart flies across the rear of the room.

PRIEST : *I'm going to ask you a simple question. I would like someone to say the Apostles' Creed . . .*

Another dart flies across the back of the room. The bespectacled PRIEST glances around and touches the shoulder of a youth sitting near STACH. The youth jumps nervously to his feet.

PRIEST : *You, perhaps. Is your name Jacek?*

The youth, hopelessly lost, looks around him, desperate for help. STACH responds.

STACH whispering : *The Apostles' Creed!*

Both JACEK and the PRIEST glance at him. STACH is still offering help.

STACH whispering : *I believe in God . . .*

JACEK, looking at STACH, repeats what he says.

JACEK repeating : *I believe in God . . . I believe in God . . .*

The PRIEST walks up to JACEK, who obviously has no idea what comes next.

PRIEST : *Courage, courage!*

JACEK blurting out suddenly : *I don't know. I can learn it if I've got to!*

He sits down defiantly. The PRIEST leans over him and rests a hand on his shoulder.

PRIEST : *In your papers there's a heading, "religion". Isn't it marked Roman Catholic?*

JACEK moves his shoulder away from the PRIEST.

JACEK : *Yes.*

The PRIEST spreads his hands in supplication.

PRIEST : *Well?*

JACEK : *What?*

PRIEST : *What is your religion, really?*

JACEK looks up at him and answers with calculated rudeness, playing up now to the class.

JACEK : *There is a space for it, so you write it in!*

There is a burst of loud laughter as the PRIEST raises his clasped hands to his mouth — a picture of theatrical desperation. A bell announces the end of the period and the class rises noisily to its feet.

VOICES : *Time, time . . .*

A general view of a small, enclosed courtyard, with a staircase leading to a gallery at the height of the first storey. A crowd of youths spill out of the school building on to the gallery and run along it with noisy exclamations. They disappear from view for a moment and reappear again, running down the staircase. A small group of young people at the foot of the staircase look up at the unruly crowd. One man detaches himself from the group and steps into the path of the running students, barring their way.

KACZOR : *Stop! Friends, we've got something to tell you!*

The youths at the front stop, behind them others are coming down the staircase and pushing forward, swelling the crowd in the courtyard. In the background a young girl from KACZOR'S group, DOROTA, appears on a platform, above the crowd.

DOROTA : *Friends . . . !*

A closer view of DOROTA, slim and bright-eyed. She is seen from a low angle. In the background more students run off the staircase and approach. DOROTA shouts above the din they are making.

DOROTA : *Friends, the Union of Fighting Youth is being formed, the combat organisation of young Poles.*

More students come down as she speaks. Among them is

STACH, picked up by the camera. It follows him, until he joins the waiting crowd in the courtyard.

DOROTA off: *We will not lay down our arms! We have blood, tears and destruction to avenge. And now! Not at some time in the future.*

A close shot of DOROTA's face, flushed and fiery.

DOROTA shouting: *They murder us! They send us to rot in camps! Let's take revenge! Let's fight for a free Poland.*

A circle of youths in the foreground, their backs to camera: STACH is among them. Further back and above them, DOROTA is shouting, her right arm raised.

DOROTA: *. . . For a just Poland! Young workers, make contact with the Union of Fighting Youth.*[1] *Join the People's Guard!*[2]

A closer view of DOROTA. As she is speaking excitedly, glancing around the crowd gathered attentively below her, she feels inside her coat and takes out a handful of leaflets.

DOROTA: *. . . The militant arm of the Polish People! Don't wait to be liberated! To arms! Death to the occupiers!*

A general view of the gathering. DOROTA throws the leaflets up in the air and, as they fall slowly, and the crowd rushes forward to pick them up, she leaps off the platform, joins her resistance colleagues and disappears. STACH, highly excited, is trying to push his way through the crowd towards her.

STACH calling out: *Miss! Miss! You! You! Listen!*

The other boys grasp the leaflets and read them avidly. STACH runs away and disappears. The crowd disperses.

Outside in the street: STACH and JACEK run out, followed by a crowd of other youths. Stuffing the leaflet into his pocket, STACH glances around, obviously looking for DOROTA. A solitary woman's figure is waiting on a pavement and the two youths move towards her, camera tracking in ahead of them. It stops, and the boys reappear: the woman is not DOROTA.

JACEK: *It's not her. Make contact, but how?*

JACEK and STACH move away. In the foreground a couple of German soldiers walk by. STACH's voice comes in, commenting

---

[1] The Union of Fighting Youth (Zwiazek Walki Mlodych) was set up in 1942 as a resistance organization and survived after the war until 1948.
[2] The People's Guard (Gwardia Ludowa) was a left-wing military resistance organization, also formed in 1942.

48

on the action over the end of this and the opening of the next shot.

STACH commentating over: *Make contact — a pretty phrase! Just try it! There was no one to help me. For a long time I had to feel in the dark for a helping hand ...*

STACH and JACEK crossing the street. STACH is holding a leaflet, and they are looking at it. A car pulls up at the kerb near them, and three Germans — two uniformed officers and a civilian — climb out. The civilian, wearing a leather coat and a trilby hat, stops and stares suspiciously at the two youths.

JACEK: *A round-up!*

GERMAN barking out: *Weg!*

The two youths walk slowly away, looking round a couple of times.

JACEK: *Weg! And cheerio! That's how it is, brother!*

STACH: *That's right! They kick us around and we do nothing! Nothing! We take it like lambs!*

JACEK: *If only we had guns!*

They stop, and STACH laughs at the very thought.

STACH: *What? Arms?*

They part, grinning knowingly at each other. Fade out.

Fade in on STACH peering through the glass panels of the work room in the BERGS' wood yard. He reaches out towards the padlock, camera moving in. His voice comes in over the image.

STACH over: *That gun in the storeroom was tempting. That would be a start!*

He opens the door cautiously.

STACH over: *I was bursting with pride at the thought that I could join them already armed ... That would make them take notice!*

Inside the storeroom: in the dark the door is seen opening silently and STACH enters, moving cautiously. He cannot avoid knocking against something and making a slight noise. His hand appears, reaching up over a pile of boxes. A dim light falls on his face as he feels inside one box. He finds what he is looking for, takes out the dark shape of the pistol, turns and moves stealthily away through the door.

STACH, leaving the storeroom, is moving across the dark

49

workroom. Suddenly the lights go on, and OLD KRONE appears in the background, walking lamely forward, leaning on his walking stick. STACH bends quickly over a bench and starts hammering on something. OLD KRONE comes up to STACH's shoulder.

OLD KRONE : *What are you knocking up there, Stach? What is it?*
STACH in the foreground occupies himself busily with some pieces of wood.

STACH : *A tool-box, for myself!*

OLD KRONE steps back and sits down by the stove. STACH pretends to measure one piece of wood against another. Behind him, OLD KRONE starts speaking reminiscently.

OLD KRONE : *Yeah! When I went into the army, I also had a tool-box, a painted one. A recruit's box. That was in the Tsar's time ... I was posted to the Manchurian border ...*

STACH, turning his back on OLD KRONE, takes the pistol out of the cloth and thrusts it inside his clothing. Relieved, he turns around and walks over to the old man.

OLD KRONE : *... Nothing but mountains, steppes ... A vast world ... I was young then ... strong as an ox!*

STACH sits on the opposite side of the brazier, closer to the camera. OLD KRONE continues, rolling a cigarette.

OLD KRONE : *It seemed then, that if I just dug my feet in, I could lift the whole world on my shoulders. I bet you feel the same now, lad, eh?*

STACH : *Where are your dogs, Krone?*

A close-up of OLD KRONE, his head lowered.

OLD KRONE : *The boss gave them away to the dog-catcher.*

STACH looks on thoughtfully, rolling a cigarette, then putting it to his lips to lick the paper.

OLD KRONE off : *Me — kicked out! Dogs to the dog-catcher.*

OLD KRONE continues sadly.

OLD KRONE : *Stach! These are my last days here! Well? ... How do you live without work?*

Light flickers over STACH's face.

STACH : *You're not having a peaceful old age, Krone.*

He raises a burning paper to light his cigarette.

OLD KRONE nods his head forebodingly.

OLD KRONE : *Yeah! It'll come to you one day. Not that I wish it on you, because I've got to like you. But things'll never change.*

He raises a burning slip of paper to light his own cigarette.

STACH contradicts him brightly.

STACH : *Go on! I'm not so sure.*

He gets to his feet.

Dissolve to STACH in the foreground, a long view of a street behind him. He is glancing down at the belt, where the butt of the pistol is sticking out. He pulls his jacket down to hide it. Then he looks over his shoulder towards the entrance of a bar. SEKULA and another man come out of the bar. STACH turns quickly and runs across to them.

STACH shouting : *Sekula! Sekula!*

The men stop and wait as STACH comes up.

STACH and SEKULA move away a couple of steps, talking while the other man remains in the background.

STACH : *Sekula!*

SEKULA : *Well? What's up? Quickly. I'm in a hurry.*

STACH eagerly : *There was a meeting at school. A girl was speaking. I ran after her . . . She stood up on a barrel and spoke . . .*

They stop and talk.

SEKULA : *What? What's all this rubbish!*

STACH : *She told us to join the People's Guard . . . I want to join the People's Guard!*

SEKULA : *Wait a moment! Slow down!*

STACH : *Sekula! I know you can help me!*

SEKULA : *I've no time now. Come on Sunday at eleven.*

STACH : *Where?*

SEKULA : *At the Bem-Wolska crossroads.*

He lowers his voice and continues in a confidential manner.

SEKULA : *You won't forget? But keep it to yourself. If anyone should ask about me in the workshop, you don't know anything. I'm not going back to the Bergs.*

STACH startled : *Yes!*

SEKULA turns to his waiting companion and calls out :

SEKULA : *I'm coming Szymon; I'm coming!*

He resumes his conversation with STACH.

SEKULA good-naturedly : *You were saying it was a girl?*

STACH grinning : *And what a girl!*

SEKULA : *Is that so?*

STACH: *Well!*

SEKULA, now all smiles, shakes hands firmly with STACH.

SEKULA: *So long then, Stach. See you on Sunday. Don't forget, I wasn't here! You haven't seen me.*

STACH: *Good!*

SEKULA: *Well . . . See you. Cheers!*

STACH: *Cheers!*

They part at last. SEKULA walks towards his companion, and STACH runs excitedly the opposite way, down the dark street. A horse-drawn cab moves down the street, away from us. STACH runs across to it, keeps up for a moment with the horse's canter, and then leaps on the cab, sitting on a ledge behind the carriage. Joyful, fairground-style music can be heard as the cab moves away down the street, receding into the background. Fade out.

Fade in on a crowd of people in front of a church: STACH and SEKULA appear, stop in the foreground, gaze around, then start moving away.

STACH: *There were two boys with her. I ran after them, but they vanished without trace.*

SEKULA: *Yes . . . yes . . .*

A close shot of a girl, her back to us. A young man is facing her, holding a paper bag with dried pumpkin seed in it. They are both eating out of it.

DOROTA: *We have to inform Kaczor.*[1]

YOUNG MAN: *I'll do it now.*

He hands DOROTA the bag and moves out of shot. STACH and SEKULA approach from the background.

STACH: *That's her! Christ, it's her!*

They stop, and DOROTA turns to face them.

SEKULA, grinning, greets DOROTA and introduces STACH.

SEKULA: *Hey, Dorota. Meet this lad. A new recruit, and not a bad one, I believe.*

DOROTA smiles and shakes hands with STACH.

DOROTA: *It'll come out in the wash!*

She speaks to STACH, still smiling.

---

[1] Kaczor means "Drake", obviously a Resistance pseudonym.

DOROTA : *What should I call you? What? Tiger? Panther? Pansy? Zoologically or botanically?*

STACH : *It's not a laughing matter! Call me something plain and human!*

DOROTA : *You have a bit of a country air about you. A Bartek.*[1]

STACH smiles approvingly.

STACH : *All right, Bartek.*

SEKULA takes out a pocket watch and checks the time.

SEKULA : *Well, cheerio, kids! Keep well!*

SEKULA shakes hands with DOROTA and prepares to leave.

DOROTA : *Now, now, not kids, if you please.*

SEKULA departs, and camera moves back. A wedding procession comes across from the church. DOROTA looks at STACH standing rather awkwardly at her shoulder.

DOROTA : *Take my arm, or something.*

STACH complies, rather clumsily. The wedding procession, led by the bride in a white dress and the groom, moves slowly across. As the last of the guests goes by, camera tracks in to a

---

[1] Bartek is a typical peasant name.

close shot of DOROTA and STACH. She turns to him.

DOROTA: *Do you know about the People's Guard? About our Workers' Party? Do you know why you want to join?*

STACH smiling shyly: *I do! . . . Well, perhaps it's not that I do know, but . . . please don't laugh . . . but . . . I feel it.*

DOROTA smiling: *I'm not laughing. I think you might do very well.*
Smiling at one another, they move away.

People outside the church: DOROTA appears in the foreground, followed by STACH. They stop, taking leave of each other.

DOROTA: *You remember our meeting place?*

STACH: *Yes.*

DOROTA: *To-night, then, my house.*

They move another step forward and stop to shake hands. We see them framed in a large heart-shaped hole in a fairground placard. DOROTA leaves and STACH stays on for a moment, clearly in a state of happy oblivion. A PHOTOGRAPHER moves forward and takes STACH's shoulders to arrange his position for a snap. Startled, STACH glances up and down the placard, and, realising his situation, dashes away.

Fade in on STACH at the door of DOROTA's house; KACZOR is standing at the open door. STACH introduces himself.

STACH rather loudly: *I'm Bartek!*

KACZOR raises his finger warningly.

KACZOR: *Shshsh! . . . Kaczor.*

He lets STACH through into a room, camera tracking in with him. A number of young people are already gathered there. STACH's entry momentarily diverts attention from DOROTA, standing at the head of a table.

A close shot of DOROTA. As she starts speaking, STACH appears, and she acknowledges his silent greeting without interrupting the speech. He stops beside her.

DOROTA: *The Germans say: "Räder müssen rollen für den Sieg" — the wheels must roll for victory.*

Camera leaves her face and pans slowly across the silently attentive faces of the other conspirators. They are smoking a single cigarette, passing it round from hand to hand, and the camera is following this movement. DOROTA's voice continues over the shot.

DOROTA off: *It's up to us to stop those wheels rolling eastward. To cripple the movement of enemy forces and his transport are our most important tasks. They say that we are only a handful. But the comments of those who gave away our country into criminal hands are of no account to us. We are the soldiers of a great army made up of all the peoples fighting the Nazi invaders in the sacred cause of freedom. No one is ever alone in a just war. The Red Army is with us. I'm using big words. I and you. But we know how to translate the words into everyday work for the Resistance. The stone walls of the city are our maquis. With pistol in hand we'll be moving inside this maquis. And if they say that this is madness, tell them: even if it is, it has to be this way. There is no other way.*

The cigarette has finally reached STACH and we see him and DOROTA together again. It is already quite dark, and DOROTA lights a candle. She turns towards the window.

STACH and DOROTA looking out of the window, which we see from outside. STACH, with an expression of innocent wonder, points towards something.

STACH: *There . . . there . . .*

Down among the ruins children are waving big sparklers about.

STACH: *They're playing . . .*

Close shot of DOROTA and STACH at the window.

DOROTA: *Saying good-bye to the day . . .*

She looks at STACH and starts pulling the blind down.

Inside the room: DOROTA pulls the blind down and turns away from the window.

STACH speaks, addressing her primarily, but also the rest of the gathering.

STACH: *I have a friend, Janek . . . but he is a bit doubtful . . . Jacek, he doesn't believe in God . . . Mundek . . . I've known him since childhood. I've only just met him again by chance.*

DOROTA: *Good, Bartek! You can set up a subsection of the people you know.*

She turns to the others.

DOROTA calling out: *Stand to attention, comrades!*

A general view of the room. A hush falls and all the youths rise to their feet. Light from a single candle burning on a table in the middle flickers over their faces.

DOROTA: *You're going to take an oath! Attention!*

They all stand to attention.

DOROTA: *I, an anti-fascist son of the Polish People, hereby swear . . .*

All the young conspirators repeat her words in unison.

DOROTA: *. . . To fight valiantly and with all my strength . . .*

The new recruits repeat her words again.

DOROTA: *. . . For the freedom of our country . . .*

She pauses again and the conspirators repeat the phrase earnestly.

DOROTA: *. . . And the sovereign power of the people . . .*

The image fades out gradually as the group repeats the last sentence of the oath.

Fade in on a general view of a street with a number of dead bodies hanging down from telegraph poles. German soldiers, spread a couple of yards apart, are lining the pavements, one of them, in the foreground, with an Alsatian dog on a lead. A German motorcyclist rides past; an officer is taking photo-

graphs. A group of people approaches from the background. JANEK KRONE comes up, glancing at the bodies and the German soldiers. He stops, but seems to be avoiding the company of other people. He pushes his way to the front and gazes at the two nearest corpses. Only their legs are visible, and notices pinned below their feet. There are railway tracks in the background and a train is just passing by.

A closer view of the crowd, stopping to read the notices, with the list of names of the executed; the German soldiers stand in the foreground. JANEK stops beside a helmeted German soldier to read the list, then draws his raincoat tightly around him and moves on. The group of grim-faced people remain reading the notices behind the line of German sentries facing them, poker-faced.

Dissolve to JANEK entering the Bergs' workshop. As he walks to his bench, STACH follows him. He glances around before approaching STACH.

A close shot of STACH leaning towards JANEK.

STACH: *Hey! Do you know about the People's Guard? I'm getting a few blokes together . . . Will you join us?*

JANEK, undoing the belt of his coat, turns slowly round to look at STACH in the foreground. He speaks defensively, obviously feeling the need to justify his refusal.

JANEK: *No . . . I can't . . . The boss's sacked my father. "Too old" —*

JANEK: *. . . he said . . . "Can't cope any longer". I'm the only breadwinner . . . If I got it through my hat, he'd have to go begging. No — I can't . . .*

He pauses, seems to be turning away, then turns to STACH once more.

JANEK: *But you don't think I'm just trying to get out of it?*

STACH: *There's no compulsion! You can join us if you want to. If don't — keep your mouth shut!*

JANEK leans over to STACH and lowers his voice.

JANEK: *No need to worry. I'm a communist, too.*

STACH glares reproachfully at JANEK.

STACH angrily: *You're a fool — not a communist. You'd better be careful what you're saying! A communist! Communists fight!*

With a final, fiery look at JANEK, he turns to go.
JANEK watches the departing STACH sadly. Fade out.

Fade in on a pair of horses drawing a cart. STACH, his back to us, is the driver, lashing the horses excitedly with a long whip. The cart clatters over the cobblestones and joyful music starts up. STACH turns round, grinning happily.

STACH : *Hup!*

A closer view of STACH standing up on the cart, a whip in his hand. An older man — the usual driver — dressed in a thick coat with a fur collar, and a fur hat, is sitting beside him. He grins at STACH, as the latter shouts encouragement to the horses.

STACH : *Get a move on, girls!*

STACH, seen once again from behind, urging the horses on.

STACH : *Hup!*

STACH in the foreground, smiling widely. The other driver, also grinning, is seen at the edge of the frame.

A longer view of the cart, with STACH in the background. They are approaching a viaduct.

STACH : *Hup! Hup!*

A general view of the cart as it moves towards the shadow of the viaduct.

STACH : *Come on, Blackie, hup!*

The exhilaration suddenly disappears from STACH's face. He pulls violently at the reins, trying to stop the cart.

STACH : *Prrrr . . .*

A VOICE off : *In die Reihe!*

A view of the cart : STACH tugs hard on the reins. Within a few steps, the horses are pulled back to a walking pace.

From under the shadow of the bridge a column of Jews comes out, guarded by armed Germans, some with tracker dogs. The Jews are carrying spades and pickaxes.

A VOICE : *Was ist los?*

The Jews walk by, pushed and jostled about by the Germans. In the background STACH's cart drives away in the opposite direction, STACH looking on grimly.

A VOICE : *Ich werde Dir den Arsch kaputt schlagen, blöde Sau.*

A pair of high wooden gates at the entrance to a wood yard are being opened. STACH's cart splashes through a pool in the gateway.

A VOICE : *The gate! Hup, hup!*

The German guard, a rifle slung over his shoulder, pushes the gate shut again. There are a couple of other Germans, some playfully throwing stones at a thawing snow man. There is a loud noise of a circular saw. STACH's cart is driven through the yard.

STACH : *Hup!*

STACH is handed a slip of paper by a uniformed attendant. In the far background open sheds in which planks of wood are piled up can be seen. JACEK appears from the background and approaches STACH, who is waiting for his cart to be loaded up. They light a cigarette, JACEK using the light from STACH's butt. They talk, but the noise of the saw drowns the dialogue. But suddenly it stops and JACEK's warning to STACH can be heard.

JACEK : *Take good care at the gate . . .*

A large sign, RAUCHEN VERBOTEN, is hanging behind them on one of the sheds.

Close shot of a diamond shaped hole in a wooden fence : the old sentry's face appears in it, a forage cap over it. The sentry is looking on suspiciously, one of his eyes opening wide.

The clatter of the cart can be heard close by.

DRIVER off : *The gate! Gate! Prrrr . . .*

We look away from the fence to a general view of the gateway. The cart comes along, with STACH driving again; the DRIVER is seated next to him. The OLD GUARD comes out and stops the cart. He comes up to STACH and takes some papers from his hands. He speaks in Polish.

OLD GUARD : *A check-up!*

He walks away round the cart and disappears.

DRIVER shouting down : *They've already checked in the yard! This is my fifth time round! You know me!*

The GUARD appears at the back of the loaded cart, counting planks.

OLD GUARD : *Don't try to teach me!*

STACH and the DRIVER are sitting on the cart, hands in pockets.

DRIVER : *Mister, I'm in a hurry! Time's money!*
STACH : *Geld!*

>The OLD GUARD appears from behind the cart. He comes close and points up at STACH, speaking now in German.

OLD GUARD : *Mensch . . . komm! Komm zum Kommandanten!*

>STACH, surprised, shows some reluctance in climbing down, and the German raises his voice angrily.

OLD GUARD : *Du! Komm! Komm!*

>At last STACH climbs down and the GUARD pushes him towards a narrow door at the side of the gate.

>Inside the office. A man — a worker — stands with his arms raised in the foreground, his face to the wall. He carries obvious signs of a beating. Another man, also with his arms raised, is standing in the background. Two Germans stand behind their backs : the big and heavily built COMMANDANT and another, younger officer. The COMMANDANT, turning round, barks a command in German.

COMMANDANT : *Rein! Gustav — Bunker!*

>The other German leads the two beaten-up men out of the room. At the same time another door opens and the GUARD enters with STACH. The GUARD pushes STACH towards the centre of the room.

OLD GUARD : *Der hat Bretter gestohlen . . .*
COMMANDANT : *Wieder ein Dieb! Lauter Banditen.*

>He approaches STACH, signalling at the same time to the GUARD to leave the room. STACH speaks in Polish, very loudly and distinctly, as if determined to make the German understand.

STACH : *I don't steal! The guard's wrong!*

>COMMANDANT's cutting answer comes in Polish, spoken with a perceptible accent.

COMMANDANT : *A German is wrong?*

>He raises a short cane he is holding in his right hand and lashes STACH across the face with it.

>A close shot of the COMMANDANT raising his cane again. Hitler's portrait can be seen hanging on the wall behind him. A close shot of STACH, one of his cheeks already marked with a weal. He raises his arm to protect himself with an elbow against more lashes, and backs away. At last he finds himself

with his back to the wall. The Commandant advances, his cane raised.

Commandant murmuring fiercely: *Du polnische Schwein . . .* He suddenly calls out: *Gustav!*

From the adjoining room comes the sound of German singing and noises of whipping.

A door is opened and we look through it as Gustav, the other German enters. He shoves Stach violently through the door, without a word being spoken.

Inside the guardroom. Stach flies in through the doorway and falls down, flat on his face. There is a number of merry German soldiers in the room, sitting around in their shirt-sleeves. A couple of them pull Stach to his feet and laughing loudly, start shoving him down the room from one to another. Finally Gustav kicks him violently out of the door in the foreground.

Stach falls to the ground outside the hut. He sits up and takes a look behind him, replacing the cap on his head at the same time. Tears — of humiliation perhaps more than actual pain — well up in his eyes and start flowing down his face. Fade out.

Fade in on a general view of a storeroom. Ziarno, accompanied by Berg I, is seen removing a lid from a concealed hiding place. A considerable number of guns are hidden there, their barrels gleaming sinisterly. Berg I is looking at the hoard despairingly.

Berg I: *Such a lot . . . Anyway . . .* Resignedly . . . *One or a hundred, it's all the same . . . I'm done for . . .*

He wipes his brow with a folded handkerchief.

Ziarno: *The fatherland . . . You agreed to take the risk. You know full well why. Anyway, it won't go off by itself. There's no danger.*

A sudden noise somewhere on the premises startles them and Stach's loud voice is heard.

Stach off: *Where's the boss?*

Hurriedly, Ziarno replaces the lid; Berg I steps off a platform on which he has been standing and turns around. Stach bursts angrily into the room and throws some tools on the floor. They land with a loud clatter.

STACH: *That's the last time I'm escorting one of your transports! I've had enough!*

A close shot of STACH in the foreground, BERG I approaching him, feeling nervously for his wallet in his breast pocket.

BERG I: *They beat you up? Who? One second . . . Bloody hell! . . . I'll compensate you in a second.*

He walks away. STACH turns to look after him.

STACH: *I'm not taking money for this!*

STACH walking out of the store-room, with ZIARNO behind him. STACH approaches JACEK and MUNDEK, who are standing in the foreground. All three of them walk away together. JANEK, walks in from the background, carrying a sack. He stops and starts tying up the neck of the sack, listening to the conversation carried on by his workmates.

MUNDEK off: *I wouldn't let him off. He did it to one of us!*

STACH, JACEK and MUNDEK are talking together.

JACEK: *And not only to him! I've seen other things there! He's a bastard!*

JANEK comes up from behind, takes hold of STACH's chin and examines the weal on his face.

JANEK: *So, they did you over?*

STACH jerks his head free.

STACH: *Feels a bit as if they did . . .*

JACEK: *It wasn't your nut, you can't really feel it.*

MUNDEK contemptuously: *He would have licked his lips and asked for more . . .*

JANEK wounded: *Eh! You . . . !*

STACH, the leader, turns sharply to admonish MUNDEK.

STACH: *Stop talking crap! Nobody's asking you!*

But when he turns to JANEK his mood is by no means friendly.

STACH: *We did have a talk some time ago, didn't we?*

JANEK: *That was a very long time ago . . .*

STACH: *So what?*

JANEK: *I'm not going to be such a swine as to look on calmly, doing nothing, while they're doing somebody over.*

JANEK glares at MUNDEK.

JANEK: *And I'll have a word with you some other time . . .*

STACH: *All right! All right! He goes to Auntie Walercia's. We'll get him there and disarm him.*

JANEK: *What with?*

STACH feels inside his clothing and brings out his pistol. JANEK takes it from him eagerly, and examines it.

STACH: *The catch's on. Stop tinkering with it, you don't know how to . . . not yet . . .*

He turns to the others, seeking their advice.

STACH: *Well? What about it?*

JACEK: *I'm for it! We can use another gun, and it'll put the wind up him.*

MUNDEK: *We'll stop his swank.*

JANEK is the first to move off.

JANEK cockily: *We'll see if I don't know how to . . .*

STACH follows him out of frame, then the remaining two boys go out.

Evening: in the gloom, the four youths led by JANEK, who is barely recognisable, climb over a fence, one by one. They stop and look towards the café.

The café is seen, fleetingly, from their point of view.

Back to the boys, standing by the fence. JANEK is still in a nervously cocky mood.

JANEK: *He's got it coming . . .*

STACH: *Wait here!*

He and JANEK go out of shot, leaving MUNDEK and JACEK behind. They look nervously around. The ticking of a clock is heard.

Inside the café: in the foreground the COMMANDANT is making up to the BARMAID. The door in the background opens and JANEK enters, followed by STACH, who closes the door after them. JANEK removes his hat as he walks towards the counter. The door bell rings again and two uniformed German railwaymen come in. JANEK and STACH stop at the counter not far from the COMMANDANT.

JANEK loudly: *Two beers!*

JANEK and STACH stand in the foreground. Further away, AUNTIE WALERCIA is quickly serving the two railwaymen.

WALERCIA: *Wieviel?*

GERMAN: *Genug?*

JANEK and STACH raise their glasses and start drinking.

A close shot of JANEK and STACH drinking.

GERMAN off : *Auf Wiedersehen, Tante!*
JANEK throws a quick glance over his glass at STACH.
In the background the two German railwaymen are leaving the café.
AUNTIE WALERCIA disappears.
Close shot of JANEK drinking his beer. His eyes flit from side to side.
The eyes of the negro-face dial of the wall clock move from side to side in time with the loud ticking.
JANEK looks tense over his beer.
JANEK and STACH at the counter : they both put down their empty glasses and turn round slowly.
The COMMANDANT is sitting in the foreground, his hand moving up the thigh of the BARMAID. She is smiling, looking down at the COMMANDANT's hand. JANEK and STACH move forward towards them, JANEK taking out his pistol.
STACH : *Hände hoch!*
The BARMAID, sitting on the table, looks round and screams. STACH moves up to take the startled German's gun. The BARMAID slides off the table.
JANEK looks round in panic, as the girl continues screaming.
JANEK points the pistol at the German and pulls the trigger. A shot rings out and the COMMANDANT throws his arms up, pitching face forward.
JANEK fires again. STACH watches at his side.
The COMMANDANT's head is slumped over the table. JANEK's hand holding the pointed pistol is in the foreground. Another shot is fired.
JANEK fires again. STACH is standing just behind him, the pistol taken from the German raised in his hand.
JANEK stops firing. STACH turns and runs for the door, but JANEK stands still, looking down towards the dead German who is out of sight, and laughing nervously. STACH, looking back from the door, turns round, runs back, grabs hold of JANEK's coat and hustles him towards the door.
A general view of the café : in the foreground lies the dead body of the COMMANDANT, his face down on the table, his peaked cap perched on his head at a crazy angle. In the background STACH shoves JANEK through the door and slams it

behind them. The door bell jingles. The ticking of the clock stops suddenly.

The four boys dash up a wooden staircase: JANEK leading, followed by STACH and the other two. JANEK stops and turns to face them, panting heavily. He raises a finger to his lips to hush them. They all stop and glance behind them, down the stairs.

JANEK to STACH: *Let them see it!*

STACH feels inside his jacket and pulls out the COMMANDANT'S pistol.

MUNDEK takes hold of it by the barrel and examines it excitedly.

The Luger is passed to JACEK and finally to JANEK.

JANEK, facing camera, swings the pistol, Wild West fashion, from hand to hand.

JANEK: *A clean job . . . Here he was . . . there she was . . . and I . . . bang . . . ! bang . . . ! And she . . . aaaah! And oops!*

With a hysterical edge in his voice he re-enacts the shooting, holding the pistol and imitating the girl's scream of panic. He repeats the same thing over again, seemingly unable to stop himself.

JANEK: *. . . And I . . . bang . . . ! bang . . . bang! aaah!*

STACH grabs the pistol from his hand.

STACH: *You bloody cowboy!*

He hides the Luger and moves off, followed by MUNDEK and JACEK. Camera pans away from JANEK to an opening door. OLD KRONE appears in it. He speaks with senile slowness.

OLD KRONE: *She screamed, you're saying? They always scream!*

He is seized by a fit of coughing, but continues.

OLD KRONE: *When I was in the Tsar's army . . .*

JANEK comes back into frame, and tries to hush the old man.

JANEK: *Be quiet, dad . . .*

OLD KRONE continuing: *. . . on the Manchurian frontier . . .*

JANEK: *Yes . . . yes.*

The old man turns back into the room, and JANEK follows. Fade out.

Fade in on a long view of a tree-lined country lane. It is obviously spring. From a deep background a bicycle

66

approaches, zig-zagging from side to side. It is ridden by STACH, with DOROTA, wearing a light summer dress, sitting in front of him on the crossbar. The singing of larks is heard. DOROTA is laughing happily as STACH tries to kiss the nape of her neck. STACH's voice is heard over the image.

STACH over: *Dorota . . . she supplied us with literature and with guns . . . She gave advice . . . My respect for her was clashing in my thoughts with a desire to stroke her hair . . . Her name was less and less frequently connected for me with her function of a political supervisor. I began thinking about her as simply . . . Dorota.*

Dissolve to a modestly furnished room. STACH is sitting in the foreground cleaning a pistol; DOROTA is moving around behind him, arranging flowers, packing leaflets. STACH's off-screen commentary continues over the opening part of the shot.

DOROTA: *Listen, it'll be curfew soon.*

STACH nods and puts his cap on, but is reluctant to move.

He looks at DOROTA without getting up, smiles and removes the cap again.

STACH: *There's still time, we can talk!*

Sitting down, she cups her chin in her hands, leans her elbows on the table and smiles across at him.

STACH and DOROTA face each other, smiling across a vase of flowers. DOROTA is the first to break the silence.

DOROTA: *Is it a night job?*

STACH: *Yes . . .*

Outside in the street there is a sound of footsteps and a male voice starts singing Schubert's *Serenade* in German. They listen for a while.

DOROTA: *Do you know what he is singing about?*

STACH: *No . . .*

DOROTA laughing: *About love . . .*

STACH: *Almost human . . .*

DOROTA laughs, looking straight into STACH's eyes, who finds it almost too much to bear.

STACH: *Eh! . . . I'd better go.*

But she leans towards him, still smiling.

DOROTA: *There's time. Let's talk. We never get the chance.*

STACH: *Dorota . . .*

The German singing and the sound of steps in the street stop.

DOROTA expectantly : *What . . . ?*

STACH gets up and grunts indecisively.

STACH : *Eh . . .*

A longer view of the room. STACH appears, seemingly moving towards the door. He stops and turns back.

STACH : *We've captured a gun.*

DOROTA approaches from the background, still smiling. She stops near him and leans against the door.

DOROTA : *That's great . . .*

STACH : *There was shooting. Janek's killed a Werkschutz.*

DOROTA sobers up at once. The smile disappears from her face. She looks up sharply.

DOROTA : *What?*

STACH : *In a café near us, in "Budy".*[1] *A German . . . A Volksdeutsch . . . He beat people.*

DOROTA sharply : *Did you give notice to anyone of this job?*

STACH : *No . . . That's why I came.*

---

[1] Literally "shacks", but here the word is applied to this particular area of Warsaw.

DOROTA : *High time ... !*

STACH : *There was no chance to talk to you ...*

DOROTA's intimate mood has now completely disappeared. She speaks cuttingly, in an authoritative tone.

DOROTA : *Have you gone mad? To do a job in your own area? Where they see you every day? It's irresponsible! It is against the basic rules of conspiracy!*

Her voice becomes a bit softer when she adds :

DOROTA : *It's curfew time. We'll talk later ...*

STACH turns for the door, glancing at her over his shoulder. Fade out.

Fade in on JANEK, MUNDEK and JACEK in the brick-kiln. They are crouching down in the brick tunnel, playing a card game. JANEK is again talking about the Auntie Walercia's café action.

JANEK : *And he called me a bloody cowboy ... ! You want to know how it really happened? He ordered him to put his hands up, and I was standing there with the Vis¹ ready.*

JANEK gestures excitedly with his right arm, which is actually holding the pistol.

JANEK : *Suddenly, the scream ... and it happened. Jerry was going all soft, like a sack of flour, like that ...*

JANEK throws himself down on his back, shrieking hysterically, his cries echoing in the kiln.

JANEK : *And here ... aaaah! Aaaah!*

The other two snigger, and MUNDEK screams suddenly, mocking JANEK.

MUNDEK : *Aaaaah! Aaaah!*

JANEK sits up, startled and offended. In the background STACH and DOROTA appear, STACH pushing a bicycle.

JANEK : *You're an idiot! What do you know?*

MUNDEK in reply screams again, laughing, and JANEK aims a blow at him.

STACH and DOROTA approach and stop, but their presence makes no apparent impression on the other three, until STACH shouts at them :

STACH : *Attention! Attention!*

¹ The VIS was an automatic pistol usually carried by officers in the pre-war Polish Army.

69

The boys rise, but don't really stand to attention.

STACH : *This is Dorota, the political officer for our area.*

He tries to sound formal, but makes no impression on the boys, who are looking over the girl keenly.

MUNDEK : *A she-political, you mean?*

The three of them laugh.

JACEK sitting down : *Not bad.*

STACH : *I said, attention! Stop talking!*

JACEK : *Stop that . . . You want to impress her, at our cost?*

STACH's assumed confidence evaporates at once. DOROTA is looking on sharply, without a hint of embarrassment.

STACH : *Well . . . at ease then . . . At ease!*

They all sit down, including DOROTA.

STACH, DOROTA and JANEK : DOROTA speaks, addressing herself principally to JANEK.

DOROTA : *We've heard of you a little bit. It seems you're good with guns? You've captured a pistol. Can I see it?*

JANEK hands it to her, butt first, but cannot resist an ironic comment.

JANEK : *Watch out, it's liable to go off.*

The other two laugh, but DOROTA looks up calmly, and then proceeds to dismantle the Luger speedily and with obvious expertise. She examines the parts.

Close up of the boys' heads looking on, obviously startled and impressed.

DOROTA glances down the barrel of the gun.

DOROTA : *As dirty as a smelly old sock.*

She assembles the pistol speedily and looks up at JANEK.

DOROTA : *One has to take care of one's gun. You know yourself how much it costs to get it.*

Close shot of MUNDEK, still speaking in a disparaging tone.

MUNDEK : *A five minute sweat and fast legs!*

DOROTA, framed by STACH and JANEK, checks the mechanism of the pistol.

DOROTA : *Our organisation is a combat group, not a gang of gun slingers.*

Having now finished with the gun and carried her point, she is speaking sharply, cuttingly. JANEK makes a grab for the gun, but STACH pulls it away from him.

STACH warningly : *Eh, mate!*

DOROTA : *. . . We are not concerned about the Jerries . . . We are concerned about you, we want you to retain your humanity through all this. You must control your nerves. And you have to get used to the idea that our guns are not private property!*

JANEK, seen in the foreground, looks round nervously.

JANEK blurting out violently : *What do you want of me, for Christ's sake! I hate all this! The Germans, the bloody war and all of you!*

He jumps to his feet and leaps a few steps away, towards the exit from the kiln. But he turns and shouts back.

JANEK : *I don't want to kill! And my guts turn inside me when I think of it!*

He starts off again towards a low brick arch, framing the exit. He stops and shouts back for a last time.

JANEK : *Up yours!*

DOROTA, STACH, JACEK and MUNDEK remain seated and silent for a few moments. A shadow appears on the wall of the kiln behind them, a sound of footsteps is heard and SEKULA approaches from the background.

71

SEKULA: *The ghetto rose to-day. I've come to say good-bye, to you, Dorota, and to my boys.*

He sits down with them, nearest to camera.

SEKULA: *Our Jewish comrades need help.*

SEKULA speaks very thoughtfully to STACH.

SEKULA: *Yes, Bartek, it's up to you to keep discipline. You must be ready for my call at any time.*

He pauses for a moment, pondering.

SEKULA: *You'll be needed, Well, see you, lads!*

He gets to his feet and moves away towards the kiln exit, with STACH and DOROTA following.[1]

A distant view of SEKULA walking out of the tunnel, his figure silhouetted against the far-off glow of a burning city — the Warsaw Ghetto, already enveloped in flames. He turns and waves.

SEKULA shouting: *Keep well, kids!*

Then he turns his back to us and starts walking away.

Dissolve to a view of the burning Ghetto: a large house, flames shooting out of all windows, a flag waving on top of it.

Another angle on the burning house, clouds of thick, black smoke billowing up.

A façade of the burning building, seen face on. Huge tongues of flame are shooting out of all the window apertures.

A more distant view of the building, surrounded by other burning houses; in the foreground, a spaced-out line of German soldiers.

Dissolve to the BERG workshop. STACH and JANEK are there. ZIARNO bursts in excitedly through the door.

ZIARNO shouting mockingly: *Gentlemen, gentlemen! Have you ever heard anything like it? The Jews have actually started fighting!*

[1] The kiln scene does not appear in the early versions of the script. Indeed, it does not fit into the original narrative, where the Auntie Walercia's Café job is carried out by Sekula and Janek, with the full support of the organisation, Stach staying out because of his obvious, personal motive for the killing. Stach's "baptism" comes later, in a scene cut out of the film, when he is asked to assist Sekula in the quiet execution of a traitor, and actually has to put a knife into the man.

STACH off : *Why do you have to be so stupid?*

ZIARNO aggressively : *What, what, what?*

A long view of ZIARNO running up angrily towards STACH, down a passage between the work-benches, other workers standing around.

ZIARNO : *What did you say, skunk?*

A worker wearing a cloth cap puts two fingers into his mouth and whistles piercingly.

STACH is obviously standing his ground. ZIARNO appears and STACH glares at him fiercely.

STACH : *See? It's not a matter for stupid jokes!*

GUBRECKI off : *Men are dying, Mr. Ziarno!*

A close up of GUBRECKI's grim face.

GUBRECKI : *When they've finished with the Ghetto, our turn'll come.*

STACH and ZIARNO : the latter's confidence is evaporating fast. A noise of machines starting up is heard. ZIARNO glances around and walks out of frame.

STACH and JANEK at the whetstone, sharpening chisels.

JANEK : *You shut him up nicely. What a pig, that Ziarno! A pig!*

They go on working, STACH glancing up gravely.

STACH : *Talking's not enough.*

He leans over towards JANEK.

STACH : *There's a job. To help the Ghetto. Coming with us?*

JANEK is silent for a second, before looking up at STACH, with a sorrowful expression.

JANEK : *Me? But you've taken my gun! I'm unarmed.*

He leans over the whetsone.

JANEK continuing : *I'm a nervous civilian! No, no, I can't do anything!*

Having finished the sharpening, he turns and walks away, into the background.

STACH watches him.

STACH calling out : *You, you . . . !*

Fade out.

Fade in on JANEK at home, working with a fret-saw on a piece of wood.

A general view of a crowd of kneeling women, chanting a

73

litany — a May evening service.

A close shot of a dark young man with a somewhat wild look about him. He glances through an iron gate and walks in, moving stealthily along a wall. He enters the courtyard where the May service is being held. The loud women's chanting continues.

The man — ABRAM — walks up a dark, dimly lit staircase.

ABRAM on a landing, knocking on a door.

Inside the room. JANEK turns from his work towards the door. A close-up of ABRAM's anxious face outside the door. He knocks again, glancing nervously around. He steps back as the door is opened narrowly by JANEK, who is obviously startled by the young man's presence.

JANEK : *Abram?*

He lets in the young Jew with some hesitation. ABRAM goes in, closing the door.

JANEK and ABRAM face each other uneasily. The litany can no longer be heard.

ABRAM : *The ghetto has risen . . .*

A rapid close-up of JANEK's anxious, staring face.

ABRAM's tense face, watching JANEK's response.

JANEK off : *You've come from there?*

ABRAM and JANEK talk together.

ABRAM : *I was going to be met here. But I got here several hours late.*

JANEK : *I see . . .*

ABRAM : *They didn't wait for me that long. I walk the streets and people stare . . .*

JANEK nodding : *That's right . . . Your looks, you know . . .*

ABRAM : *So I've come to our house . . . To you . . . But I see . . .*

Close shot of the two men : ABRAM seen in profile, JANEK facing us.

JANEK : *Well, yes . . . But what can I do?*

He moves away, as if to put more physical space between him and his Jewish friend. He stops by the window, and throws down his saw noisily, in a helpless gesture.

JANEK : *You see? I'm a civilian!*

ABRAM looks on silently.

JANEK turns around at the window, his face buried in his hands.

JANEK : *Well, what can I do?*

A close shot of ABRAM, watching.

JANEK : *It's your appearance . . .*

ABRAM lowers his eyes, turns and opens the door.

JANEK in the foreground, still standing by the window, his head bowed. In the background ABRAM is seen walking out silently.

OLD KRONE off : *You're right, keep out!*

OLD KRONE is in bed; he raises himself up on his elbow, with obvious difficulty.

OLD KRONE : *You're a carpenter now, not a hero!*

He is seized by a fit of coughing.

JANEK turns round suddenly and looks anxiously about the room.

JANEK : *Where's he gone?*

He runs across the room towards the opened door.

Out on the landing, JANEK looks both ways, and then darts down the staircase.

75

JANEK shouting: *Abram! Abram!*

He runs out into the courtyard.

JANEK is running along the wall towards the gate. He stops, gets hold of the iron bars and shakes the gate: it is locked now. JANEK steps back. There is a sound of footsteps and a German patrol walks by on the other side of the gate.

JANEK watches the Germans walk away.

In the distance, the shadowy figure of ABRAM is walking away along the pavement.

JANEK, seen through the iron bars of the gate, is still watching. He turns away from the gate.

In the distance, ABRAM can be seen walking away. Gates in the street are closing. German shouts ring out suddenly.

GERMAN VOICES: *Halt! Halt!*

Fade out.

Fade in on a general view of a fun fair. Two Germans are flying high on a swing to a background noise of children's joyful shouts. But the air is thick with grey smoke. STACH's voice comes in over, as we look to a standing group of youths: STACH, JACEK and MUNDEK are there, with JANEK some way from them, leaning against a fence in the foreground. There is a large, wheeling roundabout in the background and a church further away in the distance.

STACH'S VOICE: *Smoke from the burning Ghetto poisoned the city air. It hung as a heavy cloud over the fun fair, built by the Germans in the shadow of the Ghetto walls. Sekula's call reached us from somewhere in that flaming quarter. He asked for help. Unexpectedly Janek had turned up again. I couldn't make this boy out ...*

The three boys approach JANEK.

JANEK: *I'm coming ...*

STACH puzzled: *Well ...*

JANEK: *Why do you stare? I don't come, you stare, I come, you stare all the same! Make your bloody mind up!*

STACH: *I'm glad, mate, very glad!*

That point cleared, JACEK, standing at STACH's shoulder, asks:

JACEK: *How do we get a car?*

STACH: *Somehow, that doesn't worry me. Here's Kaczor ...*

KACZOR approaches, wearing a cap. Camera moves away as he joins the smiling group. They walk away towards the turning roundabout. A German soldier comes into frame with a girl.

GERMAN: *Meine Grossmama das ist ein Weib. Die sagt so: Ein Volk, ein Reich, ein Führer. Das ist doch unhörbar ...*

Fade out.

Fade in on the group of five youths standing together in a brilliantly sunny street. There is a parked truck in the fore-ground, its driver clearly asleep, his elbow sticking out of the open window and his head resting on it. KACZOR, a cigarette in his mouth, detaches himself from the others and moves up to the truck. He slides stealthily along its side towards the driver's cab. The other four boys also start off towards the truck. KACZOR throws his cigarette to the ground, takes out a gun and reaches towards the handle of the cab-door. At the same time the others scatter to take up positions round the truck.

The DRIVER's head is cradled in his arms. A pistol, held by KACZOR's hand, comes into shot and creeps towards the German's nose. It touches and tickles him. Reacting in his sleep as if to a pestering fly, he murmurs, without opening his eyes:

DRIVER: *Du hast schöne Beine ...*

KACZOR off: *Come on, move over!*

Prodded with the pistol, the DRIVER opens his eyes at last and finds himself staring straight into its barrel.

Terrified, the DRIVER moves over behind the wheel, KACZOR coming in to take his place. STACH sits on a wing, fending off curious children.

KACZOR starts the motor.

A general view of the street: the truck moves off. The youths climb hastily into the hooded rear part of the truck and start throwing out the contents: wooden cases full of live geese. The cases break as they hit the ground, and the geese flap about, hissing and shrieking. It is a joyful scene, the boys treating it almost in a fun-fair spirit. MUNDEK almost falls out with the geese, but JANEK grabs him and shoves him back into the truck. As the truck gathers speed and moves further away, the DRIVER is pushed out into the street, followed by more cases of geese, who fly up on hitting the ground, flapping and shrieking.

DRIVER shouting: *Hilfe! Hilfe!*

Inside the cab, looking over the bonnet of the truck: KACZOR is behind the driving wheel, with STACH beside him. STACH is grinning hugely, and playfully pulls KACZOR'S cap over his eyes. Joyful music comes in.

In the rear of the truck JANEK, MUNDEK and JACEK roll about, clearly in high spirits.

Back in the driving cab STACH is laughing at KACZOR, while the truck speeds on, bumping up and down.

A close shot, at the back of the truck. JANEK is humming a tune, JACEK and MUNDEK next to him. They are having a rough ride, and are being bounced from side to side.

JANEK: *A bloody bumpy ride!*

JACEK: *My guts are quite empty. That drop of water I drank to-day doesn't count, I hope. If you're hit on a full stomach you've had it.*

They all laugh at this.

A general view of a street, running along the high wall of the Ghetto. Thick smoke is hanging over distant buildings. The truck appears and approaches; JANEK and JACEK jump out of the back before it comes to a stop. When it does stop, STACH and MUNDEK jump out, hurry to the rear, take two crow-bars and walk hastily up to a manhole.

We are looking up a dark shaft, with just a rim of light showing at the top. The lid of the manhole is moved to one side, and the heads of STACH and MUNDEK appear, silhouetted against the sky. They peer in, and STACH whistles down.

STACH crouches down by the open manhole. He reaches down and fishes out a sub-machine-gun, putting it aside. A dark-haired young man appears, his clothes covered with slime, climbs out of the manhole, picks up the gun and moves on. He is followed by a girl, who almost has to be lifted out by STACH.

STACH: *Hurry, hurry up, comrades!*

JANEK posted as a look-out at the corner of the street, his hand resting on a lamp-post. There is a background of blasted, ruined houses, with rubble scattered over the pavements. JANEK turns round to look down the street.

STACH at the manhole, helping another man out. It is SEKULA, a bloody bandage across his forehead. He is obviously weak from his wound and cannot climb out of the hole unaided. JACEK comes over to help.

A long view of STACH and the Jewish girl fighter carrying the wounded SEKULA to a waiting truck. In the foreground JACEK is standing on a street corner, keeping a look-out.

A close shot of JANEK, looking out. Something alerts his attention, and he turns quickly. Steps on the pavement can be heard, and distant German voices.

GERMAN VOICES : *Drei mal drei is neun, sechs mal sechs ist sechsunddreissig.*

A long view of three patrolling German soldiers, walking up the street. They rhythmically repeat the same phrase all over again. There is a background of smoking buildings behind them.

JANEK watches tensely. Careful not to betray himself too soon,

79

he turns and starts walking away slowly, his back to us. Suddenly, he breaks into a sprint.

JANEK runs as fast as he can, towards JACEK hiding in a shadow. Further behind, the Germans disperse quickly, to take up positions.

A burst of shooting is heard. JANEK tucks himself in behind an electric transformer. JACEK is kneeling on the other side of it. He fires a burst, gets up and runs out of frame. JANEK stays put.

JACEK dashes across the street, under German fire, towards a corner where STACH is standing, a pistol in his hand. Bullets kick up dust around JACEK as he runs. JANEK can be seen in the background, still making no move.

Close shot of JANEK, hiding in the shadow of the transformer. The Germans shooting: one of them is crouching with his gun in the shadow of a wall. Other German soldiers appear on the scene, running up the street.

The Ghetto fighters, with SEKULA in the middle, fire from the back of the truck.

STACH, JACEK and MUNDEK stand round the street corner. KACZOR can be seen some way behind them. STACH stuffs a pistol in his pocket and takes out a hand grenade.

STACH : *Look out! Look out!*

JACEK and MUNDEK dash across the street, drawing more German fire. STACH, left alone, hurls a grenade down the street, towards the advancing Germans, and blocks his ears with his hands. JANEK, clearly visible in his white overcoat, is still in his place on the other side of the street. There is an explosion, and a cloud of smoke rises.

STACH removes his hands from his ears and peers round the corner.

JANEK glances round quickly.

STACH signals towards KACZOR.

STACH : *Off!*

The truck's engine starts up at once. STACH turns in the direction of JANEK, shouting at him.

STACH : *Under the wall! Run!*

A general view of the area: in the background the truck is moving off, picking up speed. In the middle STACH is making desperate signs to JANEK to clear off. JANEK, in the foreground, crosses himself.

JANEK : *In the name of the Father, and the Son, and the Holy Ghost ...*

STACH, across the street, urges him to move.

STACH : *Come on!*

But JANEK waves to STACH that he should not wait.

JANEK : *Go on! Go on!*

The truck has moved away and the sound of the engine fades out. STACH, hesitating momentarily, turns and disappears round the corner. JANEK, left on his own, glances around anxiously.

JANEK gets up and starts running along, crouched by the wall. As he moves into the open, there is a burst of machine-gun fire. JANEK changes direction suddenly and runs into an alley, in the opposite direction to STACH.

A GERMAN off : *Halt!*

The moving truck in the far background. A German soldier appears running in the foreground. He takes aim with his rifle, shoots in the direction of the truck, re-loads quickly and shoots again. Then he starts running after JANEK.

A general view of an empty market-place : JANEK appears in the background, out of an alleyway between some houses. He runs into the market-place, stops and takes cover behind a stack of wooden crates, filled with empty bottles. As he crouches behind them, there is another shot and a bullet whines by. JANEK feels inside his coat and takes out a pistol. There is another shot and JANEK backs out, accidentally knocking over another pile of crates with empty bottles. Camera pans with him as he turns and runs away down a narrow passage between more piles of crates and planks. Dogs start barking and a small white one runs after him, making for his legs and barking furiously. Three German soldiers appear, running in pursuit of JANEK.

A general view : JANEK runs in through a doorway from the street, pistol in hand. There is a man there, arranging religious paintings for sale. JANEK stops momentarily, hides his pistol inside his coat and, changing his pace, walks normally past the man, across the doorway.

81

A high angle view of an enclosed courtyard between high walls: JANEK is running across it, looking for a way out. In the end he makes straight for a high wall.

JANEK, taking hold of a piece of broken piping sticking down the wall, pulls himself up. As he reaches the top, a burst of fire hits the wall just below him. His peaked cap falls off his head and down to the ground.

JANEK appears silhouetted on top of the wall. A bird flies past. Another shot rings out, but he gets up and runs along the top of the wall. He jumps down, and stones are kicked up from the place he has jumped from by another burst of fire.

JANEK appears running from the back of a courtyard. He drops his pistol, and turns back to retrieve it.

JANEK runs down a wide passage towards an opened gate, a sunlit street visible behind it. German soldiers suddenly appear there, cutting off his retreat. JANEK stops, takes out a grenade and hurls it quickly at the Germans, flattening himself against a wall. As the explosion subsides, JANEK runs into a narrow doorway.

JANEK comes through a pair of swing doors into the entrance hall of a large apartment house from which a staircase leads up. He stops.

Glancing around, JANEK starts up the staircase, pistol in his hand. Down behind him, the swing doors open again and a German soldier appears. JANEK turns towards him and fires: the soldier falls heavily, obviously dead. JANEK starts running up again, while a second German comes in through the door. He glances down at his fallen comrade and, with his sub-machine-gun at the ready, starts climbing the stairs. Stopping for a moment, he fires a burst towards a landing above.

JANEK throws himself down on the upper landing. A long burst of shots hits the wall above him, picking out a line of holes in the plaster. Another burst strikes the side of the landing and the bannisters just below JANEK.

The German soldier raises his gun again and fires.

JANEK picks himself up, leans over the bannister, points his pistol down and fires.

A high angle shot, looking down the well of the stairs: the German soldier, hit by JANEK's shot, lets the gun drop out

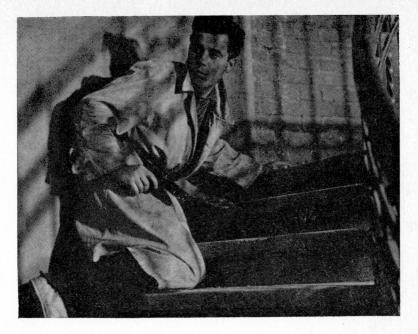

of his hands and slides down the stairs. His helmet drops
through the bannisters and down into the well, hitting the
bottom with a bang. More Germans appear there, their
helmeted faces looking up.

JANEK sets off up the stairs again, glancing down over the
bannisters as he goes.

A general view of the staircase from a high angle, looking
down into the well. JANEK, a couple of flights below, is seen
running up, with the Germans following lower down. JANEK
looks back without stopping and fires another shot.

JANEK flattens himself on the stairs as a burst of fire hits the
wall above him. He glances up at the bullet holes, gets to his
feet and runs up another couple of flights. He finds himself on
a landing at the very top of the staircase. He stops, looks down
over the bannister and fires another shot.

A closer view of JANEK at the top of the staircase : there is a
pair of wooden doors right behind him, probably leading to
a loft — the only apparent way of retreat. JANEK pulls the
door open while looking back over his shoulder, towards the

staircase. He turns, meaning to leap through the door — but his way is barred by an iron grill. Startled, he steps back, throwing a desperate glance over his shoulder.

A high angle view of the staircase, a number of German soldiers seen moving up, only a couple of flights away from the top landing.

JANEK turns back to the iron grill, secured by a hefty padlock. He takes hold of it.

JANEK's desperate face shows through iron bars. He jerks at the padlock, trying to break it, but it is obviously a hopeless task. He gives up, grasps his pistol and turns round.

JANEK stands at the top of the stairs, the iron grill behind him. He points his pistol down and shoots twice, in quick succession. He presses the trigger again, but the gun fails to fire. JANEK looks at it wretchedly, and tries again — the pistol is clearly empty.

A long, high angle view of a German soldier in a black uniform, pointing his pistol up. He fires.

JANEK is hit on the forearm. He stares at the spot, an expres-

sion of pained surprise on his face. A patch of blood is spreading over his sleeve.

Back to the high angle view of the staircase: the soldier in the black uniform is firing again. Another German runs in. JANEK glances over the bannister, his pistol lowered. Suddenly he raises it and hurls the gun down into the staircase.

We look down the staircase again as the pistol bounces down the stairs, making a metallic sound. The Germans, in a moment of panic, try to take cover.

JANEK shuts the door behind him, covering the iron bars, turns and starts to climb on to the bannister rail.

A low angle, longer view of JANEK on the bannister rail: he straightens up on the rail, balances for a moment, then raises his right hand. Slowly he lets himself topple, falling into the well inside the staircase.

JANEK'S body falls down the well of the staircase, hitting the ground with a thud. Helmeted German faces appear over the bannisters, looking down. Fade out.

Fade in on a store-room in the Berg workshop. ZIARNO, BERG I and a YOUNG MAN in jackboots are there. ZIARNO, nearest to the open cache of arms, is handing a sub-machine-gun to the YOUNG MAN, who hides it in a large sack. BERG I is standing behind them with an anxious face.

YOUNG MAN: *Is that all sergeant?*

ZIARNO kneels down and feels about inside the hide-out. The YOUNG MAN looks down at him.

ZIARNO: *It's empty . . .*

But he remains on his knees, still feeling about.

YOUNG MAN: *And the pistol . . . ?*

ZIARNO turns to a box beside him and feels inside it. He turns his face to the others.

ZIARNO: *Not there . . .*

YOUNG MAN: *Strange . . .*

ZIARNO jumps down from a pile of cases he has been standing on. He lands beside BERG I.

YOUNG MAN: *How can that have happened? It can't have evaporated? Perhaps one of you gentlemen has borrowed it? Who else knew of the hiding-place?*

ZIARNO : *With respect, sir, no one. But men come here for materials.*
YOUNG MAN : *Why do you let them in?*
ZIARNO : *The boss wanted to avoid suspicion . . .*
YOUNG MAN sharply : *Stop talking rot, sergeant! You're aware of the responsibility! There have been cases of members selling arms belonging to the organisation.*

ZIARNO takes a step towards him.
ZIARNO : *There are communists in the workshop . . .*
YOUNG MAN : *We'll discuss this in the office, sergeant! Better clear up this mess!*

He lifts up the rucksack containing the guns and puts it down beside him. Reaching up, he pulls down his jacket and starts putting it on.
YOUNG MAN : *Communists, my foot!*

STACH is approaching the glass-panelled entrance-door of the workshop. The store-room door, set at right angles to the main entrance, opens, and BERG I followed by the YOUNG MAN and ZIARNO appear. Noticing them, STACH stops at the swing door, watching, while ZIARNO turns to lock the door behind him. STACH pushes the door and walks in, at the same time removing his jacket. As they pass each other, ZIARNO watches him closely, suspiciously.

JACEK and MUNDEK: they are joined by STACH.

STACH: *What about Janek?*

JACEK: *He's not come back . . .*

MUNDEK: *Gave himself up, most probably, and now he's talking.*

STACH: *This is bad!*

JACEK: *Better clear out, mate.*

ZIARNO off: *Glue!*

MUNDEK throws his arms wide in desperation and runs off. JACEK also walks away. STACH turns to get his things, preparing to leave, when MUNDEK re-appears.

MUNDEK: *If anything happens here, I'll let you know.*

He dashes off.

STACH takes his box off a shelf. He starts packing his tools.

GUBRECKI comes and stops by him.

GUBRECKI: *Found a private job to do in the city? Do you need a partner?*

STACH, not answering straight away, hurriedly closes the box and starts walking away.

STACH over his shoulder: *Eeeh . . . ! Don't you know the way it is?*

Another worker, ZELAZOWSKI comes in, wiping his hands. GUBRECKI lays a hand on his arm.

GUBRECKI: *There's something the matter with the boy, something a bit queer. Politics, Mr. Zelazowski. They start them early, these days!*

The two men move off together. STACH with his box starts walking towards the door.

Walking out of the door STACH almost bumps into ZIARNO, who stops.

ZIARNO: *Where are you off to?*

STACH pushing on: *My mother's ill.*

ZIARNO calling after him: *What's this for? Are you going to plane off her hump?*

He walks on, but a startling thought suddenly occurs to him. He stops and glances after STACH.

A general view of a street. STACH is walking along it, carrying his box. DOROTA, on a bicycle, rides towards him from the deep background. She approaches him, stops and dismounts. They shake hands, turn and walk towards camera.

DOROTA : *I'm glad you're here. Janek's dead.*

STACH stops and looks at her.

STACH : *Jesus . . .*

For a moment they look at each other silently. STACH turns to glance up the street.

DOROTA : *Let's go . . .*

She turns away with her bicycle, followed, a few paces behind, by STACH.

Inside the living room of STACH's humble home : a search is being conducted. ZIARNO is messing about inside a large chest; the YOUNG MAN in jackboots is standing by, watching. STACH's MOTHER, highly indignant, is trying to tidy up at the same time. She is holding a dress.

MOTHER : *What do you want of him? Bothering people in their own home, carrying on like this!*

ZIARNO throws a cushion back on a chair and looks around inquisitively.

MOTHER replaces some clothing in the cupboard and slams the door shut.

MOTHER : *Haven't we got enough with the Germans, without our own people picking on one another? Why should this be going on?*

ZIARNO kicks over a chair irritably, but the YOUNG MAN steps up to it and picks it up. ZIARNO walks up to the window and looks out.

A view from the window, with ZIARNO in the foreground, looking at STACH outside, approaching the house. ZIARNO lifts his finger to his lips for silence. STACH is seen opening the outside door and going in. As he is about to enter the room, the YOUNG MAN opens the door from inside, hiding himself behind it. STACH walks in, stops, surprised, and looks around. He notices the YOUNG MAN standing behind the door, leaning casually against it.

STACH : *What's all this? What do you want here?*

ZIARNO and STACH are in the foreground of the room and MOTHER, her arms folded, in the background. ZIARNO glares across at STACH.

88

ZIARNO : *You know damn well. Stop playing the fool.*

MOTHER : *They've barged in and turned everything upside down. Who are they? Germans, or what? The police? Or rats looking for Jews to sell? I don't know who they are. In these times there's plenty of dirt of all sorts.*

STACH gestures towards ZIARNO, by way of introduction.

STACH : *That's Ziarno, from our workshop.*

ZIARNO : *Mister Ziarno!*

STACH : *Mister Ziarno. I don't know the other one.*

YOUNG MAN off : *We are soldiers of the Polish Underground Army.*

He reappears and turns to STACH.

YOUNG MAN : *And you'd better tell me, my friend, where you've put the pistol you stole.*

MOTHER : *What pistol?*

YOUNG MAN : *Have you sold it?*

MOTHER : *What do you want of him? Stach!!!*

She shouts at the son in exasperation, and the YOUNG MAN stretches out a restraining hand towards her.

The MOTHER is standing in the foreground, her back to us. STACH is facing her, flanked by the YOUNG MAN and ZIARNO.

STACH : *I don't know what they want of me. A man has to earn every penny, working hard, eating rationed bread, and even at home they won't leave him alone. Go on, fight Germans. What do you want here?*

Still speaking, he moves forward, past his MOTHER, and stops, facing us. He removes his cap and, out of view of the others, pulls the pistol from inside his belt and wraps it in the cap.

ZIARNO : *You went to the storeroom?*

STACH his back to them : *When I was asked to.*

ZIARNO : *Well?*

STACH is now standing almost back to back with his MOTHER. He turns his head and speaks over his shoulder.

STACH : *So what? All sorts of people used to go there. You've spent hours there.*

ZIARNO off : *Better tell the truth! Have you sold it?*

STACH : *Who, me? Some people trade in guns. I'd never do that!*

Close shot of ZIARNO's grim face. He addresses the YOUNG MAN.

ZIARNO : *He's well in with the communists. He used to be pally with Sekula . . .*

Back to STACH and MOTHER.

ZIARNO continuing off : *. . . When he worked at our place!*

STACH : *I keep in with those who are kind to me. You've never spoken a civil word! Now you've lost something and you want to take it out on me! Look for a sucker somewhere else, that's all I can say!*

The YOUNG MAN is still standing by the door.

YOUNG MAN menacingly : *Look here — friend!*

The door suddenly opens, knocking against the YOUNG MAN slightly, and a middle-aged woman bursts in. She starts speaking quickly, almost before she is in.

FRANUSIOWA : *Antoniowa,[1] lend me some wood . . .*

She stops, noticing the strangers, and grins amiably.

FRANUSIOWA : *Sorry! Wrong time for it . . .*

STACH off : *Mrs. Franusiowa! Call your hubby and a couple of others. These ruffians are bothering us here!*

Franusiowa turns at once.

FRANUSIOWA : *I'm off!*

The YOUNG MAN tries to grab her, but she evades him and runs out. Immediately her voice is heard shouting outside.

FRANUSIOWA off : *Franek! Franek!*

The YOUNG MAN closes the door and takes out a huge pistol. ZIARNO moves over to his side. Outside more voices are heard.

A WOMAN off : *Kazio, get to it! Antoniowa's in trouble!*

A general view of the shacks — the "Budy". The poor community wakes up at once to FRANUSIOWA's shouts. KAZIO — a huge man with an impressive belly — removes a child from his knees, gets up and picks up a piece of piping from the roof of his shack. Other people start rushing about, disapearing and reappearing. Voices rise.

WOMAN'S VOICE : *Men! Here! Come here! Bandits!*

Inside STACH's house : the YOUNG MAN and ZIARNO are standing side by side. The YOUNG MAN, pistol in hand, is looking anxiously towards the window; ZIARNO gazes up at his superior. STACH's taunting voice can be heard.

---

[1] Antoniowa — the wife of Anthony, Franusiowa — the wife of Frank; not common usage, but perhaps usual among the Warsaw working class of the time.

STACH off : *Well? Are you going to start shooting? Just try it. You won't come out alive! Down here we don't frighten easily.*

The YOUNG MAN puts his pistol away, opens the door and walks out quickly, followed by ZIARNO.

STACH and his MOTHER look at each other silently, relieved. But as STACH opens the cap he has been holding in his hand, and takes out his pistol, MOTHER gives out a little shriek of horror and puts up her hands to her face.

MOTHER : *Jesus!*

STACH is standing at the window, watching what is going on outside. A sizeable crowd has gathered outside their house. They stand their ground as ZIARNO and the YOUNG MAN come out of the shack, forcing the two men to push their way through them.

The YOUNG MAN, obviously shaken, and ZIARNO push their way through a hostile crowd. They emerge from the crowd and lengthen their stride. The neighbours, led by the big KAZIO, follow them for a bit, some shaking fists or shouting abuse.

Some way out of the area : the YOUNG MAN and ZIARNO

appear and stop. The YOUNG MAN hides his pistol and speaks to ZIARNO, glancing at him venomously.

YOUNG MAN : *Well, Mr. Ziarno! You've had it, as far as I'm concerned.*

They move off, going away over a field. Fade out.

Fade in on DOROTA at the window of her room, with STACH sitting in the background.

STACH : *I'm in trouble now, hopelessly. Ziarno's going to watch me.*

He walks up to DOROTA and stands by her.

STACH : *They know where I live.*

DOROTA : *You can't imperil other people — that's a fact. You must go underground. You'll get false papers and move.*

STACH : *Where to?*

DOROTA : *What about here, for the moment?*

She turns to face him, but after a second looks away.

DOROTA : *Comrades tell me that after the recent arrests I ought to move too, but I'll wait for a bit.*

STACH walks back and sits on a chair in the background.

DOROTA : *I've grown used to this little place.*

She turns and smiles at STACH.

DOROTA : *Listen, Stach.*

STACH sits on his chair in the foreground. DOROTA picks up another chair and sits close to him.

STACH looks on, his face breaking into a slight smile.

DOROTA off : *We meet to-morrow, at the brick-yard.*

DOROTA brings her face close to STACH, raises her finger and speaks smilingly, in a low, confidential voice.

DOROTA : *This is the sign. The password: "Do you sell feathers?" "Yes, I do sell feathers". You'll meet new members, take over as a platoon leader.*

STACH looks at DOROTA, genuinely startled by the promotion.

STACH : *Is it true? Dorota ...*

DOROTA is smiling, yet pensive.

DOROTA : *You're a strange one. Comrades say you're brave, and yet you're such a child.*

She laughs, affectionately.

STACH looks very earnest.

STACH : *I'm not brave? I get frightened, very frightened. When I*

92

*stop to think that I might also get a bullet before the end. And
never live to see it happen . . . and because, should I get killed, I'd
never see you again.*

Their faces are very close to each other. DOROTA smiles and
strokes STACH's hair.

DOROTA : *A big job awaits us. And each holiday'll be like a fairground. Bright lights and music, and dancing all the way!*

She laughs, and lays his head on her shoulder, like a child's.

DOROTA : *Perhaps, this is only our imagination? Perhaps it is easier
to die for the cause than to live for it?*

Raising his head, STACH takes DOROTA in his arms. He lays
her across his lap and they kiss. At last DOROTA breaks the
embrace and gets up, smiling down at him.

STACH : *Dorota . . .*

DOROTA : *My name is Eve . . .*

STACH remains in the foreground, while DOROTA walks towards
a mirror behind them. She adjusts her hair, turns back and
returns to STACH.

STACH : *Bloody hell . . . it's worth fighting for . . . worth living.*

He puts his cap on and wheels around from her, laughing.
The clock strikes just then. The smile fades from STACH's face
but he repeats :

STACH : *It's worth living . . .*

DOROTA, standing behind him, removes the cap from his
head. STACH's smile returns, becoming even more radiant.

DOROTA : *It's curfew . . . You can't go out into the street . . .*

STACH turns towards her and they kiss again. Fade out.

Fade in on a little courtyard, looking up the staircase leading
to DOROTA's apartment. STACH appears on the staircase,
walking down stealthily in his stockinged feet, his shoes in
his hands. At the foot of the stairs he stops, sits down on the
last step and puts his shoes on. This done, he tiptoes on, past
the caretaker's door. As he passes it, the caretaker, carrying a
broom, comes out and glances first at STACH and then up at
the staircase.

The interior of a small delicatessen shop : a blonde woman,
her back to us, is opening the entrance door. She stands back
to allow STACH to enter. He comes in looking very happy,

93

and greets her brightly.

STACH: *Good morning!*

BLONDE WOMAN: *It is good, isn't it? I can see that! You're an early bird! What can I do for you?*

She smiles, obviously attracted to STACH and pulls her gown tightly around her breasts. STACH glances around the shelves, uncertain what to ask for, but keen to get something that would give pleasure to DOROTA. A crying child is heard in the adjoining room.

STACH: *Let me have . . . a rye cookie . . .*

She goes behind the counter to get the loaf, shouting at the same time towards the other room.

BLONDE WOMAN: *Maniek, belt up, or else . . . ! God, the milk!*

She runs away and disappears for a moment. Left alone, STACH takes some marmalade on his finger out of a jar on the counter and tastes it. The woman returns and looks confidingly at STACH.

BLONDE WOMAN: *Hell of a life!*

A car passes somewhere outside. STACH points at the jar.

STACH: *Let me have a quarter of a kilo!*

The woman returns behind the counter.

BLONDE WOMAN: *Pleasure. It's all because my man's been run in. Business affairs, you know. He wasn't careful. You understand? You know the way it is nowadays. Now I haven't got enough to buy him out. They are all leeches — the police. Here you are.*

She passes the goods to him and calculates the total price on a piece of paper. Raising her eyes she gives him a meaningful glance and sighs.

BLONDE WOMAN: *It's no life without a man!*

STACH, hardly listening, gives her a banknote in payment, and then makes a cavalier gesture, as if he had decided to stake everything.

STACH: *Let me have that sunflower head!*

BLONDE WOMAN: *Pleasure.*

STACH pays up and turns to go out.

STACH, his back to us, walks in through the doorway of DOROTA'S apartment house. The CARETAKER is looking out through a window of his lodge. Noticing STACH, he starts beckoning furiously to him. As STACH comes closer, the CARE-

94

TAKER opens his door.

CARETAKER whispering: *Young man! Gestapo!*

STACH stops and looks at him, and the CARETAKER grabs him and pulls him into his lodge.

Inside DOROTA's room, DOROTA is standing, erect and proud, surrounded by Germans: three in Gestapo uniforms and a civilian, standing by an unmade bed. The officer barks a short order and they lead DOROTA to the door.

The Germans, escorting DOROTA, come down the staircase: the civilian walking ahead, the uniformed men closing her retreat. At the foot of the stairs she glances quickly aside, then walks on calmly.

STACH's desperate face appears at the window of the CARE-TAKER's lodge.

The Germans lead DOROTA down a shadowy, covered passage. They are silhouetted against the light coming in from the street, where a car is parked. DOROTA climbs into the car, followed by the Germans. The car moves off. Fade out.

Fade in on STACH sitting on a stone in the foreground in a reflective posture, his fist under his chin. Behind him is the kiln-works, with the brick chimney sticking out. A short, stocky youth appears in the distance and approaches STACH across the field, watching him expectantly. Closing in, he peers at STACH from behind and finally leans towards him.

YOUTH : *Do you sell feathers?*

STACH half turns towards him and answers without changing his position, slowly and with a hint of irony.

STACH : *Yes, I do sell . . . feathers.*

The YOUTH turns back, whistles piercingly and waves his arm. Only then STACH turns to look at him.

A group of youths appears in the background : three on foot and one on a bicycle with a girl in front of him, holding a bunch of flowers.

STACH turns his head quickly away from the approaching group. Tears run from his eyes and down his cheeks. He brings up his hand to brush them away and looks back again.

The youths approach and stop. The girl with the flowers

jumps off the bicycle. The first, stocky youth walks back to them, taking hold of the bicycle from the girl. The sun shines bright on their faces as they wait, expectantly. Fade out.

CREDITS:

Director	Andrzej Wajda
Screenplay	Jerzy Stefan Stawinski, adapted from his own short story of the same title
Produced by	Film Authors' Unit KADR for FILM POLSKI
Assistants to the director	Kazimierz Kutz, Janusz Morgenstern, Maria Atarzenska, Anna Janeczkowa
Photography	Jerzy Lipman
Camera	Jerzy Wojcik
Assisted by	Andrzej Gronau, Czeslaw Grabowski
Art direction	Roman Mann
Assisted by	Halina Krzyzanowska, Roman Wolyniec
Interiors	L. Mokicz
Wardrobe	J. Szeski
Music	Jan Krenz
Sound	Jozef Bartczak
Assisted by	R. Branski, J. Dabrowski, A. Okapiec
Editing	Halina Nawrocka, A. Rut
Make-up	Halina Sienska, H. Turant
Production manager	Stanislaw Adler
Floor managers	T. Bierczynski, Z. Brejtkopf, A. Orlowski
Shot in	Lodz Feature Film Studio, 1956

CAST:

Stokrotka	Teresa Izewska
Korab	Tadeusz Janczar
Zadra	Wienczyslaw Glinski
Madry	Emil Karewicz
Musician	Wladyslaw Szeybal
Smukly	Stanislaw Mikulski
Halinka	Teresa Berezowska

KANAL

An aerial view of war-shattered Warsaw. Burnt-out shells of buildings, some still smoking. The opening credits appear over this image.

Dissolve into a closer view of the ruins, a river in the background. The title KANAL fades in, followed by the credits. Dissolve to a more distant view of the war-ruined city, credit titles continuing.

Dissolve to a closer view of burnt-out buildings. Continuation of the credits.

Shells of ruined houses, gaunt against the dark sky. The screenplay credit.

Dissolve to terraces of apartment houses, all gutted, smoke and flames still shooting out in places. The music credits.

A couple of helmeted German soldiers, carrying a flame-thrower, move among the ruins.

Dissolve to a view of a rubble-strewn street, lined by gutted apartment houses. Two German soldiers walk swiftly down the street, tongues of flame shooting spasmodically out of their flame throwers. Camera credits.

The façade of one of the apartment houses suddenly collapses. A cloud of dust rises and rubble spills out on to the street. The director's credit.

Another row of burnt-out, windowless houses, black rings around the window apertures. The final production credit.

Fronts of a couple of buildings collapse suddenly, as if dynamited. In the background a cloud of thick black smoke rises up into the sky.

A closer shot of the house caving in.

Ruins: the sky behind them darkened by a rising cloud of black smoke. In the foreground some barbed wire entanglements, smashed brick walls, broken pieces of furniture and shattered glass. Immediately behind rises the hump of a small hill. A number of human figures appear from behind it, silhouetted against the bright horizon, some carrying guns.

COMMENTATOR off : *Late September of 1944. The Warsaw Rising nears its tragic finale.*

More armed men come over the hill.

COMMENTATOR continuing off : *The Old Town, Riverside, Czerniakow and Sadyba fell long ago. The City Centre, Zoliborz and Mokotow,[1] cut off and surrounded by superior German forces, are in flames.*

The men, coming down the hill, approach the barbed wire and rubble in the foreground.

COMMENTATOR continuing off : *This company now numbers forty-three men. Three days ago there were seventy.*

The men reach the wire and the rubble, but continue walking alongside a fairly high brick wall, providing shelter from the enemy fire. A Home Army emblem — a stylised representation of an anchor — is whitewashed on it. An officer in a worn battledress is walking ahead of the rest.

COMMENTATOR continuing off : *Lieutenant Zadra,[2] their Commanding Officer. He recruited these men and is responsible for them. And that's his second-in-command, Lieutenant Madry.[3] He drilled his boys with an iron hand.*

ZADRA, a rather thick-set man of middle height, with a forage-cap pushed to the back of his head, walks past. He is followed by a bigger man carrying a sub-machine gun. Some soldiers walk past in double file, and then a very young girl, slim and dark, with the face of a Renaissance Madonna. Closely-cropped hair and a tight-fitting uniform make her look a bit like a graceful boy.

COMMENTATOR continuing off : *Halinka, the messenger girl. Leaving home, she solemnly promised her mother to keep herself warm. Probably the others have made similar promises. All mothers are the same.*

A rather stocky man in a light shirt, wearing a beret, walks past the camera.

COMMENTATOR continuing off : *Sergeant-major Kula[4] writes in a perfect hand. Carries all the company records in his document-case.*

---

[1] Zoliborz is in the north of Warsaw, Mokotow in the south.
[2] All the soldiers' names are Resistance pseudonyms. "Zadra" means "splinter".
[3] "Madry" means "wise".
[4] "Kula" means "bullet".

A young man, looking very neat in his uniform, walks past the camera.

COMMENTATOR continuing off : *Officer-cadet Korab[1] pines for his daily bath. But the boys of the Third Platoon have bigger troubles.*
A tall, blond young man wearing a corporal's insignia on his dark uniform goes by.

COMMENTATOR continuing off : *Smukly,[2] Korab's aide. He dreams of building aeroplanes when the war's over.*
Most of the detachment has now gone past. Among the miscellaneous rubble, a black wing of a pianoforte comes into frame. The last man in the file is a civilian, unarmed, with a long face and staring eyes. He is walking, apparently unconcerned and oblivious to danger.

COMMENTATOR continuing off : *Lastly, the artist. He's not a soldier. He turned up only yesterday.*
Two men carrying an ammunition box go past. The COMPOSER, following, stumbles over some rubble and has to quicken his step to catch up. The column ahead of him comes to a halt.

COMMENTATOR continuing off : *These are the tragic heroes. Watch them closely in the remaining hours of their life.*
A part of the column, led by KORAB, starts advancing slowly again along the wall. A wide breach in the wall comes into view. There is a sudden burst of machine-gun fire. The men stop and crouch down. The firing seems to draw closer. Only the COMPOSER stumbles on, his shoes in his hand, his jacket thrown over his shoulder, unconcerned or perhaps too weary to care. At last he stops by a group of crouching men. The firing continues. A few of the men run quickly forward, taking cover behind the brick wall. They stop at the edge of the breach. Suddenly, one by one, they dart forward, across the open ground, where they are met by a loud burst of machine-gun fire; a hail of bullets kicks up dust around them. Having crossed the open ground, the men jump, one by one, into a trench, which gives them cover. They move away, to emerge finally in a barricaded street, bordered by a few ruined houses.

---

[1] "Korab" signifies heraldic arms, shared by several old landed families.
[2] "Smukly" means "slim one".

They reform ranks at a distance and move away in a loose column formation.[1]

The heads of the men in the column can be seen moving along behind a mound of rubble. ZADRA is the first to emerge onto the open ground in front of the burnt-out shells of houses. In the foreground there is a cross on an obviously fresh grave. A LIEUTENANT with a bandaged head is standing in front of it. He takes out of his pocket a Cross of Valour and hangs it on the wooden arm of the cross. ZADRA approaches and the LIEUTENANT turns to face him.

ZADRA : *Hello!*

LIEUTENANT : *Hello, Zadra! Dead on time!*

ZADRA stops right in front of the LIEUTENANT.

ZADRA : *What's that? You've been hit?*

LIEUTENANT : *Just caught the draught.*

ZADRA looking around : *What's the position?*

LIEUTENANT gazing into the distance : *You can see. The Stukas were here. Germans tried to push three times. Lucky, they sleep at night. You are not going to have an easy life tomorrow.*

ZADRA : *An easy death, more likely. Never mind, we'll try to stay for a while.*

LIEUTENANT : *I wish I could stay.*

ZADRA offers the LIEUTENANT a cigarette.

ZADRA : *Till the Last Judgement?*

LIEUTENANT : *But we'll be hailed by posterity.* He pauses momentarily. *They won't take us alive.*

ZADRA strikes a match rather nervously. The LIEUTENANT looks up at him.

ZADRA : *That's right, the Polish way!*

LIEUTENANT : *What's wrong, you've always been so steady.*

ZADRA : *I've had enough, do you understand? What am I to tell my men? They trust me!*

LIEUTENANT takes a long draw on his cigarette.

LIEUTENANT : *You're losing your nerve. You won't have time to brood here. Bartek has almost abandoned the advance positions today. As if there was anywhere to bolt to, the shit-pants.*

He looks around.

---

[1] This entire introductory scene is shot in one continuous take.

ZADRA: *It's getting very tight.*

LIEUTENANT: *They're anxious to finish off Mokotow and concentrate on the City Centre. Damn it, to think we are in the fifty-sixth day of the Rising. It's hell.*

ZADRA: *Hmm. That's always open for us.*[1]

We see the rest of the group again. HALINKA is being embraced by a blonde girl; SMUKLY, festooned with bandoliers, is walking slowly away from the others. He approaches a group of wounded men, sitting or lying on the ground. He stops and looks down smilingly. The voices of HALINKA and the other girl are heard off.

HALINKA off: *Bozena!*

BOZENA off: *Halinka!*

HALINKA off: *Bozena, what news?*

SMUKLY: *We've met, remember? You gave them to me on the first day of the Rising.*

He points at the boots he is wearing.

A young woman is lying motionless on a stretcher on the ground. SMUKLY's boot is visible in the corner of the frame. Her eyes move up and she smiles gently.

GIRL: *Do they fit?*

SMUKLY off: *Don't they?*

SMUKLY looks down smilingly. The COMPOSER comes up from behind and stops at his shoulder.

SMUKLY cheerfully: *To think they might pull it off my corpse. But I see that you have joined the Rising.*

The GIRL listens, calm and motionless.

SMUKLY off: *What does your mother say to that?*

She pauses before replying, and turns her head slightly to one side.

GIRL: *She's dead.*

The COMPOSER in the foreground, his back to us, is looking down at the girl. SMUKLY's legs are visible by the stretcher.

SMUKLY: *Is the wound bad?*

GIRL shaking her head: *Nothing much.*

SMUKLY: *A pity you already . . .*

The stretcher is lifted up, though we don't actually see the

---

[1] In the screenplay the scene ends with the arrival of a boy-messenger with news that ZADRA's wife has given birth to a son.

bearers. A blanket covering the GIRL slips off, revealing that her right leg has been amputated at the knee; the stump is heavily bandaged. SMUKLY breaks off in mid-sentence, and both he and the COMPOSER stand and look as the stretcher is borne away. The COMPOSER moves away and SMUKLY remains, staring with a grave face after the GIRL.

Two soldiers are laying out a cable in the rubble. They are approached by the COMPOSER.

COMPOSER: *Excuse me. Is there a telephone around here?*

SOLDIER: *There will be.*

COMPOSER: *Can I phone Rakowiecka Street?*

SOLDIER: *Are you mad? Germans are there.*

COMPOSER: *I know . . . but . . . my home is there . . . Please let me phone, won't you?*

SOLDIER: *Ask the Commander.*

COMPOSER: *There?*

The COMPOSER turns and moves away. SMUKLY joins him and they walk off together.

Looking through the door of a house on to the rubble outside. Men are moving along a path there. A number of them pass through the doorway, followed by SMUKLY and the COMPOSER. SMUKLY, impressed, whistles.

SMUKLY: *Some people used to live in style in Warsaw.*

COMPOSER: *A middle-class, bourgeois drawing-room. Monstrous!*

They move across the room, which is furnished with the trappings of bourgeois comfort: panelled walls, a chandelier of wrought iron, heavy curtains and wide windows. Several men are sitting on chairs and armchairs, or lying around on the carpets. ZADRA approaches with MADRY from the opposite side of the room, wiping the back of his neck rather nervously with a folded handkerchief.

ZADRA: *With small arms and hand-grenades against tanks and planes. We'll never learn.*

MADRY: *Orders are orders. Stop rationalising.*

He sticks a cigarette in his mouth.

ZADRA shouting: *Korab!*

KORAB appears in the frame and stands stiffly to attention.

KORAB: *Yes.*

ZADRA: *Post sentries and send a patrol out.*

104

Korab : *Right, lieutenant!*

He clicks his heels, then turns and looks around the room.

Korab : *Six volunteers come forward!*

Soldier I : *Yes sir!*

Boy Soldier : *Yes sir!*

They spring to attention in front of Madry and Korab. Korab pushes the boy gently away.

Korab : *I'll have a special assignment for you.*

He goes out, his arms around the two soldiers.

The Composer wanders in. Madry stops him, taking his arm.

Madry : *Wait! You're a composer?*

Composer : *Yes.*

But he wants to go on, and tries to free himself from Madry's firm grip.

Madry : *Come on, play something decent, there's a piano.*

Composer : *But I . . .*

Madry : *Come on.*

Composer looking towards the grand piano : *Christ, a Bechstein!*

He walks swiftly over to the grand piano in the corner of the room : there is a machine-gun on top of it. He runs his fingers over the keyboard, stops, sits down and removes a boot.

Composer : *Take that foul thing off. It rattles too much.*

A soldier on the opposite side of the piano removes the gun. Madry has come to stand nearby. The Composer plays the opening chords of Chopin's *Revolutionary Study,* but it fails to impress Madry.

Madry : *You know, La Comparsita! It's much better.*

The Composer groans painfully but complies and starts playing an old tango tune. Madry walks away from the piano, nodding his head in time to the music.

The Composer, momentarily absorbed in his piano, suddenly looks up with a blank look and stops playing.

Madry is drawing reflectively on his cigarette.

In another part of the room Halinka sits down, smiling with relief, and removes her cap. She is joined by a young, dark-haired soldier, who sits down behind her, leaning slightly over her shoulder. He is holding an ocarina in his hand.

Soldier : *I dreamt of you today, Halinka.*

Halinka looks round briefly, then turns her head and stares

straight ahead.

SOLDIER: *We were dancing a tango, and . . .*

She gets up and leaves him, obviously intending a brush-off.
MADRY smoking his cigarette, deep in some disturbing thought.
HALINKA comes into the shot and smiles up at him.

MADRY: *Well? What's new, Halinka?*

HALINKA: *You promised me a gun, lieutenant. I don't want to be
left unarmed. They all have something . . .*

MADRY nods and fishes out of his breast pocket a small, toy-
like automatic pistol. HALINKA looks at it rather contemptuously.

HALINKA: *It's so small, I was hoping for a Luger.*

MADRY, looking down at her, roars with laughter.

MADRY: *A Luger? You'd strain yourself. This number six is just
right for you. It'll kill a man at six feet. Take it.*

HALINKA walks away, MADRY gazing after her. He turns his
head to look towards the COMPOSER, who has been providing
background music with snatches of Chopin, finally breaking
into his own improvisations.

MADRY: *Stop that row. Play something with a bit of feeling.*

HALINKA resumes her seat near the young SOLDIER with an
ocarina. She is holding the pistol with both hands. Off-screen,
the COMPOSER continues drumming the piano, taking no
notice of MADRY's request. The SOLDIER grins amiably at the
girl.

SOLDIER: *I could get you a real gun, not that cap pistol.*

HALINKA maliciously: *A cap pistol? And why do you keep your
antique?*

She gestures at the SOLDIER's old-fashioned gun.

The COMPOSER is still at the piano, improvising.

KORAB briefs two young soldiers for patrol duty.

KORAB: *Everything clear?*

SOLDIERS: *Yes, sir!*

KORAB: *Don't take risks.*

KORAB, a sub-machine-gun slung over his shoulder, is seeing
them out of the door. He closes the door after them, walks back
into the room, stops and leans against the wall, listening.

MADRY leaning against the piano; the COMPOSER at the keyboard behind him. KORAB, coming over, stops on the opposite

106

side of the piano. Suddenly the COMPOSER stops playing and looks up as though something has caught his attention. He bends down, puts his boots back on, rises from the piano stool and walks across the room, staring fixedly straight ahead.

ZADRA is standing by the window, consulting a small notebook. A field telephone is silhouetted against the window. The COMPOSER appears and stops. He speaks anxiously.

COMPOSER : *Lieutenant, can I telephone my flat, my home, in Rakowiecka? My family may be there.*

ZADRA puts his notebook away in an inside pocket and listens.

COMPOSER : *Can I use this telephone?*

There is a sound of a loud explosion somewhere outside, and ZADRA glances briefly through the window. The COMPOSER continues.

COMPOSER : *Just ask the exchange to put me through to 4-0-2-1-8.*

ZADRA agrees readily and picks up the receiver.

ZADRA : *All right, let's check what's going on there.* Speaking into the receiver. *Zadra here. How are you? Still surviving.*

A VOICE in the receiver : *No window panes.*

ZADRA : *No window panes? I forgot what they look like. You're lucky to have a roof. Listen, can you try number 4-0-2-1-8?*

He looks at the COMPOSER for confirmation.

A VOICE in the receiver : *Our side?*

ZADRA : *No, German. Rakowiecka.*

A VOICE in the receiver : *There's no one there.*

ZADRA : *That's what we want to find out.*

A VOICE in the receiver : *I'll try.*

ZADRA : *All right, I'll hold on.*

ZADRA turns to the COMPOSER and hands him the receiver.

ZADRA : *They're saying there's no one there.*

A woman's voice comes over in the receiver. The camera moves in, eliminating ZADRA from view.

WANDA off : *Hallo?*

COMPOSER : *Wanda? Wanda? Wanda? It's me . . . Michal . . .*

WANDA off : *Michal . . .*

COMPOSER : *Are you safe? I've been trying to find you . . .*

WANDA off : *Where are you ringing from?*

COMPOSER : *From the Resistance. I got attached to one party . . .*

WANDA off : *Is there still a Resistance?*
COMPOSER : *I don't know by what miracle, but there is. What about you?*
WANDA off : *They are in our house.*
COMPOSER : *Deporting?*
WANDA off : *Don't think so. Rounding up into cellars and burning. I'm glad you've left, Michal.*
COMPOSER : *Wanda, my God!*
WANDA off : *Here is the little one.*
COMPOSER moved : *Zosia. Zosia. Zosienka.[1] It's me, it's your daddy.*

A child's high-pitched voice comes from the receiver.
ZOSIA off : *Daddy, come back soon. Why do they . . . keep . . .*
COMPOSER : *Zosia . . .*
ZOSIA off : *. . . shooting?*
COMPOSER : *Zosia! Zosia! Zosia!*
WANDA off : *They're coming, Michal!*
COMPOSER : *Wanda! Hallo! Wanda! Wanda! Wand . . . Hallo.*
He rattles the telephone rest anxiously, then turns to look desperately towards ZADRA.
COMPOSER : *Jesus, Holy Mother! They're cut off.*
ZADRA looks up grimly from his position by the window. He rises, without a word.
ZADRA crosses the room to meet KORAB, walking towards him.
KORAB : *All sentries posted, sir!*
ZADRA : *Thank you . . . Smukly!*
ZADRA walks away, and a messenger boy, ZEFIR,[2] runs up to KORAB.
ZEFIR : *What do I do now?*
KORAB : *Get some sleep.*
ZEFIR : *Come on . . .*
KORAB pushes the boy off, then follows him.
VOICE off : *Get ready for supper!*
MADRY is standing in the middle of the room, looking around, his thumbs in his belt.
MADRY : *Halinka, let's find somewhere to sleep.*

---

[1] Diminutive forms of Zofia (Sophia).
[2] "Zefir" means "zephyr".

HALINKA walks past him and MADRY, placing his hand on her shoulder, goes out with her. Fade out.

Fade in. Dawn. An aggressively heavy silence. We are looking across a rubble-strewn stretch of ground with a deep trench running towards the house in the background. On a mound a wooden cross sticks up at a crazy angle. The ground is littered with pieces of paper stirred by a breeze. The lonely figure of ZADRA is standing in front of the fortified brick building, gazing out, a pair of field glasses slung around his neck, a coat draped over his shoulders. He stands almost motionless for quite a long time. Sergeant KULA climbs up towards him from the direction of the house. He salutes the officer breathlessly.

KULA anxiously: *Lieutenant! Lieutenant sir! I haven't got the records of Korab's platoon.*

ZADRA rather irritably: *Stop bothering me with your records. It's going to start soon.*

KULA: *But we must keep records, sir. There'll be men killed.*

ZADRA: *Of course there'll be men killed. Stop bothering me now.*

> KORAB, stripped to the waist, is walking across the waste ground towards a hand pump. He works the handle up and down, trying to draw some water into a cup. He raises his head towards the house.

KORAB shouting: *Smukly, can you see anything?*

> SMUKLY leans out from behind some sandbags in the upper window embrasure of the gutted building.

SMUKLY: *Nothing. Potato-diggers have only just come off the field.*

> KORAB, still pumping, draws some water. He speaks, half to himself.

KORAB: *Devil knows if they'll live to eat them.*

> He stops pumping and, holding the cup gently so as not to spill any of the water, walks away from the pump, crouching. ZADRA is still in the same spot, when KORAB approaches him and stops. Following ZADRA's gaze he looks up at the sky.

KORAB: *I hope the Stukas won't come, or this wreck'll really fall apart.*

ZADRA: *Are you ready, Korab?*

> KORAB signifies with a nod and a grunt that he is.

ZADRA: *They'll surely start before eight.*

KORAB : *Just let me shave. I've got ten ammunition belts.*

ZADRA looks away from KORAB.

ZADRA suddenly : *How old are you, Korab?*

KORAB : *Twenty-three.*

ZADRA smiling : *At this age, life doesn't seem all that precious.* He becomes serious. *You know these are the last days?*

KORAB moving on : *I know. But we'll make them bleed first.*

He walks away down the path leading to the house.

ZADRA off : *Is Stokrotka[1] back?*

Inside the house : the COMPOSER is sitting rather restlessly in an armchair, looking through a portfolio of Botticelli reproductions. KORAB approaches, still carrying his precious water. The COMPOSER gets up.

KORAB : *What's wrong?*

COMPOSER sharply : *Nothing.*

He picks up some hand grenades rather carelessly, hooking them up to his belt.

KORAB : *Do you know how to handle that? Careful!*

COMPOSER : *Are you mad? It's dead easy.*

KORAB : *Just be careful.*

COMPOSER : *I'm off. The Germans'll soon finish their breakfast.*

The COMPOSER walks towards the door while KORAB, standing by the piano, leans over the keyboard and strikes a few chords. On the first note the COMPOSER turns sharply in the doorway.

COMPOSER : *What are you playing?*

He walks back and takes over from KORAB, but after a few notes slams the cover down angrily.

COMPOSER : *Out of tune! Too many musicians here.*

But he starts playing again.

The COMPOSER at the keyboard, KORAB watching him. The COMPOSER closes the piano once again and touches a hand grenade.

COMPOSER : *I'm going.*

KORAB, in a friendly gesture, lays a hand on his arm.

KORAB : *Just don't get silly. It would be a pity to lose an artist.*

COMPOSER : *What do you know about that?*

He turns and walks away. KORAB picks up his cup left on the piano and goes through another doorway in the corner of the

---

[1] "Stokrotka" means "daisy".

room. We see him mounting the first few steps of a staircase. KORAB at the top of the staircase.

A small bare room with a boarded-up window: MADRY and HALINKA are in bed together, MADRY with a cigarette in his mouth. KORAB opens the door and sticks his head in. They both spring to a half-sitting position, HALINKA pulling the bed-clothes up to her neck.

KORAB: *Oh! Sorry!*

He means to withdraw, but MADRY grins at him.

MADRY shouting: *It's all right . . . well, come in . . . Come! What is it?*

KORAB, looking down at them, becomes suddenly angry.

KORAB: *Better get up! It's hardly time for this!*

MADRY off: *Is that the way to speak to your superior?*

MADRY embraces HALINKA, pulling her closer.

MADRY: *This is just the right time. We're in love.*

KORAB withdraws, closing the door behind him. He crosses a landing, opens another door and enters a room. MADRY's booming voice reaches him.

MADRY off: *And how's Stokrotka?*

Inside the room, KORAB wets his face using a shaving brush, prepares his razor and starts shaving in front of a large wall mirror. The door behind him opens and a big, pretty, blonde girl comes in. Her reflection appears in KORAB's mirror.

STOKROTKA: *Here I am, Jacek.*

She comes up close to KORAB who continues shaving, pretending unconcern.

STOKROTKA: *I hope I don't stink. I left my shoes outside.*

KORAB: *Time you'd stopped loitering in those sewers. Anyway, you were supposed to come back yesterday.*

STOKROTKA stands right behind KORAB, smiling knowingly. She nuzzles against the nape of his neck.

STOKROTKA: *Worried about me?*

KORAB: *I stopped worrying long ago. But Zadra was asking about you.*

STOKROTA: *Jealous?*

KORAB is still shaving, taking great care over it.

KORAB: *Me? What else! But you won't spare anyone.*

STOKROTKA faking innocence: *I do nothing bad. I just give Zadra*

111

a smile, like anyone else.

KORAB turns his head slightly.

KORAB : *It looked as if you had a soft spot for him.*

STOKROTKA : *That's the way I am. Can't be helped.*

KORAB moves out of her way, and STOKROTKA, now facing the mirror, produces a stick of lipstick and moves it along her lips with obvious coquetry.

KORAB : *Too bad! You should have stayed in the City Centre. You've got all those . . . friends there. We're finished here.*

STOKROTKA : *I know.*

She moves out of shot, while KORAB comes back to the mirror and recommences shaving. She returns, coming up behind him again, and holds out some packages towards him.

STOKROTKA : *Look what I've brought you. Genuine English tea and cigarettes.*

KORAB takes one look at the packets, and turns back to the mirror.

KORAB : *You know I don't smoke. Where did this stuff come from?*

Moving closer, STOKROTKA adopts a childish manner.

STOKROTKA : *My auntie!*

KORAB : *Some auntie . . .*

She touches his shoulders caressingly.

STOKROTKA : *Jacek, I came back only for you.*

KORAB : *For me? That's interesting. And why?*

STOKROTKA brushes her lips against KORAB's smooth cheek. He turns his face slightly.

STOKROTKA : *Why? . . . Because I'm your messenger.*

She lets go of him and moves away, but her reflection remains in the mirror. She now speaks in a changed, serious tone.

STOKROTKA : *You know that the main attack is going through here?*

KORAB just smiles and continues shaving.

STOKROTKA : *Why don't you stop this shaving!*

He turns round suddenly.

KORAB : *You'd better get washed! You stink!*

He moves away and STOKROTKA comes closer to the mirror, now reflecting her full face. KORAB is also seen in the reflection, in the rear of the room, watching her. Making up her mind suddenly, STOKROTKA unbuttons her blouse and removes it. She is wearing a black slip underneath. KORAB, reflected in

112

the mirror, comes up from the back of the room and takes hold of her naked shoulders.

KORAB : *Sunbathing in the nude?*

Her voice becomes heavy with excitement.

STOKROTKA : *I've spent the whole of July in Zalesie, and on the first of August got back to Warsaw — God knows what for . . .*[1]

KORAB draws her firmly towards him, but MADRY's loud, jocular voice outside interrupts him.

MADRY off : *Did you stay with your auntie in Zalesie, too?*

KORAB pauses only briefly, smiles, then returns to his embrace. He slides the straps of her slip off STOKROTKA's shoulders. Suddenly, there is a whining noise of flying shells and a loud explosion. A shower of plaster falls on the couple from the ceiling.

KORAB : *We're off!*

He lets go of STOKROTKA and dashes across the room, grabbing his sub-machine-gun on his way. Just as he opens the door there is another loud explosion, and plaster showers on the landing.

Outside the house, a group of men are running from the house along the trench in the middle of the waste ground. Explosions throw up mushrooms of earth around them. Discordant music adds to the clamour.

Men carrying sub-machine-guns are running up a staircase in the fortified brick building. The force of the explosions shakes the building time after time.

KORAB is helping another soldier to mount a heavy machine-gun at one of the embrasures.

Looking down at the series of explosions on the open ground outside. KORAB takes aim with the machine-gun. Suddenly STOKROTKA's head appears beside him. He turns to her angrily.

KORAB : *Go away! Get out of here, damn it!*

STOKROTKA : *Don't be an idiot!*

KORAB gives up and fires a burst with the gun.

The defenders' point of view : a cloud of smoke rises, obscuring the ground outside.

---

[1] The Warsaw Rising began on that date.

113

MADRY, in another embrasure, is gazing out through a pair of field-glasses.

Another view of the approaches. Explosions and thick smoke everywhere. But a single, gaunt tree is still somehow surviving the blasting on the centre of the stretch of waste land.

MADRY's embrasure. A huge explosion, and a shower of plaster falls on MADRY and another soldier. They duck, covering their heads with their hands. As the smoke clears slightly, MADRY puts the field-glasses to his eyes again.

MADRY encouraging the soldiers : *Go on!*

The soldier beside him takes aim with his machine-gun.

MADRY : *The left machine-gun lower!*

Another explosion scatters dust and rubble over a wide stretch of waste ground.

ZADRA, standing in front of a low wall of sandbags, scans the field through his glasses.

A shell breaks a tree in two.

ZADRA, looking anxious, is moving around. A helmeted soldier mounts a bazooka on the sandbags and places a shell in it. SMUKLY with a machine-gun takes up a position beside him, with the COMPOSER on the other side of the soldier. Another screaming shell comes over.

ZADRA : *Look out! Take cover!*

There is a deafening explosion somewhere behind them.

ZADRA, inside the house, is trying desperately to get through on the field telephone.

ZADRA : *Hallo! Hallo, Bartek! Hallo, Bartek! Damn it. Both the phones are dead. They'll take us from the rear. Zefir!*

ZEFIR : *Yes, sir!*

ZADRA : *Zefir, run along to the headquarters, report that we are holding the Red House, but the Germans have broken through Bartek's section. We need a counter attack, or they'll cut us off. Be off.*

ZADRA : *Got it?*

ZEFIR : *Sure.*

ZADRA : *Run along.*

The waste land is still torn by explosions. In the smoke a number of crouched figures — German soldiers — are seen moving towards the house. They are followed by the lumbering mass of a tank.

In the bazooka embrasure, SMUKLY, the COMPOSER and the SOLDIER have been joined by ZADRA.

The tank is now clearly visible, moving down a hillside. There is a sudden flash as its gun is fired.

In the embrasure, the SOLDIER fires the bazooka.

SOLDIER shouting desperately: *Scrap-iron! Stupid load of piping!*

ZADRA takes over the bazooka, flanked by SMUKLY and the COMPOSER.

ZADRA anxiously: *They'll do us in ten minutes. Withdraw.*

SMUKLY and the COMPOSER turn and look at ZADRA, who seems on the verge of cracking up.

ZADRA: *We can't stop them with our fists. Enough, damn it!*

SMUKLY gets up quickly, takes the bazooka from ZADRA and starts loading a shell into it.

SMUKLY is silhouetted against the bright sky as he rams the shell home. The COMPOSER stands, curiously detached, just behind him.

SOLDIER off: *That's the last shell, Smukly.*

SMUKLY mounts the bazooka on the sand bags and takes aim. Seen from the outside, SMUKLY swivels the bazooka round while ZADRA and the COMPOSER watch. There is a loud bang and a flash from the bazooka.

Almost simultaneously the advancing German tank swerves off course and suddenly explodes.

Back in the house there are cheers and laughter from the men around the bazooka.

VOICES: *Men, Smukly's got him! Bravo! Bravo!*

But ZADRA's face remains grim. He is listening to the din outside, to which a new note, almost like animal howling, is added.

ZADRA: *Goliaths.*

The cheers fade out. The group falls silent and draws back slightly.

Two small, tracked vehicles, apparently unmanned, advance towards the house, dragging thick cables after them through the waste ground.

KORAB lowers his machine-gun. STOKROTKA and a soldier near him look suddenly quite desperate.

115

In the other embrasure the Composer and other soldiers draw back behind the sandbags. But Zadra remains standing, with a hopeless, desperate expression on his face.

The Goliaths,[1] their engines clattering, come up quickly over the waste ground. One of them changes direction, heading straight for the house.

Korab, watched by Stokrotka, starts hastily pulling on a pair of gloves. Turning round, he picks up a short shovel.

Outside, men are fleeing the house, running down the trench towards the other building. Zadra, Smukly and the Composer are among them.

They emerge in front of the other fortified building. One soldier stops, turns round and fires a short burst. Behind, the white-shirted Korab is seen jumping from a first-floor window to the ground. Shovel in hand, he dashes across to the trench. Behind him, there are two massive explosions, and a cloud of dust obscures the view. Shovel raised, Korab advances down

---

[1] Electrically-driven, remote-controlled track vehicles, joined to a mother tank by a thick cable.

the trench.

Emerging out of the trench, KORAB throws himself to the ground. A burst of machine-gun fire, obviously directed at him, kicks up the dust. KORAB lies still as the small vehicle comes up closer and closer, seemingly heading straight at him. It rumbles past him, the caterpillar tracks missing him by inches. The cable is dragged through the rubble behind the midget tank. KORAB grabs it firmly, allowing the vehicle to pull him along for a bit. He raises the shovel and hacks at the cable again and again. It resists, but finally KORAB succeeds in severing it, and the engine cuts out at once.

KORAB lies grinning on his back, the end of the cable in his hand. He casts the cable away after a second, but before he can start back there is a burst of fire and blots of blood appear on the shoulder of KORAB's shirt. He looks at the spot with an expression of surprise on his face, turns round and starts crawling back.

MADRY, gun in hand, runs crouching along the trench. He clambers out and looks round.

KORAB is crawling over rubble towards the trench: the knocked-out Goliath tank is in the foreground. He turns over onto his back and grins again looking at the vehicle. MADRY springs up and runs, crouching, towards him. He reaches KORAB, pulls the wounded man onto his broad shoulders, and, stumbling, carries him down into the trench. Once there, KORAB slides off MADRY's back.

KORAB in an apparently normal voice: *Stop it, I'm all right.*

He takes a few steps by himself, but suddenly his knees buckle and he falls flat on his back. MADRY picks him up again and carries him in his arms, like a child.

MADRY, carrying his burden, staggers in through the rubble. STOKROTKA[1] rushes out to meet them. There is another deafening explosion somewhere behind. STOKROTKA helps MADRY and they carry KORAB together to a sheltered spot behind the wall of the building. Once there, KORAB stirs again.

STOKROTKA: *Keep still.*

---

[1] In the original screenplay it is Stokrotka, not Madry, who saves Korab.

HALINKA rushes in to meet MADRY, and leads him away.

HALINKA : *You're not hurt? I'm glad you're all right.*

The COMPOSER joins KORAB and STOKROTKA, bringing water and wound dressings. He pulls KORAB's shirt open and applies the dressing. The wounded man gasps with pain and sinks back against STOKROTKA.

KORAB : *What's happening here? Where are my men?*

ZADRA and MADRY are looking over the top of the embrasure wall. ZADRA passes his field-glasses to his deputy, who gazes out while he drums his fingers nervously on top of the sand-bags.

ZADRA : *What are the Jerries waiting for?*

Looking along the trench : the recently-vacated house is now enveloped in flames.

Back with ZADRA and MADRY — still gazing through the field-glasses.

ZADRA : *Is Zefir back?*

MADRY : *No.*

He hands the glasses back to ZADRA.

MADRY: *We're surrounded.*

ZADRA glances nervously at him.

ZADRA: *How's Korab?*

MADRY: *He'll survive.*

ZADRA raises the glasses to his eyes again.

ZADRA: *They've wasted my men!*

MADRY: *It's no time to get sentimental.*

A helmeted soldier, stripped to the waist, is waiting tensely behind a heavy machine-gun. Another, right behind him, fits cartridges into a machine-gun belt. Down below, other soldiers lie about, reading, preparing food or just resting. ZADRA is standing by a shattered brick wall, on the other side of the dugout. Some way above him SMUKLY'S position can be seen through a hole in the wall. There is a strange calm and silence.

SMUKLY: *This silence makes my ears ring.*

ZADRA: *Only a short lull.*

SMUKLY: *They're scheming how to finish us off. No good from the front, so they'll try the kitchen door.*

He leans out through a hole in the wall towards ZADRA.

SMUKLY: *It's a good time to withdraw, lieutenant, sir.*

He offers a cigarette from a packet. ZADRA takes one and places it between his lips.

SMUKLY: *You didn't smoke before. Nerves?*

He also takes a cigarette and strikes a match.

ZADRA: *Fear. It's eating through us.*

SMUKLY dragging on his cigarette: *Not me. I've smoked since I was a kid.*

A different group of soldiers lying around, most of them wounded. KORAB is there, tended by STOKROTKA. KULA is also at his side, half-turned away, a pen and notebook in his hands.

KULA: *When did you join the Resistance?*

STOKROTKA wipes KORAB'S brow with a handkerchief.

KORAB wearily: *July 1941.*

KULA: *Decorations?*

KORAB: *Cross of Valour for the Blank's Palace . . . ah . . .*

He speaks with difficulty, groaning with pain and stammering.

KORAB : ... *Blank's Palace action ...*

KULA glances at the wound and writes something down.

KULA speaking to himself : *Wounded in the right ... yes, in the right chest, twenty-sixth September, 1944 ... Next of kin?*

KORAB looks up at him and says nothing.

KULA after a pause : *Thank you.*

He notes down something and gets up. STOKROTKA, bending forward, wipes KORAB's lips and helps him to get down to a reclining position. Throughout this scene there is a musical background of a Home Army song, played on an ocarina.

ZADRA and SMUKLY together; ZADRA takes a quick drag on his cigarette and looks up anxiously. The rumble of approaching aircraft becomes audible.

ZADRA : *They've found a way.*

The sound of the aircraft passes overhead and seems to recede, then comes closer again.

SMUKLY : *I've changed my mind. I don't want to build planes after the war.*

MADRY off : *Zadra! Zadra! Zabawa[1] is looking for you. Something's happened.*

ZADRA climbs down and walks across the room, past MADRY. He climbs down over girders as ZEFIR, the boy messenger appears, leading a balding, older man through a doorway in the wall. ZADRA salutes the man and reports.

ZADRA : *Sir! The company in the Red House!*

They shake hands.

ZABAWA : *Hello, Zadra!*

ZADRA : *Take off, Zefir.*

The boy goes out.

ZABAWA : *Your losses?*

ZADRA : *Twelve dead, ten critically wounded.*

ZABAWA gravely : *You will leave this house at dusk. We're crossing to the City Centre.*

ZADRA astonished : *What? How? Which way?*

ZABAWA : *Through the sewers.*

ZADRA : *I'm not going.*

ZABAWA : *Are you mad? There are only a couple of streets left.*

---

[1] "Zabawa" means "game", "fun", or "play".

They'll finish us off to-morrow.

    ZADRA bites his lip and speaks with nervous resolve.

ZADRA : *I'm not going. All that blood spilled and we crawl away, like rats. How can I face them?*

    ZABAWA looks grimly at ZADRA who turns his face away.

    A view from the window, over the waste land.

ZABAWA off : *That's an order, Zadra.*

    ZADRA turns round furiously.

ZADRA : *Sod your orders!*

ZABAWA off : *You're a damned civilian, after all. Don't you want to rescue your men?*

    ZADRA looks down, then raises his head but looks away, smiling bitterly.

ZADRA : *They believed me . . .*

ZABAWA : *We all did.*

    He moves closer, feels inside his pocket and produces a crumpled piece of paper.

ZABAWA : *Here's your pass to the sewers. Take care, Zadra!*

    ZADRA looks on silently as the Commandant takes his leave.

A room with resting, weary soldiers; HALINKA is sitting close to one soldier. The COMPOSER picks himself up wearily and pushes his hair back. The man with an ocarina enters the room. He looks round and grins.

SOLDIER calling out : *Gentlemen, why so glum? For God's sake!*

MADRY : *Why don't you play us a tune?*

The SOLDIER takes an ocarina out of his pocket and starts playing a cheerful Home Army tune. The COMPOSER, standing by an organ and playing with the stops, looks round irritably.

COMPOSER : *Stop it! Don't! Stop it!*

The SOLDIER somewhat offended, stops playing.

SOLDIER : *You want me to perform a symphony? You do it.*

He hands the ocarina to the COMPOSER who looks it over, laughing to himself.

COMPOSER : *On this?*

But he tries a few notes, before returning the instrument to the SOLDIER who turns and walks out.

SOLDIER murmuring : *The know-alls.*

The COMPOSER starts playing with the organ again.

ZADRA, clutching the pass for the sewers, enters the room, passing MADRY and a couple of soldiers on his way. He makes an effort to sound cheerful.

ZADRA : *Well, children, good news.*

He folds the paper and tucks it in his breast pocket.

SMUKLY looks down excitedly through the hole in the wall.

SMUKLY : *What is it, Lieutenant, reinforcements?*

ZADRA glances around, buttoning the flap of his breast pocket. He seems to be gathering courage.

ZADRA : *We are crossing to the City Centre. Through the sewers.*

The men around look blankly at him. The SOLDIER with an ocarina addresses himself to ZADRA.

SOLDIER unbelievingly : *What? Leave here?*

ZADRA'S eyes are cast down. SMUKLY is visible in the gap in the wall, just above and behind ZADRA.

ZADRA : *We can't hold Mokotow. There are only a few streets left. They'd crush us.*

SMUKLY jumps down from his hole, holding his gun, and

124

appears beside ZADRA.

SMUKLY : *There you are, boys. So that's why we've been messing around in this coffin.*

He throws his gun on the floor where it lands with a clatter. The assembled company look on in silence. Somewhere in the background the COMPOSER at last produces some soft notes out of the organ. ZADRA looks around at them, very uneasy. Finally he turns and walks back towards the doorway. He pauses there, glancing back.

ZADRA : *It's an order, from headquarters.*

He goes out.

The COMPOSER, seated at the keyboard of the organ. He plays a few notes on it, quite loud, listening carefully. He stops, as if in disgust at himself.

COMPOSER : *Nothing. A void. All I do is make up hollow sounds, even now.*

MADRY off : *Then don't.*

HALINKA off : *Stop drinking, enough.*

The COMPOSER plays a few more notes, stops and leans his elbows on the keyboard. He looks despairingly away.

COMPOSER : *I'm impotent, do you understand? A pitiful hireling.*

He now plays a few more notes from Bach : the angle of view opens and we see HALINKA and MADRY with a bottle of vodka, in front of the organ.

COMPOSER : *This is a real tragedy.*

HALINKA : *Please don't drink . . .*

But MADRY, the bottle at his lips, gulps another large measure of the vodka. The COMPOSER stops playing.

COMPOSER : *I'm glad this misery is ending.*

HALINKA : *Give it to me. I want some.*

MADRY gets up, holding the bottle, stumbles past the COMPOSER and goes to sit by the wall, where he can drink alone. The COMPOSER leaves his organ and crouches by the girl.

COMPOSER : *He loves you, the handsome trooper, does he? Your first?*

She nods her head slightly.

COMPOSER : *I feel that we won't live through this night.*

HALINKA her eyes upturned in rapture : *It's easier to die when you're in love.*

COMPOSER: *Nonsense! Melodrama!*

He pauses for a second to pick up a sheet of music from the organ top.

COMPOSER: *Don't get carried away!*

Very deliberately he tears the sheet of paper to pieces.

ZADRA comes through an opening in the wall by the spot where MADRY is lounging. MADRY grins drunkenly.

MADRY: *Make room for the company commander!*

MADRY's hand appears, thrusting the bottle towards ZADRA.

MADRY off: *Drink, Zadra!*

ZADRA looking away from him: *They've gone mad! You too, Halinka?*

HALINKA looks up innocently from her place by the organ. The COMPOSER is tearing the piece of paper into ever smaller and smaller pieces.

HALINKA: *I'm not drinking. I'm listening to music.*

The COMPOSER turns round to look at ZADRA, who sounds really enraged.

ZADRA off: *Music! You feel like music now! And you're playing!*

COMPOSER: *It's for the last time!*

MADRY is still dangling the bottle in front of ZADRA. His speech is becoming rather slurred.

MADRY: *Drink, Zadra. This'll help you through the sewers.*

ZADRA: *That's your sense of discipline! At your post till the end! But dead drunk!*

MADRY: *It's a long way to the City Centre. Plenty of time to sober up.*

The COMPOSER walks over to join MADRY and ZADRA.

COMPOSER to ZADRA: *What happens when we get there?*

ZADRA: *We fight on.*

The COMPOSER glances sharply at ZADRA. Laughing sarcastically he takes the bottle and sits down next to MADRY.

COMPOSER: *Fight on! They'll crush us like bed-bugs, all of us. Nothing'll be left of the city, anywhere.*

He raises the bottle to his lips. ZADRA, enraged and indignant again, turns sharply towards him.

ZADRA: *Shut up! You can't even die like . . . a man!*

Reacting angrily, the COMPOSER rises.

COMPOSER: *On the contrary. I know how to die now.*

126

Laughing again, he hurls the bottle to the ground. It lands with a resounding crash.

ZADRA, getting himself under control, looks down at MADRY and gives an order in a dry, firm voice.

ZADRA : *Company roll-call!*

MADRY, reacting at once, staggers to his feet.

MADRY : *Yes, sir!* But he cannot resist a comment. *It's a platoon now, not a company.*

Dusk. The remainder of the company is assembled against a dark wall. The only light is provided by distant fires. In front of the company, MADRY, slightly unsteady on his feet, speaks in a low, somewhat slurred voice.

MADRY : *Let no one as much as fart once we're off. Silence, like in a family tomb. And if anybody's frightened, come to me. I'll hold your hand. Heads up, then.*

Through a gap in the wall — where the cross can be seen silhouetted against a distant flame — ZADRA appears, emerging from the shadows.

MADRY : *Attention!*

There is a shuffling of feet in the darkness.

MADRY stretches himself to attention and ZADRA has no option but to march up to him and receive the formal report.

MADRY : *All present and correct, sir! Two officers, five non-com-officers, twenty other ranks!*

ZADRA in a low voice : *You're drunk! It's no time for drill!*

Then he turns towards the company.

ZADRA in his conventional officer's tone : *Thank you. At ease! Forward march!*

In the shadows the column starts moving forward. MADRY lets a few men past, then he himself joins the column. The wounded KORAB ends the column, leaning for support on STOKROTKA.

ZADRA : *Can you do it, Korab?*

KORAB : *I'll go. Let me, let me try. I'm not risking much.* He moves on, his arm in a sling.

ZADRA : *He needs two strong men.*

STOKROTKA quickly : *I'll take care of him, rest assured.*

But ZADRA is not happy with that.

ZADRA : *You'd better come wih me, to show us the way.*

STOKROTKA insistently: *The way is easy. Lieutenant, please let me stay with Korab.*

ZADRA nods briefly, and STOKROTKA walks quickly after KORAB. ZADRA glances around, turns and goes after the column.

The dark column moves forward silently — the men crouching, their guns at the ready. Some light from distant fires falls on them. Suddenly, the dark-haired soldier — the one who plays the ocarina — crashes blindly into a pile of cans and refuse. A terrific din resounds in the silence of the night. Almost at once, flares go up, illuminating the sky, and revealing the crouching company. German machine-guns open on them immediately.

In the trench STOKROTKA is crouching at KORAB'S side. Her face is partly lit by the flares. In the momentary lull in the shooting she gets up quickly and, taking KORAB, runs forward with him.

ZADRA calling out from somewhere in the shadows: *Now!* . . . *Madry, give us covering fire.*

Other men run forward, following KORAB and STOKROTKA. The clatter of machine-guns continues, but MADRY stays behind with three other men and replies with fire.

The men run forward over the stretch of open ground, disappearing into smoke and darkness. Dying flares still partly illuminate the scene of devastation.

MADRY, SMUKLY, the COMPOSER and the dark-haired soldier are left behind in the trench. Another burst of machine-gun fire kicks up the dust on the parapet just above their heads. German voices are heard, coming closer and closer. On the parapet just above the men a helmeted head appears. The German fails to spot them and is about to move on when SMUKLY suddenly jumps up, seizes the German's neck and pulls him down violently into the trench. The COMPOSER jumps in to help SMUKLY, while MADRY fires a burst over the edge of the trench.

Close shot of the German's blood-stained face as he is clubbed to death.

Leaving the trench, MADRY, SMUKLY and the COMPOSER run forward, but the dark, upright figure of the SOLDIER remains, leaning against the parapet.

The COMPOSER runs back across the rubble, the sound of firing all around him.

The COMPOSER touches the silent SOLDIER's shoulder, and suddenly the upright figure falls stiffly backwards. The SOLDIER is obviously dead. Pausing for a split second, the COMPOSER grabs the dead man's gun, notices his ocarina and takes that too. The COMPOSER runs out of shot.[1]

It is morning; a street full of panicky, shouting, screaming people, some carrying bundles, running in all directions. The street is littered with paper and rubbish. Shells are exploding all around, starting small fires in the surrounding houses. A loud clatter of machine-gun fire starts up nearby.

ZADRA is standing in a doorway, looking at the apocalyptical

---

[1] This scene doesn't appear in the original screenplay. On the other hand, fighting for the Red House is developed there at a considerably greater length, including some fierce hand-to-hand combat. Zadra is forced to withdraw — before orders to cross to the City Centre ever reach him — and the company find shelter in a church which has been turned into a field hospital. The organ is obviously a relic of that setting.

scene. He turns and beckons behind to his men, who come out one by one and run quickly along the street. In the end ZADRA himself ducks and runs towards a brick barricade built across the street.

A BOY of no more than twelve is seated on a sandbag on the barricade, a rifle at his side. Wholly unconcerned with the horrors around him, he is calmly pulling his long boots off. A heavy rumbling of tanks comes from somewhere beyond the barricade, and the BOY, looking out, speaks quietly to ZADRA who has just appeared.

BOY SOLDIER : *Tiger tanks.*

ZADRA, his back to us, peeps over the barricades : at a distance, two heavy tanks are seen approaching along the smoke-shrouded street. Complete chaos reigns in the street on the other side of the barricade. There are bodies lying about or being borne away on stretchers, men and women rushing apparently aimlessly in all directions, to the background accompaniment of chattering guns and explosions.

ZADRA is still peering over the barricade, watching the advancing tanks. There is a flash from one of them, as its gun is fired. Just below ZADRA, the BOY SOLDIER, now barefoot, is calmly emptying grit out of his long boots. ZADRA steps down and crouches beside him.

BOY SOLDIER with nonchalant familiarity : *This is the last barricade. Get into the sewer, mate.*

KULA comes up to ZADRA.

KULA : *Lieutenant, sir, may I report respectfully, it's our turn . . .*

BOY SOLDIER : *Report respectfully into the hole, go on.*

The men move out, but the BOY remains, supremely calm, unaffected by the screaming panic and explosions around him. Slowly, he reaches for the rifle.

A long, unruly queue is being formed around the corner. All ZADRA's men are there, in a file against the wall. ZADRA himself appears, walking past his company and looking at the men as if checking that they are all there, or considering their fitness for the task ahead. A middle-aged WOMAN, a black shawl around her head, obviously frantic with fear, tries to stop him.

WOMAN : *Gentlemen, haven't you seen my daughter? A blonde . . .*

But ZADRA walks past her, with hardly a glance.

ZADRA : *Let's go.*

The WOMAN continues to try to accost the men as they move past her.

WOMAN : *Gentlemen, gentlemen, gentlemen, wait! Gentlemen, wait a moment . . . My daughter, a blonde . . . tall, in a brown coat . . . a brown coat . . . with a belt . . . Wait! . . . Have a heart, for God's sake! Gentlemen, don't go away . . . Gentlemen, my daughter, a blonde . . . Tall . . .*

The men ignore her and move on. KORAB goes past, his good arm around STOKROTKA's shoulders. There is a deafening explosion close by. It makes the WOMAN jump, but she continues to shout imploringly, as the men rush past her in the smoke and dust.

WOMAN : *Gentlemen, have pity . . . Don't leave us. Gentlemen, don't go . . . Don't go away . . .*

A soldier, a sub-machine-gun hanging round his neck, disappears into a manhole. HALINKA follows him, then MADRY who lowers himself slowly into the hole. With only his head out he takes a last glance round and disappears.

It is a narrow sewer, no more than two feet across, and not high enough to stand upright, a trickle of dirty water at its bottom. ZADRA, his crouching figure partly lit by an electric torch he is carrying, is walking forward at the head of his men. Those behind him are barely visible in the murk : the tall SMUKLY and KULA with the company document-case. They go past crouching, carrying their burden like porters. Complete silence reigns, disturbed only by faint footsteps and heavy breathing, as two dark figures with linked arms come closer. Suddenly violent coughing, reverberating in the sewer, shakes one or two : it is KORAB. He stops and crouches down, with STOKROTKA standing over him.

COMPOSER : *What was that?*

STOKROTKA : *Shit!*

COMPOSER : *My God, what marvellous acoustics!*

His dark figure moves past.

COMPOSER reciting resonantly : *"I see a land of heavy dreams and*

131

shadows . . ."[1]

MADRY's voice answers him from the darkness.

MADRY : *Stop playing the fool! Get a move on, maestro!*

Light from a small torch flickers briefly over HALINKA's face.

HALINKA : *Silence! The orders were, no talking.*

MADRY, following her with a torch, suddenly hits his head against the vaulting, and his shoulder against the curving wall. He groans painfully.

MADRY : *I'm too big . . . bloody hell! You're better off, Halinka.* MADRY is standing, flashing his torch around; HALINKA crouches at his side. The sewer goes down steeply, almost like a children's slide, running into a much larger sewer down below. Human voices are heard somewhere ahead of them, echoing strangely and growing in volume. Suddenly people appear, obviously in extreme panic, running in the opposite direction to HALINKA and MADRY.

MEN'S VOICES : *Gas! Gas! . . . Germans let in gas! Gas . . . Gas . . .*

They dash past and MADRY watches them go, helplessly.

HALINKA : *Madry, let's go back. There's gas ahead.*

MADRY : *The Germans are there now, at the manhole. We must catch up with the company.*

They start moving down again.

The underworld still reverberates with strange and frightful sounds. Dark figures appear running forward trying to jostle their way through.

MADRY : *Halt! What is it?*

A young man in a German camouflage jacket stops and speaks, panting with panic.

YOUNG MAN : *The Germans let in gas! Is that the way back?*

MADRY : *I suppose so. Although the devil knows . . . All the sewers look alike.*

His confidence is clearly evaporating. The man next to him is now seen to be the COMPOSER. The YOUNG Man moves on, but another runs out of the shadows and bumps into the men. He shouts, the sentence ending in a hysterical howl.

MAN : *I'm going from the Old Town. That's enough of these*

---

[1] The composer's quotations are from Dante.

sewers, and all that shitty blind man's buff!

Leaving them, he starts frantically up the shaft leading from the main sewer to the street. He reaches an iron ladder at the top, fastened to the brickwork of the shaft.

Looking up the shaft: a circle of brightness at the top is obscured by the man's body as he presses on the iron rungs. Below the shaft: the stream of diffused daylight brings out the faces of HALINKA and MADRY. Another face, that of the COMPOSER, enters the frame. They all stare upwards, with foreboding. Suddenly, there is a burst of machine-gun fire and an agonised cry.

The body falls down the shaft and lands at the foot, slumped in a sitting position. It writhes for a moment, then becomes still.

The faces of HALINKA, MADRY and the COMPOSER look on in mute horror.

The head of the dying man slumps to one side. His clothes are filthy, his face and arms covered with a thick slime.

Dark figures run down the main, intersecting sewer — which

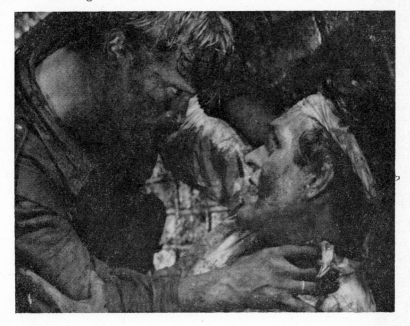

is about a couple of yards high and wide. There are echoing cries of panic, and the clatter of running feet and splashing water.

MAN off : *Go back! Gas!*

KORAB and STOKROTKA halt by the side of the sewer. STOKROTKA tries to stop a man running in the opposite direction.

STOKROTKA : *Men! Where are you going?*

The features of KORAB and STOKROTKA are streaked with sweat and slime.

KORAB echoes her efforts in a weak voice.

KORAB : *Men . . .*

Torchlight plays over the slimy brickwork of the sewer.

Miasma rises from the foul liquid flowing along it.

KORAB and STOKROTKA : KORAB swallows hard, as if choking and slides his hand over his face.

KORAB : *I feel dizzy. It must be gas.*

STOKROTKA tries to arrange his wounded arm more comfortably.

STOKROTKA : *You're feverish, Jacek. There's no gas.*

KORAB : *We'll never catch up. Perhaps we should call Michal?*

STOKROTKA : *There's no need to. I know this sewer. The way is not difficult. We'll make it slowly by ourselves.*

They move off again down the sewer. In the murky light KORAB's arms gleam with sweat and slime. He is walking ahead, STOKROTKA following just behind him. He sighs deeply.

KORAB : *Let me rest, Stokrotka.*

STOKROTKA firmly : *Keep going, damn it!*

She repeats her exhortation in a gentle tone.

STOKROTKA : *Keep going, Jacek. You'll rest at home.*

KORAB : *At home. Has anyone got a home, still?*

She puts her arm around him, supporting him from behind, and they edge painfully along — like a big, clumsy four-legged creature.

KORAB : *But you're strong, Stokrotka. You could have been a porter.*

Their faces emerge out of the gloom. STOKROTKA is peering anxiously ahead.

STOKROTKA : *Oh, I've never been a porter!*

KORAB : *I hardly know you, really.*

134

STOKROTKA glancing at him: *We fought in the Rising together.*

KORAB stops, making her stop, too.

KORAB: *I know that, Stokrotka, but . . .*

STOKROTKA sharply: *Now you want me to tell you the story of my life?*

But KORAB, in his half-conscious state, remains gently inquisitive. And STOKROTKA is obviously torn between the need to keep a tight rein on the difficult situation, and a desire to respond to his intimacies.

KORAB: *Is it a long story?*

STOKROTKA looks at him and nods slightly.

STOKROTKA: *Longer than the sewer. Keep going.*

Painfully, slowly, they move forward again, two dark figures, with only a faint light given off by STOKROTKA's torch. Suddenly they both plunge into water, gasping and shouting.

STOKROTKA: *Jacek! Jacek!*

KORAB coughs again.

KORAB: *What is it . . .?*

The light from their torch plays over black, slimy fluid, which reaches up to KORAB's chest. At a distance, ahead of them, another light flickers, reflected dimly in the sewer.

KORAB: *Look . . .*

STOKROTKA flashes the torch ahead.

STOKROTKA: *A lamp at the junction, or what the devil . . .*

KORAB: *Maybe it's Germans . . .*

STOKROTKA: *They wouldn't dare come down here.*

KORAB: *You think so?*

STOKROTKA: *Uhm, certainly.*

They wade forward through the water again, hardly visible behind the round beam of their torch. STOKROTKA sighs with relief.

STOKROTKA: *Jacek, it's just an ordinary candle. This is the first barricade. You can rest here.*

They move a bit quicker down the sewer towards the light. A few human figures, seated on planks at various levels, become dimly visible. They stare indifferently at the approaching couple. STOKROTKA tries to hoist KORAB up.

STOKROTKA shouting sharply: *Help me lift a wounded man!*

One of the seated soldiers whispers:

SOLDIER : *Quiet!*

Another, the nearest one, rises lazily, takes KORAB's arm, pulls him half-way out of the water, leaves him and goes back to his place. STOKROTKA climbs out of the water and gives a hand to KORAB. Her clothes cling tightly to her body and the men stare silently.

STOKROTKA sharply : *What are you gaping at?*

With a lot of splashing and kicking, KORAB manages at last to haul himself out of the water. He is panting heavily, and then is suddenly seized by a fit of violent coughing, which reverberates down the sewer. One of the seated soldiers abuses him in a furious whisper.

SOLDIER : *Quiet! You stupid son-of-a-bitch!*

STOKROTKA gazes wide-eyed around her.

The filthy, sweaty face of a soldier glares out of the darkness. Suddenly, a blinding stream of light falls on it from above : somebody has evidently opened a ventilation shaft. At the side of the shaft a couple of iron rungs become visible. The SOLDIER flinches and, grimacing strangely, draws his head into his shoulders. An object flashes past him and a blinding explosion follows immediately.

KORAB's and STOKROTKA's faces are spattered by the wave of foul water. The filth turns STOKROTKA's light blonde hair suddenly black. Two other explosions follow, and the violently disturbed water splashes against the side of the sewer. Fade out.

Fade in on a man's wrist, with a large watch strapped to it.

ZADRA off : *It's seven already.*

The hand is raised and the camera follows the movement till we see the anxious faces of ZADRA and SMUKLY behind him. ZADRA raises his eyes.

ZADRA : *To think it is day up there.*

He pauses and glances around.

ZADRA : *Call Lieutenant Madry.*

SMUKLY calling out: *Lieutenant Madry to report to Lieutenant Zadra!*

KULA, following the leaders, turns to look down the line of men.

KULA : *Lieutenant Madry to report to Lieutenant Zadra!*

But the only answer to KULA's loud call are distant, panicky voices.

VOICES : *Gas! Gas!*

A group of men, gasping, run past ZADRA and SMUKLY still shouting.

MEN : *Gas! Gas! Jesus, gas!*

ZADRA watches them go, in grave silence.

SMUKLY anxiously: *Lieutenant, sir, it'll be difficult to enforce discipline in here . . .*

ZADRA takes a cigarette from his case and puts it between his lips.

SMUKLY : *. . . but we must try to keep control. What now?*

ZADRA offers an open case to SMUKLY, who helps himself to a cigarette. ZADRA snaps the case shut, takes out a box of matches and tries, unsuccessfully, to strike one.

ZADRA : *Let's wait for Madry. We can't leave them behind. Damn matches!*

KULA, his eyes wide with fear, butts in nervously.

KULA : *It's not matches, Lieutenant, sir. Too many feet churn this mush. It's fumes. This is killing us, not the grenades. I used to dabble in chemistry. Don't you feel weak, sir?*

ZADRA angrily: *No!*

KULA : *But there's no oxygen in this air. Let's get out, lieutenant, sir.*

SMUKLY : *What about it, lieutenant? Leave the men to die like this?*

A feeling of helplessness makes ZADRA even more angry.

ZADRA : *Is that my fault?*

ZADRA : *Why isn't Madry here? Call them!*

He glares towards the waiting men.

ZADRA : *Don't sit down. It's foulest near the water. You won't get up.*

There is a stirring among the line of men, as they try to raise their weary bodies a little higher. Their arms laid aside, they no longer look like soldiers. In the foreground, a wounded man is being helped by a colleague.

ZADRA's torch illuminates his set features. KULA, standing next to him, tries again.

137

KULA : *Let's go, lieutenant, sir. We mustn't stay here.*

ZADRA doesn't answer, but his grim face shows that he is resolved to wait.

KULA sighing : *I'm going then, to call Madry.*

KULA, splashing ankle deep in water, moves along past the line of men, too weary to take any notice. One of them slumps forward into the water, but is caught by the man sitting next to him.

KULA, holding a lighted torch in front of him, splashes his way along the sewer.

The beam falls on a canteen flask floating, half-submerged, in the foul liquid. The sewer is empty, as far as one can see.

KULA looking out, fear reflected clearly in his expression. He turns and makes his way back down the sewer. He rushes down it, stumbling and falling at one point, then picking himself up.

KULA comes out of the gloom, the beam of his torch lighting up ZADRA's features.

KULA : *Lieutenant Madry asks us to go ahead.*

He crouches down, closer to the resting ZADRA.

KULA : *They've stopped to give a rest to Korab.*

ZADRA still looks anxious and unconvinced.

KULA : *Stokrotka knows the way, after all. They can catch up. Let's go lieutenant, sir.*

ZADRA is not easily persuaded. He glances at KULA, then round at the men. KULA and SMUKLY, standing over them, wait anxiously for his decision. Reluctantly, ZADRA makes up his mind.

ZADRA : *Let's go, boys.*

Picking up their arms wearily, the men move slowly, one by one, after ZADRA.

MADRY, with HALINKA behind, splashing forward through another part of the sewer.

HALINKA panting hard : *Slow down, Madry.*

MADRY : *Faster! Faster! Zadra is probably out in Aleje[1] by now.*

He flashes a torch back.

---

[1] Aleje Ujazdowskie and Jerozolimskie are two famous streets in the centre of Warsaw.

MADRY: *Give me the flask.*

HALINKA: *It makes you weak . . .*

MADRY: *Give it to me, come on.*

In the gloom MADRY can just about be made out, raising a flask and taking a drink from it. The COMPOSER'S face appears faintly behind him. MADRY coughs and splutters, then tips the flask back to drink again. He turns to the COMPOSER.

MADRY: *Do you want to?*

COMPOSER: *Yes. It's cold. I'm all out.*

He takes the flask and drinks.

HALINKA: *Enough.*

COMPOSER: *It's the waters of Lethe, the river of oblivion.*

MADRY: *An ordinary, home-made brew. But it makes you feel livelier, doesn't it?*

The COMPOSER peers anxiously through the darkness, his eyes growing wide.

COMPOSER: *Did you hear those sounds?*

He listens, the echoing music replying to his straining ears.

MADRY hurls the flask away and moves forward again.

MADRY: *Hurry, hurry!*

There is a sudden, loud rumbling noise. HALINKA looks round in panic.

HALINKA: *Christ, what is it? Madry! Jesus, Jesus!*

A terrifying howling noise swells up, rolling through the sewers. Suddenly, a number of people appear, apparently swept along by a swirling wall of water. The deafening din is punctuated with human cries of horror. For a moment the wave submerges MADRY and HALINKA.

HALINKA: *Madry. Ah . . .*

MADRY: *Are you alive? Halinka!*

A woman's voice rings out desperately in the darkness.

WOMAN: *Witold, Witold! Where are you? Where is my child?*

MADRY's attempts to calm the woman prove ineffectual, as he is himself carried away by the general panic, and his voice rises to a hysterical shout.

MADRY: *Shut up, shut up, shut up you damn fool!*

HALINKA, her eyes closed, is holding her tiny pistol against her head. Her face is covered in slime, as if she has only just surfaced. The uproar and cries of terror, multiplied by echoes, still reverberate in the tunnel. The same WOMAN's cries can be heard again.

WOMAN off : *You've sold us out ... murderers!*

Confused fighting breaks out among the men in the tunnel. More come along, the lights of their torches bobbing up and down.

HALINKA raises her face up, her pistol poised.

Men shout and shove each other in the water; a half-naked man hauls himself up out of the sewer; several people push and jostle for a place beneath a ventilation shaft, at the top of which the bright sky is visible through the rungs.

The face of the COMPOSER peers wearily through the gloom. Shouts and screams are still audible, though they seem to have moved away somewhat.

COMPOSER : *A moment. One moment. "There, in the depths of the pit as we stand, I see the people in a river ..."*

He is reciting to himself rather than any audience. We cut on his words to men wrestling in the foul slime.

COMPOSER off : *". . . of excrement that seemed the overflow of the world's latrines".*

Resume on the COMPOSER and HALINKA.

HALINKA : *What are you saying, Michal?*

COMPOSER : *It's not I, child. It's Dante.*[1]

He raises a finger to his mouth, meaning to silence her.

Confusion still reigns in the shaft; a number of dark, half-naked bodies are wrestling towards the light. Parts of bodies appear momentarily; a glimpse of a face contorted with fear. Some men try to climb up the staples, which stick out of the wall.

MADRY makes a desperate attempt to control the crowd.

MADRY : *Get down at once, damn you! You'll get the Germans on our head.*

He stands with drawn revolver, threatening the panic-stricken people.

MADRY : *Now!*

HALINKA, standing just behind him in the shadows, starts whimpering.

---

[1] Composer's quotations from Dante do not appear in the original screenplay.

HALINKA : *Madry, save us! I'm afraid!*

MADRY, holding his torch, turns round towards her.

MADRY sharply : *Stop snivelling! Do you think I don't want to get out? We're going back.*

He starts off back down the sewer.

Total darkness in the tunnel, punctuated by sharp pin-points of light. Dim figures move by in the gloom.

STOKROTKA : *You look bad, Jacek. You need a shave.*

KORAB gasping : *I don't care.*

STOKROTKA worriedly : *You must be really ill.*

Faces appearing from the gloom : that of the COMPOSER in the foreground, HALINKA and MADRY behind. HALINKA is sobbing unrestrainedly. Strange, ethereal sounds echo down the tunnel.

MADRY anxiously : *What's that again?*

COMPOSER : *Raining? The spatter of rain. Be quiet.*

HALINKA keeps on sobbing.

COMPOSER : *Don't cry, child. Can't you hear? . . . Everything's singing.*

MADRY coarsely : *Yes. Perhaps you're seeing angels, too. . . . Get on, keep going, don't stop.*

COMPOSER: *Be quiet! Do you hear? Do you hear? Listen.*

He stops and raises his hand.

MADRY: *Nonsense. It's only the water.*

The COMPOSER's face assumes a dreamy, strangely peaceful expression.

COMPOSER: *I can hear it! At last, I can hear it! You know? I can hear it!*

He raises the ocarina to his mouth and starts playing softly. MADRY appears beside him, obviously shaken.

MADRY: *Shut up, damn you! Have you gone mad?*

HALINKA's sobs grow in volume. MADRY takes hold of the COMPOSER and shakes him violently, then slaps his face, himself almost hysterical.

The COMPOSER frees himself calmly, looking at MADRY with an air of blank surprise.

COMPOSER: *Ridiculous, squealing little man! How could you understand?*

With a last look at MADRY he turns away, raising the ocarina to his mouth again.

MADRY's features express helpless anger.

MADRY shouting: *Come back, you! Stop playing the fool!*

The COMPOSER moves away, producing mournful tones out of the ocarina.

MADRY draws his Luger and levels it in the direction of the COMPOSER.

MADRY: *Halt! Or I shoot!*

But his fury, and the threat, peter out suddenly. He drops his gun arm and looks around despairingly.

The COMPOSER, ignoring him completely, walks slowly away, without as much as a backward glance. HALINKA continues sobbing. The COMPOSER is playing the ocarina, dragging his feet through the slimy water, from which a faint miasma rises.

MADRY, torch in hand, stalks forward in front of the seated HALINKA, making a last attempt to stop the COMPOSER.

MADRY shouting: *I order you to come back, at once!*

But the order is answered only by the tones of the ocarina. MADRY, accepting defeat, turns round helplessly.

HALINKA embraces MADRY, clinging to him tightly, amidst sobs.

HALINKA: *Madry!*

MADRY wearily: *Why am I so weak? We won't reach the Centre, anyway. . . . There's no way . . .*

With a sudden, new lease of desperate determination he wrestles himself free of her embrace.

MADRY: *This bloody sewer must end somewhere . . .! Let's go.*

HALINKA's sobs grow and explode into uncontrollable crying.

The light of a torch appears in the darkness, moving towards us. Two shadowy figures can be seen behind it, as the beam falls on the filthy water underfoot. More figures emerge from the shadows: it is ZADRA at the head of his men. Behind him, holding the torch, come SMUKLY and KULA. A monstrous howling, painful, tense, broken into a regular pattern and growing in volume, echoes through the underground tunnels. ZADRA, obviously shaken, stops.

ZADRA: *What is it?*

SMUKLY: *A wounded man, I suppose.*

ZADRA: *Can that be a human voice? . . . Come on!*

KULA: *Lieutenant, sir, it's impossible to make anything out of these noises.*

The howling, amplified by the echo, grows still louder.

SMUKLY: *I'll go and see. Wait.*

He moves forward, past ZADRA.

The sweat on SMUKLY's cheek and the steel of his sub-machine-gun glint in the dark as he moves cautiously down the tunnel. The terrifying, yet monotonous, howling still grows in volume.

ZADRA, standing with his torch at the head of a line of men, waiting for a signal from SMUKLY.

SMUKLY is advancing down the tunnel. As he comes closer, the amplifying effect of the echo disappears and the howling subsides into recognisably human groans. A vague, prostrate shape appears in front of SMUKLY. He turns his head.

SMUKLY shouting: *Here's your howler!*

A uniformed officer's body is floating in the sewer, his head resting against the wall, his long, grey beard partly submerged

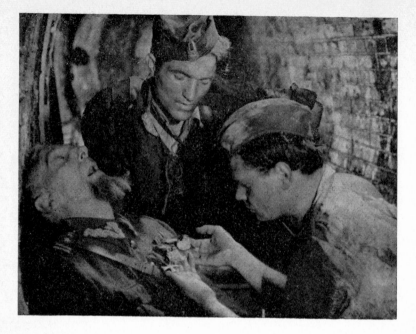

in the fluid. There are medals on his chest. His eyes are closed, but the mouth still opens at regular intervals, as he groans.

ZADRA approaches, crouching, peering forward, followed by KULA.

KULA : *A man! Let's get out of here, lieutenant, sir!*

ZADRA : *I know him. He's a colonel. I've seen him at headquarters.*

He turns to the men behind.

ZADRA shouting : *Who'll carry him, men?*

ZADRA moves off. The men behind hesitate. The last soldier throws his gun into the sewer. No one takes any notice. At last two men attempt to lift the officer out of the water. Someone stumbles, making a splash.

SOLDIER : *What's the matter with you?*

A couple of men slump down, groaning, at the side of the sewer.

ZADRA off : *Forward!*

ZADRA, SMUKLY and KULA walk down the tunnel, looking round. They approach a junction with a narrower sewer.

SMUKLY : *Where? Where is that sign?*

144

ZADRA worried: *There ought to be the sign for Wilcza,*[1] *here on the left.*

KULA: *Stokrotka should have been here. She knows the way.*

ZADRA: *Stokrotka is taking care of Korab. We can read.*

KULA voice quivering: *There's nothing we can do, lieutenant, sir. Let's get out, or we never shall! Holy Mother . . .!*

SMUKLY: *There is no sign.*

ZADRA is seen close up — the other two appear as shadows.

ZADRA: *Call the men, Kula!*

KULA: *Yes, sir!*

Men sit wearily by the side of the sewer, torchlight playing over their exhausted features. The dark water glimmers below them. KULA appears.

KULA: *Get up! The lieutenant is waiting.*

SOLDIER: *Go ahead. Go on.*

ZEFIR, the messenger boy, is obviously all in.

ZEFIR weakly: *Wait a moment. I'm weak. Let's rest.*

KULA, with a parting glance at the seated men, goes back. Ahead of him, the splashing steps of ZADRA and SMUKLY can be heard.

KULA, gasping, breaks into a run, splashing, afraid of being left behind.

A junction off the main tunnel: the two dark figures of ZADRA and SMUKLY can be seen.

ZADRA shouting at the top of his voice: *There! There! There should be a sign! Wilcza! Wilcza!*

The torch beam flashes up the wall. There follows a pause.

SMUKLY wearily: *No. There is no sign.*

ZADRA and SMUKLY start to move on. ZADRA looks suddenly exhausted and staggers. KULA comes up from behind.

ZADRA: *Well?*

KULA: *They're coming, catching up.*

SMUKLY: *Lean on me, Zadra.*

KORAB and STOKROTKA moving on slowly down the tunnel, its roof gleaming darkly with slime.

KORAB gasping: *Well, that's enough.*

---

[1] Wilcza Street (Wolf Street) is in the centre of Warsaw.

STOKROTKA : *All you have to do is to move your legs.*
KORAB : *Aren't you tired, Stokrotka?*
STOKROTKA : *Why should I be? I'm not wounded.*
KORAB : *It's calm and misty! We're walking through a dark and fragrant forest.*
STOKROTKA : *We're stumbling through stinking shit!*
KORAB manages a faint laugh which develops into a cough.
KORAB : *You're always to the point, Stokrotka.*
STOKROTKA : *Hmm!*
KORAB : *You couldn't ever fall in love, could you?*
She only sighs deeply in reply. But KORAB seems to be awaiting an answer. They walk on for a few paces.
STOKROTKA : *Keep moving those legs, or we won't get there in three days. You're running a high temperature. We'll die of hunger here.*
KORAB groans and staggers suddenly. STOKROTKA grips his arm firmly.
STOKROTKA : *What's the matter?*
KORAB : *Nothing. What is it?*
STOKROTKA flashes her torch ahead of them.
The beam falls on the dead face of the bearded colonel, floating in the sewer.
STOKROTKA off : *He was old . . .*
KORAB and STOKROTKA are only faintly visible in the light of their torch.
STOKROTKA : *He probably died of fear during that gas panic. Stupid people, they don't know the sewers.*
They wade on, KORAB panting heavily.

ZADRA, SMUKLY, and KULA, all three very tired and breathing heavily. They flash the torch on the wall, trying to find the sign.
SMUKLY : *Nothing! I can see nothing!*
ZADRA shouting joyfully : *There! There it is, men. Here!*
SMUKLY strikes a match and lights up an indistinct, chalked sign.
SMUKLY reading slowly : *I love . . . Jacek.*
Cut to the crude lettering on the wall, the match flickering in front of it.

Back on the three men; ZADRA's face registers his shock.

ZADRA whispering : *My God . . .!*

Suddenly, he breaks into wild, hysterical laughter, which echoes down the tunnel.

Back with KORAB and STOKROTKA, breathing heavily, moving laboriously forward. KORAB's voice is hardly above a whisper.

KORAB : *My head is spinning. Maybe there is gas . . . Look at that fog.*

STOKROTKA : *You're a child, Jacek. You're seeing things, it's your temperature.*

They take a few more slow steps.

STOKROTKA : *Wait! Here's our sewer. See? Wilcza!*

The beam from STOKROTKA's torch lights up the sign, crudely chalked on the brickwork of the tunnel.

At the entrance to the narrow tunnel, leading up to the street, STOKROTKA turns to KORAB, standing wearily.

KORAB : *I could never have noticed it. I can hardly see it now.*

STOKROTKA firmly : *Let's go up there. Give me your hand.*

KORAB grabs her outstretched hand and she pulls him into the entrance of the tunnel.

It is a narrow, steeply-sloping shaft, with a trickle of dirty water at the bottom. STOKROTKA, for all her strength, finds it very difficult to pull KORAB up, and he is too weak to help much. They climb a couple of yards, but his hand slips.

KORAB crying out : *My hand . . . hold it!*

STOKROTKA : *Jacek!*

We are looking up the shaft, as KORAB hurtles down backwards, landing with a splash in the main sewer.

STOKROTKA off : *Jacek!*

STOKROTKA's point of view. KORAB is visible at the foot of the shaft, looking up at her.

KORAB : *I can't come up that tube. Go yourself, Stokrotka.*

He waves to her with his good arm.

STOKROTKA's face at the top of the shaft is suddenly lit up by her torch as she looks round with a fleeting expression of regret in her eyes. Her hair is matted and her shoulders thickly coated with mud and slime.

STOKROTKA : *Idiot!*

She starts to descend the shaft.

STOKROTKA crawls, panting, down the shaft. She reaches KORAB who is leaning against the brickwork at the entrance to the main tunnel.

KORAB : *You won't be able to pull me up. Better go and get help, Stokrotka. I'll rest here, and wait.*

He gazes up the wall, STOKROTKA's eyes following his.

KORAB : *What's that writing? Large letters . . .*

The light picks out the letters and KORAB tries to read.

KORAB off : *I lo . . . love . . .*

KORAB and STOKROTKA side by side. She switches the torch off.

STOKROTKA : *We must save the battery.*

KORAB : *That writing up there . . . What does it say?*

STOKROTKA : *I love . . .*

She pauses, before continuing, resolutely.

STOKROTKA : *. . . Jacek.*

KORAB : *I lo . . . Who could have been writing such nonsense?*

STOKROTKA : *It's not nonsense. Empty sewers, Germans overhead. It is fear . . . you understand?*

KORAB groans again, as if meaning to articulate the sign, then gives up.

STOKROTKA: *Someone wrote . . . and someone felt better at once . . . I used to pass this way, too.*

KORAB: *And what did you write?*

STOKROTKA suddenly matter of fact: *Kiss my arse!*

KORAB: *What?*

STOKROTKA: *. . . and things like that.*

She gets to her feet.

In the foreground KORAB is still seated. STOKROTKA has moved a few steps away.

KORAB: *And . . . and . . . who was Jacek?*

STOKROTKA: *A bloke someone loved . . .*

KORAB: *Much . . .?*

STOKROTKA, now standing over him, leans forward and brushes his hair with her lips. She answers in a whisper.

STOKROTKA: *Very, very much.* More briskly. *Well, let's go.*

She turns to face the shaft.

KORAB: *No. We won't be able to make it there, Stokrotka. Really, I'll wait here. You'll bring help soon. Won't you?*

STOKROTKA sharply: *Get up!*

KORAB: *No.*

STOKROTKA: *Quiet!*

She listens for a moment to distant sounds.

STOKROTKA: *No. It's an illusion.*

KORAB staggers to his feet.

KORAB stands, very weak, his eyes almost closed. The sound of the ocarina comes closer.

KORAB: *My head is whirling. I hear music.*

He raises a hand, gleaming with perspiration, to his mouth.

KORAB: *It's fever, isn't it? . . . No, I can really hear it.*

The sound of the ocarina approaches. STOKROTKA's head appears beside his. Wide-eyed, she looks along the sewer.

Out of the gloom of the tunnel the COMPOSER emerges, playing the ocarina. Completely engrossed in his playing, he walks past STOKROTKA and KORAB.

The COMPOSER walks away slowly.

KORAB off: *Who was that?*

KORAB and STOKROTKA gaze in the direction of the COMPOSER.

KORAB : *Is he mad, or am I?*

STOKROTKA : *He is, and has been for some time. Don't you remember?*

KORAB : *Strange . . . No, I don't.*

KORAB puts his hand to his brow.

KORAB whispering : *Michal . . .? Michal?*

Suddenly, he moves forward and shouts after the COMPOSER.

KORAB : *Michal! Come back!*

The tunnel stretches away, empty. There is no sign of the COMPOSER. Only the dying tones of the ocarina.

KORAB off : *Michal . . .!*

Back to KORAB and STOKROTKA.

STOKROTKA : *Be quiet. He can't hear you, anyway. Jacek! Jacek! Stop this damned whining. Let's go.*

KORAB still doesn't move.

KORAB : *I won't manage it up there. But I want to live.*

STOKROTKA, looking around, now turns and looks straight at him.

STOKROTKA : *That's good, Jacek. Don't worry, you're going to live.*

She looks down the main sewer.

STOKROTKA : *We're going straight ahead here. This intersecting sewer has got to run into the Vistula not far from here.*

A shot of the empty, narrow shaft leading to Wilcza Street.

MADRY and HALINKA alone in a narrow sewer. They can hardly be seen.

HALINKA'S panting voice comes from the darkness.

HALINKA : *It's dry here. There must be an exit somewhere. Switch on the torch.*

MADRY : *The battery's weak. We'll get there anyway.*

But he switches the torch on and flashes it over the solid brickwork. It seems that this particular sewer ends in a cul-de-sac.

HALINKA : *Ah!*

MADRY : *No, it's not possible!*

HALINKA resignedly : *I don't have the strength. We won't come out. That's the end.*

Suddenly we see MADRY'S desperate face against the brick-work. He is half-sobbing but enraged at the same time.

MADRY : *What do you mean, the end? What end? I don't want to. I've got someone to live for.*

HALINKA weakly off : *I'm with you. Who do you want to live for?*

MADRY shouting : *What do you mean who? My wife and my child!*

HALINKA looks up blankly.

HALINKA : *Wife and child? Funny. You've said nothing. But you wear no . . .*

MADRY fumbles in his breast pocket.

HALINKA off : *. . . wedding ring.*

MADRY : *So what? I've got it on me. Look!*

He pushes a wedding ring on his finger. The gold of the ring gleams. He is also holding a photograph, which is lit up by his torch.

HALINKA looks up silently, like a wounded animal.

MADRY is standing over her, shouting almost hysterically.

MADRY : *You see? I've got to live. We're going back, up the sewer. Now, while I've got some life left!*

HALINKA watches him.

HALINKA in a strangely calm voice : *A moment. Put out the torch, Madry.*

MADRY off : *Get up! Get up! Get up!*

But he does switch the light off and the tunnel is plunged into almost total darkness. There is a click of a pistol being cocked and a muffled shot, which echoes in the tunnel.

A glimpse of MADRY's horrified face.

KORAB and STOKROTKA stagger forward. He is leaning with all his weight on her arm.

KORAB : *Stokrotka, let me sit down for a second.*

STOKROTKA : *No.*

KORAB : *I must. I must rest.*

KORAB leans against the wall of the tunnel, groaning. STOK-ROTKA's arms are around him.

STOKROTKA : *Jacek! We are near the river now!*

KORAB : *No. I can't open my eyes. They're painful.*

STOKROTKA soothingly : *Don't try. It's fever. You'll have to go into hospital.*

KORAB : *A hospital? What hospital?*

Herself desperately tired, she pulls him off the wall almost by force and they stagger off again.

STOKROTKA: *What . . . Do you think there'll never be a normal life?*

KORAB: *Never . . .*

STOKROTKA: *Jacek . . .*

KORAB: *To live, Stokrotka . . .*

STOKROTKA: *I promised you.*

KORAB: *And I used to be rude to you . . .*

STOKROTKA: *We'll settle that later.*

KORAB: *I've been bad . . . I've been bad . . .*

They struggle on, the torch-light flickering over STOKROTKA's arms and shoulders. Suddenly, she shouts excitedly.

STOKROTKA: *I can see it! I can see a light, Jacek!*

Some diffused light is apparent further on down the tunnel.

KORAB and STOKROTKA embrace and kiss with a painful passion. Breaking the embrace smilingly, she looks out.

The outlet of the sewer is blocked by an iron grill. Beyond it, in bright daylight, runs a wide river with green meadows on the other side, in the distance. A trickle of foul water runs out of the sewer and into the river. As the camera tracks quickly towards the iron grill, one can almost feel a gentle breeze on the other side.

STOKROTKA appears in the frame, dragging KORAB along. They stagger towards the outlet.

KORAB: *We're going to live . . .*

They stop by the grill, panting heavily.

STOKROTKA: *Don't open your eyes . . . The glare is too strong.*

She turns and grasps the iron bars.

KORAB's feverish face, the eyes closed, is seen through the bars of the grill, from outside the sewer.

KORAB: *Is it much further?*

Light reflections from the water flicker over his face.

STOKROTKA, seen from outside, grasps the bars and stares out hopelessly. She pushes her head between the bars.

STOKROTKA: *I see water, Jacek . . . and green grass.*

KORAB: *Let's go there, Stokrotka.*

She glances in the direction of KORAB.

He is still in the same position, his eyes closed. But suddenly

he slumps down to the floor. STOKROTKA leaves the bars, takes KORAB in her arms, and tries to make him comfortable.

STOKROTKA : *You can rest now. We'll come out soon, on the grass.* She pauses and looks down on him tenderly. He tries, unsuccessfully, to raise his head.

STOKROTKA : *No, no. Don't open your eyes, because . . . the sun's come out.*

She looks up. The camera moves slowly past her to the grill, looking towards the Vistula and the far shore.

MADRY crawls with feverish haste up a narrow shaft. His knees slide on the slippery slope, but he presses on with all the strength and resolution he can muster. Suddenly, a stream of bright light falls from above, as if someone has opened the shaft. MADRY looks up, removes his sub-machine-gun to gain greater freedom of movement, and starts climbing the rungs embedded in the side of the shaft. He climbs step by step towards the bright circle of light.

Outside the manhole : MADRY's black face, covered in mud, appears out of it. Blinded by the light, he shoves his gun away from him, and with painful slowness drags his big body out of the manhole. As he kneels at the edge of it, a pair of jackboots can be seen behind him, the owner apparently standing with his legs wide apart. MADRY finally climbs to his feet and staggers, rubbing his eyes. A German SS officer — the wearer of the boots — comes forward covering MADRY with a Luger.

GERMAN OFFICER shouting: *Hände hoch!*

MADRY raises his hands. The officer strides up to him, takes his sub-machine-gun and throws it on a pile of other arms. It lands there with a clatter. MADRY looks around miserably. A detachment of German soldiers is standing, well-spaced, around a group of Polish freedom fighters who have their hands raised around their necks. The state of their clothing and their air of weariness testifies that they, too, have come out of the sewers and have been trapped on exit. In the background an armoured personnel carrier is parked. Two white-coated cooks walk by in the background, carrying a food can. In front of the Polish prisoners are two piles of equipment — mostly rifles and sub-machine-guns. By the wall enclosing the yard a pile of dead bodies can be seen.

MADRY's shoulders begin shaking with heavy sobs. Choking and coughing, he raises his arm to his face. The German officer, impassive, impeccably clean and wearing gloves, pushes him back and starts searching him with great speed and expertise. He removes MADRY's ammunition pouches, throws these on the pile, pulls out personal documents and the family photograph from his breast pocket.

GERMAN OFFICER calmly, in good Polish: *The wedding ring.*

MADRY doesn't react, and the OFFICER takes hold of his finger and wrenches the ring off with one brutal pull. Then he pushes MADRY towards the other prisoners. The lieutenant staggers heavily towards the pile of corpses and falls on his knees, his back to the German soldiers. He raises his arms.

On the wall of the building, behind the OFFICER, there is a silhouette of a man with "PST!!" whitewashed beside him. Some way below, the letters "LSR" are written in white. The SS OFFICER, pistol in hand, walks over to the open manhole and shouts down it in Polish.

GERMAN OFFICER: *Come out! Come out!*

ZADRA, SMUKLY and KULA splash through the narrow sewer. SMUKLY, leading the way, catches the wall with the barrel of his sub-machine-gun. He stumbles once, and the bolt of his gun hits him in the face. He raises his hand to the painful spot.

ZADRA : *Smukly, throw that bloody gun away. We've got to save people. You're killing yourself.*

SMUKLY : *Bloody hell, it stunned me.*

KULA : *Throw it away . . . Let's get out, get some fresh air, quick.*

SMUKLY : *Piss off!*

KULA suddenly shouting : *Light! The air, lieutenant, sir!*

ZADRA and SMUKLY look in the direction he is pointing. ZADRA grins.

ZADRA, SMUKLY and KULA approach the inlet. The light is getting stronger. ZADRA turns gleefully to the sergeant.

ZADRA : *We're going to the inlet. Tell the men, Kula. We're going to the inlet.*

KULA turns back reluctantly, glancing momentarily at the officer.

A fleeting shot of the empty sewer : no one is following.

A close shot of KULA's face, dirty and sweating. He speaks into the empty space.

KULA : *We're turning left, going to the inlet.*

KULA smiles, as he addresses ZADRA.

KULA : *They're coming, lieutenant, sir!*

ZADRA smiles with relief.

ZADRA : *They're coming!*

The inlet is blocked with girders and barbed wire, with a couple of grenades hanging there for good measure. SMUKLY stops, and ZADRA goes forward to inspect the booby-trapped obstacle.

ZADRA : *No good, it's blocked.*

He turns round and, with an anguished face, looks down at SMUKLY and KULA. He stifles his sobs.

ZADRA : *We turn back, if we've got the strength? I must get my men out.*

KULA : *Sir, lieutenant, sir! We must have some air. It's death back there!*

SMUKLY suddenly moves forward, passes under one of the

girders and starts inspecting the booby trap closely.

SMUKLY'S mud-stained face is seen from outside, looking up through a tangle of barbed wire and girders.

SMUKLY : *They've hung grenades there, the dirty swine! But just you wait.*

Climbing up, slimy water running down his arms, he reaches slowly to where a stick grenade is delicately suspended from the barbed wire. For a long while his muddy hand remains poised just an inch from the grenade.

Below, one foot rests precariously on a slimy piece of rubble, the other suspended in mid-air.

SMUKLY'S tense face draws even closer to the grenade. He takes hold of it, and with the barrel of his sub-machine-gun, succeeds in unhooking the stick from the barbed wire. He lowers the grenade gently, screws the safety catch on and passes it back to ZADRA. He now looks up grimly towards the second grenade, hanging directly over him. He stretches his hand out and takes hold of it.

His boot below loses its grip on the stone and suddenly slips.

The grenade swings over him, but nothing happens. SMUKLY's slimy hand reaches out again and his face appears, watching the grenade tensely. He smiles as he successfully lowers the grenade and defuses it.

SMUKLY : *Good. Just one more and we're off.*

He takes hold of the last grenade and pushes the barrel of his gun to unhook it.

Below, the stone he is standing on wobbles precariously and suddenly his foot slips completely from it.

SMUKLY's face suddenly disappears from view, while the grenade swings violently. SMUKLY's nervous laugh is heard, as his hand appears again, reaching out. Suddenly, there is a bright flash and a terrific explosion.

Smoke fills the inlet. Two other explosions follow the first. ZADRA and KULA peer fearfully from round the corner of the sewer.

KULA anxiously : *Let's go, let's go, lieutenant. Let's go up.*

ZADRA starts to crawl on all fours to the exit.

He looks up through the girders and barbed wire, which have been blown away from the exit, and down at the remains of SMUKLY's body. Rivulets of blood run down it, trickling audibly down.

Seen from outside, ZADRA's head appears from the manhole. The ground around is strewn with rubble, and fire is spreading silently through the buildings in the background. There are no people around. He slowly hauls himself out of the hole, remaining on his knees for a while, his field-glasses dangling from his neck. At last he gets to his feet and staggers towards the burning buildings. An arm appears in the manhole, as KULA begins to haul himself out. He stops halfway up.

KULA : *Thank you, Holy Mother of God. Where are we, lieutenant, sir?*

There is an expression of utter weariness on ZADRA's face.

ZADRA : *Why aren't they coming out? Call them, Kula.*

KULA, half lying by the manhole, looks up with a frightened grin.

KULA : *We are safe! Fresh air at last! Let's get away, lieutenant!*

He crawls away from the hole. ZADRA gives him a tired grin, but continues pressing KULA about the others.

ZADRA : *Kula, call them. They may have walked on.*

KULA, covered in slime, looks up from his kneeling position. He tries to smile ingratiatingly.

KULA : *They've stayed behind; they stayed long ago. I only pretended they were catching up . . .*

ZADRA's face stiffens at once with a terrible anger.

ZADRA : *You scoundrel!*

He backs away a few steps, and his hand moves to his holster. KULA shuffles away on his knees, then rises and tries to back away.

ZADRA shouting : *And my company?*

ZADRA, his gun in his hand, fires one shot.

KULA, hit, crashes to the ground.

ZADRA fires two more shots.

ZADRA shouting : *My company's in there!*

KULA half-raises himself on one arm, but another shot hits him and he falls down.

ZADRA, pistol in hand, looks down in a mixture of anger and anguish.

KULA lies sprawling in the rubble. One of his legs is twitching slightly.

ZADRA glares in the direction of KULA's body, and then, with a bitter face, averts his eyes to look elsewhere.

ZADRA weakly : *My company . . . my company . . . my company.*

He closes his eyes, swaying and swallowing hard.

Pistol in hand, ZADRA walks slowly towards KULA's still body. He stops and stands for a moment over it. KULA's document-case is lying at his side, its flap undone. A strong breeze blows some papers from the case and makes them dance around. Slowly, ZADRA moves off, walking past the body towards the black pit of the manhole. He steps into it and lowers himself gradually, step by step. Only his head and shoulders are still visible when he stops for a moment and takes a last, bitter look around. Then he disappears completely into the narrow manhole, raising his pistol arm above his head. The pistol in his hand is the last thing sticking out above the hole. A breeze continues blowing the pile of company records away from KULA's body.

159

CREDITS:

Director	Andrzej Wajda
Screenplay	Jerzy Andrzejewski and Andrzej Wajda, based on the novel by Jerzy Andrzejewski
Produced by	Film Authors' Unit KADR for FILM POLSKI
Photography	Jerzy Wojcik
Camera	Krzysztof Winiewicz, Wieslaw Zdort, Zygmunt Krusznicki, Jerzy Szurowski, Bogdan Myslinski
Art direction	Roman Mann
Assistants	Jaroslaw Switoniak, Leszek Wajda, Marian Kowalinski
Music	Jan Krenz
Performed by	Wroclaw Radio Quintet, conducted by Filip Nowak
Sound	Bogdan Bienkowski
Editing	Halina Nawrocka
Assisted by	Irena Chorynska
Assistants to the director	Janusz Morgenstern, Andrzej Wrobel, Anita Janeczkowa, Jan Wlodarczyk
Production manager	Stanislaw Adler
Assisted by	Zygmunt Wojcik, Michal Sosinski
Wardrobe	Katarzyna Chodorowicz
Make-up	Halina Sienska, Halina Turant, Halina Zajonc
Shot in	WFF Lodz and Wroclaw, 1958

CAST:

Maciek Chelmicki	Zbigniew Cybulski
Krystyna	Ewa Krzyzewska
Szczuka	Waclaw Zastrzezynski
Andrzej	Adam Pawlikowski
Drewnowski	Bogumil Kobiela
Porter	Jan Ciecierski
Pieniazek	Stanislaw Milski
Slomka	Zbigniew Skowronski
Kotowicz	Artur Mlodnicki
Mrs. Staniewicz	Halina Kwiatkowska
Waga	Ignacy Machowski
Stefka	Barbara Krafft
Swiecki	Aleksander Sewruk

ASHES AND DIAMONDS

TITLE : *It is May 7, 1945 — a small provincial town in Poland is enjoying its first days of liberty. In a few hours the greatest war in the history of mankind will be over. Germany has already surrendered unconditionally. But on this, the last night of the war, there are many who will not sleep peacefully . . .*

It is a fine late spring day; the air seems heavy with the promise of summer. In the tall grass on a bank below a small roadside chapel, MACIEK CHELMICKI, a dark-haired stocky young man, lies stretched out lazily. His companion, an older, slimmer man called ANDRZEJ, is leaning on one elbow and looking nervously around. There is the sound of a bird whistling close by.

MACIEK : *God, I'm sleepy. I can't keep my eyes open.*

A LITTLE GIRL enters behind the two men and goes towards the door of the chapel and tries to open it. ANDRZEJ looks round sharply on hearing the noise.

MACIEK : *That bloke, what's his name? I forget . . .*

ANDRZEJ : *Szczuka.*

MACIEK : *Who is he?*

ANDRZEJ : *A Secretary of the Regional Party Committee.*

The LITTLE GIRL approaches the two men from behind; she is carrying a small bunch of wild flowers in her hand.

LITTLE GIRL : *Please sir, can you open this door?*

ANDRZEJ gets up and goes with the LITTLE GIRL to the door.

ANDRZEJ : *You see. It's locked.*

ANDRZEJ lifts the LITTLE GIRL up, enabling her to look over the door and place her flowers in the embrasure above it. The sound of a car engine comes closer and ANDRZEJ is listening to it while holding the child up.

A third man, JULEK DREWNOWSKI, who has been left as a look-out near the chapel, turns and whistles. At the bottom of a ravine below him a road can be seen, along which a jeep is approaching.

ANDRZEJ quickly puts the child back on the ground.

ANDRZEJ sharply to the child: *Run away now!* He turns in the direction of his companion. *Maciek!*

MACIEK is still lying in the same position, spreadeagled in the grass.

MACIEK calmly: *Yes? What's up?*

ANDRZEJ off: *They're coming!*

MACIEK: *So what! I've waited for bigger things.*

ANDRZEJ off: *Hurry up!*

MACIEK gets up, still showing no urgency, and starts to pick up two sub-machine-guns lying in the grass beside him. He drops them at once, as if finding them burning hot.

MACIEK: *Bloody ants!*

He brushes something off the guns, then passes one to ANDRZEJ who pushes the LITTLE GIRL away.

ANDRZEJ sharply: *Go away, now!*

DREWNOWSKI comes up to the two men; he is extremely nervous.

DREWNOWSKI: *Hurry up! Hurry up! They're here!*

For a moment, MACIEK is seen in a strange posture, suspended in mid-movement, his machine-gun pointing in the air, before

164

he runs down the grassy slope and crosses the road. The jeep suddenly appears quite close on the road and MACIEK immediately fires a burst at it. The vehicle, now out of control, darts up the bank, its engine whining. A man, one of the occupants of the jeep, half-leaps and half-falls out of the car.

ANDRZEJ fires a burst of shots at the car and at the other occupant.

MACIEK continues firing at the car.

The heavily-built, middle-aged man behind the wheel is dead. There is some blood on his face. The firing has stopped.

ANDRZEJ and DREWNOWSKI look on at the scene of destruction.

ANDRZEJ : *Get his papers!*

DREWNOWSKI, very nervous, runs forward and pushes his hand inside the dead man's jacket. He searches about despairingly.

DREWNOWSKI almost sobbing : *He hasn't got any . . .*

MACIEK is standing over the other, younger man, who lies face down on the ground, apparently lifeless. MACIEK removes the empty magazine from his gun, meaning to replace it with a full one, when the man's eyes open suddenly. He jumps to his feet and runs away up the bank.

The man, probably wounded, staggers towards the chapel; DREWNOWSKI, who is in a position to intercept him, makes only ineffectual, pawing gestures.

The man reaches the door of the chapel and starts thumping on it, trying to break it open.

MACIEK and ANDRZEJ run after him. MACIEK raises his gun and fires a burst.

A cluster of little holes burst open in the back of the man's jacket; small flames shoot out of them, licking the fabric of the coat. At that moment the door gives way under the weight of his body and the screaming man falls face down into the chapel, in front of a large crucifix.

MACIEK starts firing another burst, but ANDRZEJ knocks his gun off-target.

Looking out from the interior of the chapel : the dead body is lying on the threshold. MACIEK and ANDRZEJ are standing in the background, while DREWNOWSKI scurries about worriedly, anxious to get away. When DREWNOWSKI sees the corpse in the chapel doorway, he raises his hat and seems to

whisper a short prayer to himself.[1]

DREWNOWSKI : *For God's sake, let's get out of here.*

MACIEK : *Wait, you stupid ass! Where do you think you're going?*

DREWNOWSKI comes running down a tree-lined avenue, leading away from the chapel. MACIEK and ANDRZEJ hide their sub-machine-guns in a large hold-all held out by DREWNOWSKI. He rushes away with the bag; his hat falls to the ground, but he leaves it lying there. MACIEK picks it up nonchalantly and walks away with ANDRZEJ.

A freshly-ploughed field : we are looking from a low angle up an easy slope cut across with hundreds of ridges. A ploughman and his horse are silhoutted on the horizon against the evening sun. A lark is singing somewhere nearby and the distant sound of bells is heard.[2]

---

[1] The episode with the wounded man does not appear in the original script, where the ambush lasts for a much shorter period and is more immediately effective.

[2] In the original script this sequence begins with a general view of the assassination scene : the overturned jeep, its wheels still turning slowly, the two bodies in the grass. A little girl appears and stops to look at the two corpses.

The two dead bodies have been laid out in the grass; there is another jeep parked in the background. Two men are climbing out of it: SZCZUKA, a heavy, middle-aged man leaning on a walking-stick, and PODGORSKI, of a similar age, but tall and lean. They walk forward from the jeep. Another WORKER appears as they approach the bodies.

SZCZUKA: *What happened?*

WORKER: *They killed two of our men.*

PODGORSKI: *Smolarski, member of the cement factory council.*
SZCZUKA points towards the other body.

SZCZUKA: *And that one?*

PODGORSKI: *Gawlik. A young lad, not more than twenty.*
Another WORKER climbs up the slope towards them.

SECOND WORKER: *Twenty-one. Just back from Germany.*
A group of workers holding bicycles look on at the scene.

THIRD WORKER: *Poor devil. Fancy coming back to this . . .*

FOURTH WORKER: *The bastards were firing from there.*

FIFTH WORKER: *We'd better call the police.*

SIXTH WORKER: *If only I could . . .*

The two bodies lie on the ground, their faces stony in death. SZCZUKA and PODGORSKI look on and converse in low voices.

SZCZUKA : *I think it was us they meant to kill . . .*

PODGORSKI looking up sharply : *You think . . .?*

SZCZUKA : *Certainly. But it doesn't matter.*

The sound of church bells reaches them again. This is joined by the sound of the ringing of bicycle bells, as more workers, on their way home from the factory, arrive on the scene.

SZCZUKA and PODGORSKI walk back to the jeep. A WORKER appears and stops SZCZUKA.

WORKER : *Excuse me, comrade.*

SZCZUKA : *My name is Szczuka.*

WORKER : *Are you the regional party secretary?*

SZCZUKA : *That's right.*

WORKER : *Can I ask you something? Not just for me, for all of us. Can you tell us how long we have to watch our people being killed? This isn't the first time . . .*

SZCZUKA : *Nor the last. Are you afraid?*

VOICE off : *Sure! Everybody wants to stay alive.*

A group of WORKERS stand round listening.

WORKER : *We've lost a lot of our people ...*

SZCZUKA looks thoughtfully at the workers.

WORKER continuing off : *... during the occupation.*

A man is pushing his way through the crowd of workers.

SECOND WORKER : *Don't forget Smolarski lost his two sons.*

SZCZUKA walks slowly along the front line of workers.

THIRD WORKER : *One was killed in 1939, and ...*

SECOND WORKER : *... the second one was shot by the Germans in 1943. And he died here today. And why? Who killed him? Poles!*

A group of listening workers.

SECOND WORKER : *Just tell us! How long is this going to go on?*

SZCZUKA is walking up and down, leaning heavily on his stick.

SZCZUKA : *I'd be a bad communist if I tried to comfort you as if you were children.*

SECOND WORKER looks attentively at SZCZUKA.

SZCZUKA : *The end of the war doesn't mean the end of our fight.*

Close shot of SZCZUKA's grave face.

SZCZUKA : *The fight for Poland, the fight for what sort of country it's going to be, has only just started. And each one of us may be killed ... any day.*

The WORKERS listen in attentive silence.

SECOND WORKER : *We understand ... But what are we going to tell his wife?*

Close shot of SZCZUKA drawing close to his jeep.

SZCZUKA very gravely : *Don't think I'm not grieved, because I know full well that these bullets were intended for me ... And now pull yourselves together, and get on with your work ... while you're still alive.*

The sound of the lark singing is audible again; bells ring faintly in the background.

It is early evening. We are looking at a church spire, from which the sound of joyously ringing bells is coming; then we look down to the market square below, in which a loudspeaker has been prominently installed. The square is filled with Polish and Soviet troops, while civilians crowd the pavements, watching and listening to the loudspeaker announcements. A column of artillery drives noisily by. DREWNOWSKI, conspicuously not sharing the crowd's cheerful mood, is pushing through the people, looking round anxiously.

LOUDSPEAKER COMMUNIQUE : *You are listening to a special news bulletin. Today, the 8th of May, an unconditional act of surrender was signed in the ruins of Berlin, the capital of Germany, by the German Supreme Command. The act of surrender was signed by Keitel, Friedeburg and Stumpf on behalf of the German Supreme Command, by Marshal of the Soviet Union Zhukov on behalf of the Red Army Supreme Command, by Air Marshal Tedder on behalf of the Supreme Commander of the expeditionary Allied Forces. The signing was witnessed by the Commander of the U.S.A. Strategic Air Force, General Spaatz, and the Commander-in-Chief of the French Army, General Delattre de Tassigny.*

MACIEK and ANDRZEJ are standing among the crowd. A newsreel is being shown on a temporary open-air cinema screen. The reflected light from the screen shows up the men's faces in the early evening murk. MACIEK is carrying an old rucksack thrown over his shoulder. He glances at his watch.

MACIEK : *What's keeping him?*

ANDRZEJ : *I've no idea. He should be here.*

MACIEK : *Where does he get all the information from?*

ANDRZEJ : *From his boss.*

MACIEK : *His boss? Who's he?*

ANDRZEJ : *The Mayor! The idiot is his secretary.*

MACIEK : *That close! I hate that two-way game!*

ANDRZEJ : *So do I. But he can be useful.*

MACIEK : *Reliable?*

DREWNOWSKI is pushing his way through the crowd. On the cinema screen in the background is a film of people marching and celebrating : it is May 1 in Warsaw.

MACIEK and ANDRZEJ are standing in the crowd; the beam of the projector is in the background.

ANDRZEJ : *Is anything?*

MACIEK and ANDRZEJ in the foreground; we are looking towards the screen, on which can be seen film of Soviet tanks in the streets of Berlin. MACIEK is watching avidly.

MACIEK : *Look! Not bad, those tanks.*

MACIEK and ANDRZEJ with the beam of the projector light behind them.

171

MACIEK : *There he is!*
DREWNOWSKI appears and joins MACIEK and ANDRZEJ. He is
now dressed differently, wearing a dark morning jacket and a
bow-tie, though he has kept his long boots. MACIEK clamps
DREWNOWSKI's hat on his head.
DREWNOWSKI : *How are you, gentlemen?*
ANDRZEJ : *Anything wrong?*
DREWNOWSKI : *No, I've had to change.*
MACIEK : *Getting married?*
DREWNOWSKI : *Worse. The old man is throwing a banquet tonight.
I'm running the whole bloody show.*
MACIEK : *Pass me the bag.*
DREWNOWSKI passes him the hold-all, in which the guns were
placed after the shooting. At the same time he looks critically
at the screen.
DREWNOWSKI : *Not too good, is it? Too much light. Another thing,
Andrzej. As I've been saying, don't count on me in future for that
sort of thing.*
ANDRZEJ : *All right. All right.*
DREWNOWSKI : *I don't mean . . . information. I'm not backing out,
of course. But for the other thing . . .*
ANDRZEJ : *Don't be such a bore. Maciek?*
ANDRZEJ clearly wants to leave. MACIEK, who has been watch-
ing the screen, reacts, and so does DREWNOWSKI.
DREWNOWSKI : *Where are you going?*
MACIEK : *To your banquet. We've just been invited.*
DREWNOWSKI : *Stop joking, please . . .*
ANDRZEJ : *Don't be afraid. I know what I'm doing.*
DREWNOWSKI : *Don't take any risks.*
ANDRZEJ : *Stop bothering me!*
DREWNOWSKI : *See you!*
MACIEK : *See you.*
MACIEK and ANDRZEJ leave; DREWNOWSKI remains looking in
the direction of the screen.

A detachment of infantry marches down a street. DREWNOWSKI
appears, crosses the street, watching the soldiers move away.
A line of workers pass behind him, carrying easy chairs above
their heads. DREWNOWSKI approaches the Monopol Hotel,

172

from which strains of dance music are coming; light shines brightly through the glass panels of the main entrance door. Inside the entrance-hall of the Monopol Hotel, which also serves as a lounge: the line of workers carrying the chairs passes through the hall, watched by the PORTER. DREWNOWSKI enters after them and the PORTER greets him at the door with a slight bow.

PORTER: *My humble respects, sir.*

DREWNOWSKI: *Good evening.*

KOTOWICZ, a tall, middle-aged, very smooth gentleman enters from the restaurant; he is wearing a light jacket, white shirt and bow-tie. He greets DREWNOWSKI with a show of cordiality.

KOTOWICZ: *Who do I see? How are you? What brings you here?*

DREWNOWSKI: *Duty, Mr. Kotowicz.*

KOTOWICZ: *I understand. I know. The banquet. Are you looking for Mr. Slomka?*

DREWNOWSKI: *That's right.*

KOTOWICZ points to the door leading to the banqueting room. A waiter carrying a tray passes between the two men. DREWNOWSKI walks slowly over to the door of the banqueting room to watch the waiters setting the table.

MACIEK and ANDRZEJ are standing in a corridor, apparently wiping their hands on a towel. DREWNOWSKI enters through a a door and passes them by without a sign of recognition, on his way to meet SLOMKA. MACIEK is whistling softly. The two men pass the lavatory, as DREWNOWSKI addresses SLOMKA, a big, powerfully-built man with rather coarse features.

DREWNOWSKI: *Good evening. How are things?*

SLOMKA: *Good evening. I hope the Mayor will approve.*

DREWNOWSKI: *The Mayor is particularly anxious about tonight.*

SLOMKA: *I understand. The end of the war. A memorable moment.* He gestures towards the lavatory door. *The toilets. Quite convenient.*

The lavatory door opens and JURGELUSZKA, an old, shrivelled woman-attendant comes out.

SLOMKA: *How are you doing, Mrs. Jurgeluszka?*

JURGELUSZKA: *All right, thank you. It's pretty quiet.*

DREWNOWSKI and SLOMKA walk away and the old woman looks suspiciously after them.

173

In the banqueting room, SLOMKA and DREWNOWSKI are in the foreground looking down a long table, which is already laden with dishes. DREWNOWSKI sits at the head of the table, clearly impressed.

DREWNOWSKI with assumed nonchalance: *It doesn't look bad at first sight.*

SLOMKA: *Rest assured, Mr. Secretary, it will look even better when you eat it.*

MACIEK has stopped in front of a large wall mirror and is pushing his hair back over his ears.

MACIEK: *Wait!*

The hotel bar, with a pretty blonde girl behind it, is reflected in the mirror, and MACIEK's attention is immediately taken by her. He is joined by ANDRZEJ.

MACIEK: *Wait. Isn't she pretty? Look!*

ANDRZEJ looking round sharply: *Where?*

MACIEK and ANDRZEJ approach the bar from the background — MACIEK eagerly, ANDRZEJ with reluctance.

ANDRZEJ: *Don't lay it on.*

MACIEK: *Come on, let's have a drink.*

They sit on stools at the bar. MACIEK fixes his gaze on the blonde, KRYSTYNA, as she walks up to the coffee machine and turns the tap on.

MACIEK: *Good evening. What can we have to drink?*

KRYSTYNA: *Sorb vodka? Old?*

ANDRZEJ: *Two small plain, please.*

KRYSTYNA walks down the bar towards MACIEK and ANDRZEJ and sets two glasses before them, then reaches for a bottle on the bar counter near the only other customer at the bar — PIENIAZEK.

KRYSTYNA leans over MACIEK's glass to pour the vodka in. But at the last moment MACIEK, quick as a flash, grasps the glass and darts it away from the bottle.

KRYSTYNA, entering into the game, leans over the glass again, aiming for it with the bottle and watching MACIEK for any movement. He repeats his manoeuvre of snatching the glass away.

The next round: ANDRZEJ is watching the game closely as

174

MACIEK once again darts the glass away from the bottle. At the same time, with his other hand, he pulls out a battered and bent old German mess cup, which he substitutes for the glass. He shows with his fingers how much vodka he wants her to pour into it.

KRYSTYNA, with a hardly perceptible smile, pours vodka into the cup.

ANDRZEJ thaws out sufficiently to exchange a smile with MACIEK. KRYSTYNA pours vodka into ANDRZEJ's glass and walks away.

ANDRZEJ and MACIEK are in the foreground, with PIENIAZEK, already showing the effects of drink, behind. KRYSTYNA approaches him with a bottle, refills the glass and starts to go away, but PIENIAZEK calls her back.

PIENIAZEK : *Miss Krystyna . . .*

KRYSTYNA : *Yes sir?*

MACIEK : *Krystyna. A pretty name.*

ANDRZEJ : *Stop acting the fool.*

MACIEK : *I'm not acting the fool.*

KRYSTYNA comes back and ANDRZEJ takes out a wad of paper money. MACIEK is still watching her smilingly, but she pretends unconcern.

ANDRZEJ : *Drink up and let's go.* He turns to KRYSTYNA. *Two large plain . . .*

He gets up from his stool and places a small pile of notes on the bar counter. MACIEK, however, is reluctant to leave.

MACIEK : *Nice. The bar, I mean, not you.*

KRYSTYNA goes up to the beer tap and starts to fill a glass of beer. MACIEK appears and switches the tap off. KRYSTYNA switches it on again and the game restarts.

MACIEK : *How long do you stay open?*

KRYSTYNA : *We close at three.*

A small vase of violets is standing on the counter near the beer tap. MACIEK picks it up.

MACIEK : *Do you like violets?*

KRYSTYNA with mock intensity : *Very much!*

MACIEK, sniffing the violets, assumes the same manner.

MACIEK : *Me too!*

ANDRZEJ off : *Maciek!*

Maciek, showing by his expression that he has to tear himself away, replaces the violets on the counter surface and leaves at last. Krystyna glances after him with a flicker of interest.

Two girls are standing in a corridor, adjusting their hair. Andrzej comes up from behind them; Maciek catches him up, turning round and staring at the two girls.

Maciek : *Did you see that?*

Andrzej : *What?*

Maciek : *Those two. They were almost like Warsaw girls. Do we have to leave?*

Andrzej : *Stay if you want to.*

Maciek : *It's easy for you to say stay.*

Andrzej : *No one is waiting for you, as far as I know.*

Maciek : *That's just it. Why stay if no one is waiting?*

Andrzej : *I don't follow you.*

Maciek laughs suddenly.

Maciek : *Neither do I.*

They walk away.

Andrzej enters a telephone booth under the staircase in the entrance-hall of the hotel. Maciek remains outside. Andrzej starts to dial a number.

A large portrait of a man on a white horse fills the screen; he is wearing a major's uniform. A telephone is ringing somewhere in the background.

Through an open door we see Mrs. Staniewicz, seated, holding a handful of cards. The rest of the company is out of sight.

An old woman servant is cleaning a naked sabre; the portrait of the cavalry major is in the background.

Woman Servant : *It's probably the master ...*

The Servant continues cleaning the sabre, while Mrs. Staniewicz gets up to answer the phone.

On her way to the telephone, she takes the sabre from the Servant, almost absent-mindedly, and places it with another sword beneath a holy image of Our Lady of Czestochowa.

Mrs. Staniewicz speaking into the telephone : *Hallo? Mrs. Staniewicz speaking. I'll put you through. Excuse me.*

176

MRS. STANIEWICZ unplugs the phone, picks it up and carries it away down the hall.

MRS. STANIEWICZ calling: *Telephone for you, major!*

The door opens and a bald-headed man, WAGA, appears and takes the receiver. MRS. STANIEWICZ discreetly retires.

WAGA taking the receiver: *Hallo? Hallo?*

ANDRZEJ is talking into the receiver of the telephone in the booth. MACIEK is visible in the entrance-hall, lounging at the reception desk.

ANDRZEJ: *Andrzej speaking. Just to let you know that the matter's been successfully settled.*

SZCZUKA and PODGORSKI enter the hall through the main door. PODGORSKI stops at the reception desk.

ANDRZEJ continuing: *Everything's O.K. No complications.*

PODGORSKI is talking to the PORTER at the desk.

PODGORSKI: *Good evening. Have you got a room for Comrade Szczuka? Reserved by the City Hall?*

MACIEK is startled by the name. He raises his head quickly,

glances at the new arrivals and walks towards the telephone booth, leaving his newspaper behind.

PORTER : *Certainly. Everything's O.K. Number eighteen has been reserved. First floor.*

ANDRZEJ is still speaking into the telephone. MACIEK appears outside the booth, making desperate signs to ANDRZEJ.

ANDRZEJ agitated : *Yes . . . Yes . . . Yes. Hold on a moment.*

WAGA at the telephone, the portrait behind him.

WAGA anxiously : *Hallo! Hallo! . . . What happened to you? Did you have to go away? One moment, I don't understand. You failed? Yes . . . Yes, it's clear now. Can't be helped. All right, come along here. At once.*

ANDRZEJ and MACIEK are now both in the telephone booth. MACIEK opens the door and gets out. ANDRZEJ lingers behind for a moment, nervously toying with the telephone receiver.

SZCZUKA is filling in a form at the reception desk. Having finished, he hands it to the PORTER. MACIEK appears just beside SZCZUKA.

PORTER : *Thank you.*

SZCZUKA : *Have you got any cigarettes?*

PORTER : *Yes, sir. American, Hungarian?*

SZCZUKA : *Let's have American.*

ANDRZEJ passes by behind SZCZUKA and looks quickly towards MACIEK, who has started reading his paper again, lounging against the reception desk.

ANDRZEJ : *Wait for me in the bar. I won't be long.*

MACIEK : *All right. I've waited for bigger things.*

Meanwhile SZCZUKA, having obtained his cigarettes, speaks to the PORTER.

SZCZUKA : *Do you know the Staniewicz family?*

PORTER : *I do, sir.*

SZCZUKA : *Do they live where they used to, before the war?*

PORTER : *Yes sir. The same place. Just round the corner.*

He points towards the window.

SZCZUKA : *Thank you.*

PORTER : *Shall I put you through? They're on the 'phone: 12-14.*

SZCZUKA tears open the new packet of cigarettes and takes one out. MACIEK, himself meaning to have a cigarette, strikes a match and offers a light to SZCZUKA. The latter draws on

his cigarette and looks pleasantly at the young man. The
PORTER hands a slip of paper bearing the telephone number
to SZCZUKA.

SZCZUKA : *Thank you.*

He takes his room keys, walking stick and brief case, then turns
to PODGORSKI.

SZCZUKA : *What time is that banquet again? Ten?*

PODGORSKI : *That's right. There's a car at your disposal.*

PODGORSKI goes out; SZCZUKA, limping slightly, walks towards
the staircase. MACIEK gazes after him, before turning back to
the reception desk. MACIEK leans over it, picking his teeth
with a matchstick.

PORTER : *Can I help you?*

MACIEK : *A packet of cigarettes, please.*

PORTER : *American, Hungarian?*

MACIEK : *Hungarian. They're stronger.*

MACIEK takes out a fifty zlotys bank note and lays it on the
counter.

MACIEK in the foreground, the PORTER standing behind the
counter.

MACIEK : *It's all right. Keep the change. Smoke?*

MACIEK leans over the counter, holding out a packet of
cigarettes.

PORTER brightening up : *Too strong. At my age, you know, the
cough . . .*

MACIEK : *What age? How old are you?*

PORTER : *Sixty. A good sixty.*

MACIEK : *Wouldn't give you fifty.*

PORTER : *Are you by yourself?*

MACIEK : *For the moment.*

PORTER : *A blonde?*

MACIEK : *Very likely.*

PORTER : *It's really difficult with the doubles, believe me.*

MACIEK : *Doesn't matter. A single will do. The closer, the better.*

PORTER : *You're from Warsaw, aren't you?*

MACIEK : *Where else?*

The PORTER leans over the counter, smiling. MACIEK is in
the foreground, his back to us.

179

PORTER : *I'm from Warsaw. I used to work in the Savoy, you know.*

MACIEK : *Nowy Swiat Street?*

PORTER : *Just two months short of twenty-five years. Quite a stretch, isn't it?*

MACIEK : *Were you in the Rising?*

PORTER : *Of course. In the Centre, till the last day. And you?*

MACIEK now facing camera.

MACIEK : *Here and there. First in the Old Town, then in the Centre.*

PORTER : *Yes . . . you become a different kind of man here.*

The PORTER, now swept away by his own sentimentality, is facing camera.

PORTER continuing : *It's like losing an arm, not having Warsaw. Worse.*

MACIEK : *That's right. If you could see the chestnuts blooming in Ujazdowski Park.*

PORTER : *Blooming, are they?*

The PORTER makes a come-what-may gesture.

PORTER : *I meant to give you a room on the third floor, but it's not nice . . . bugs!*

The PORTER turns and reaches towards the pigeon-holes behind him, takes out a key and hands it to MACIEK and shakes his hand at the same time.

PORTER continuing : *Take number seventeen, first floor. You deserve it. Here's the key.*

MACIEK : *Thank you.*

PORTER : *We've got to stick together. Any luggage?*

MACIEK points to his rucksack.

MACIEK : *That's all.*

MACIEK, now facing camera, takes out a German identity card.

PORTER : *That's not much.*

MACIEK : *Enough. I've had less.*

He hands his identity card to the PORTER, who adjusts his glasses and looks at it.

PORTER : *Maciek Chelmicki?*

MACIEK : *That's right.*

PORTER : *Born Warsaw, 1921. Occupation . . . worker?*

180

MACIEK : *That's for the Germans. I'm a student. Thank you.*
MACIEK takes the key and slings the rucksack over his shoulder and walks towards the staircase.

SZCZUKA is in his hotel room, sipping tea. He approaches a telephone, and seems to hesitate. It is a large double room, furnished with the remnants of provincial, bourgeois comfort. SZCZUKA takes out the slip of paper the PORTER has given him, then crumples it up disgustedly and starts to sip his glass of tea again.
MACIEK enters his own small, dark room next door. He stops at the locked door in the partition which separates him from SZCZUKA's room and listens for a second. Then he walks to the window.
We are outside the hotel; MACIEK comes to his window and opens it. He takes off his battle-jacket and pullover, unbuttons his collar and looks around.
Through a window, exactly opposite from MACIEK across the courtyard, a girl can be seen weeping. SLOMKA enters the room.
SLOMKA : *What are you blubbering for? Have they been saying things in the kitchen? You're stupid! They're all jealous of you!*
MACIEK looks out from his darkened room; he is now shirtless. He leans forward as the girl's weeping becomes louder.
STEFKA, a peasant girl, is seated on the bed and wailing unrestrainedly, and SLOMKA is standing over her. STEFKA is shaking her head to deny SLOMKA's suspicions.
SLOMKA : *What then?*
STEFKA crying : *Stasiek's been murdered! The bastards shot him!*
SLOMKA : *What Stasiek? Who shot him?*
STEFKA turns towards the bed and slides to her knees.
STEFKA : *Stasiek Gawlik! Oh God, kill the bastards!*
SLOMKA : *Sit down.*
She complies, sitting on the bed.
SLOMKA : *Why should they kill him?*
STEFKA : *How should I know?*
SLOMKA pours vodka into a glass.
SLOMKA : *Probably it's not true.*
STEFKA : *I know it's true! Jeziorek came just now . . .*

SLOMKA: *The cop? I expect he was just after vodka. I bet he got it all mixed up.*

STEFKA: *He said they shot two workers from the cement works this afternoon. I knew there was something wrong. Who did they shoot, I asked. And he says, Smolarski and Stasiek Gawlik. My God, I thought I was going to die; I felt it in my insides. Seems they were after someone else and killed these two by mistake.*

She holds her head in her hands and starts rocking and wailing again.

SLOMKA: *Drink up. It can't be helped if it's happened. Stop crying. I'll give you a pair of stockings.*

STEFKA gulps down the vodka at one go and SLOMKA at once pushes her down on to the bed and starts to pull her skirt up. She resists a little, but without conviction.

STEFKA: *You've got a cheek! Don't be in such a hurry!*

SLOMKA: *Why not?*

STEFKA: *Because! Come on. Let's see the stockings.*

MACIEK closes the window and pulls the blind down.

Inside the room: he finishes pulling the blind down, then

182

turns and walks over to the centre of the room, his clean, white shirt still unbuttoned.

MACIEK sits down, takes out a pistol and pulls out the magazine, which is empty. He takes a fistful of cartridges from a pocket and loads the magazine. The sound of footsteps pacing up and down comes through the walls from SZCZUKA's room. SZCZUKA is pacing up and down in his room, limping slightly and leaning heavily on his stick.

A view of a street through an open window. Tanks are moving along the street with detachments of foot soldiers. It is too dark to see much, but the troops are singing a Russian song. WAGA appears and closes the window.

ANDRZEJ off : *Innocent people have died needlessly.*

He walks from the window; ANDRZEJ is now visible in the foreground.

WAGA watching him : *Conscience stricken?*

ANDRZEJ : *Do you think that's wrong, major?*

WAGA : *Do you know who was killed?*

ANDRZEJ : *Workers from the cement works, I imagine.*

WAGA moves forward towards ANDRZEJ.

WAGA : *The position is clear: a mistake has been made and it must be put right.*

ANDRZEJ hesitantly : *Major, I meant to ask . . .*

WAGA : *Yes?*

ANDRZEJ : *My question may surprise you, but let me ask you frankly. Have we got to kill Szczuka?*

WAGA : *Lieutenant, you're too experienced a soldier not to realise that I have a right to ignore your question, as your superior officer.*

WAGA starts pacing the room.

ANDRZEJ : *I think . . .*

WAGA : *I don't want to know what you think. I'm waiting for an answer.*

ANDRZEJ : *Yes.*

WAGA : *I'm glad we're of the same opinion. Nevertheless, I'll give you your answer.*

WAGA walks out of shot.

WAGA continuing off : *I understand your doubts. I'd be surprised if you had none. The situation is complex and difficult. But the war has taught us that all difficult matters should be approached from a simple, single viewpoint. No compromises. It's one thing or the other.*

He reappears on the other side of ANDRZEJ.

WAGA : *When did you join the Resistance?*

ANDRZEJ : *In 1940.*

WAGA stops pacing for a moment, then takes two steps towards ANDRZEJ.

WAGA : *And what have you been fighting for? For a free Poland, wasn't it? But was this how you imagined it? You must be aware, lieutenant, that in Poland as it is, the only chance for you and thousands like you is to fight on. Where can you go with your record? In this country everything is closed to you. Except prison.*

ANDRZEJ : *I know.*

WAGA : *And now for this gentleman who is proving rather troublesome.*

SZCZUKA is pacing up and down his room at the hotel.

Resume on ANDRZEJ and WAGA; the latter is pacing about slowly again.

WAGA: *Who is Szczuka? Well, he's a civil engineer, a graduate, a communist. An excellent organiser. A man who knows where he's going. He's just come back from Russia after several years away. He went to work for the Regional Committee. And you are aware, lieutenant, of the power of the First Secretary. The skilful removal of such a man should have considerable impact; it would be very effective propaganda for us. In any case, the situation in our sector has seriously deteriorated.*

ANDRZEJ looks questioningly at WAGA. A heavy rumble of tanks can be heard again, coming from the street outside.

WAGA: *I've just had a report that Captain Wilk's[1] detachment was surrounded by the army and security police last night. There were heavy losses. Only a handful managed to get away.*

ANDRZEJ: *That's bad news. Though if I know Wilk, he'll find his way out.*

ANDRZEJ moves closer to WAGA.

WAGA: *I'm afraid the captain was killed.*

A sideboard with pieces of china arranged decoratively on it; MRS. STANIEWICZ enters, picks up a piece and turns back and walks towards KOTOWICZ and PUCIATYCKI seated at the table.

PUCIATYCKI: *I must say, madam, that it's really easy to relax at your place. You can forget all that . . .*

MRS. STANIEWICZ accepts the compliment with a smile; PUCIATYCKI gestures towards the window.

MRS. STANIEWICZ: *I'm glad my dear count. But remember, there are no Colonels' ladies here.[2]*

PUCIATYCKI: *Quite right. This is not the time to use titles.*

KOTOWICZ passes on the piece of china for inspection to PUCIATYCKI.

KOTOWICZ: *Here . . .*

PUCIATYCKI addressing MRS. STANIEWICZ: *Thank you. And how's our business going?*

MRS. STANIEWICZ: *Everything's going smoothly.*

MRS. PUCIATYCKI, also sitting at the table, comes into shot.

---

[1] Polish for "wolf"; here used as the pseudonym of a guerilla leader.

[2] In conventional Polish usage, the wife of an army officer, especially a high-ranking one, is addressed by a form of her husband's title, used here by PUCIATYCKI.

185

MRS. PUCIATYCKI : *Are you certain, darling?*

KOTOWICZ : *In these times, nothing is certain.*

MRS. STANIEWICZ : *What a pessimist! Don't worry! Our friends won't let us down.*

PUCIATYCKI : *Well, our fate is in your lovely hands.*

MRS. STANIEWICZ : *Rather in my husband's hands. I'm certain he won't spare any efforts to get us out of here.*

Camera pans to portrait of STANIEWICZ and back.

KOTOWICZ : *Well, it's getting late. Let's drink to the Colonel's health at the Monopol.*

The old woman SERVANT enters.

THE SERVANT : *Mr. Szczuka to see you, ma'am.*

MRS. STANIEWICZ very startled : *Who? What did he say?*

THE SERVANT : *Mr. Szczuka.*

The SERVANT goes out and MRS. STANIEWICZ gets to her feet, trying hard to cover her confusion.

MRS. STANIEWICZ : *Forgive me, but I'll have to leave you for a minute. I have to attend to some rather boring business.*

MRS. PUCIATYCKI : *Poor darling, business is always boring.*

PUCIATYCKI : *But it is becoming impossible to live without it.*

MRS. STANIEWICZ : *Exactly.*

SZCZUKA is waiting in the corridor outside the door of the flat. He pulls back the sleeve of his coat and glances impatiently at his wrist-watch.

Inside the flat, MRS. STANIEWICZ walks along the hall towards the door. Her mood has changed completely, becoming cold and hard.

As MRS. STANIEWICZ reaches the door, she shuts the creaky door of a hall cupboard which has swung open. She turns to a mirror on the opposite wall and pushes a few stray locks of hair back into place.

She opens the door and SZCZUKA steps into the hall. MRS. STANIEWICZ turns away from him, very annoyed, then turns round towards him. When SZCZUKA sees her expression, he begins to look worried. The cupboard door swings noisily open again.

SZCZUKA : *How are you Catherine?*

MRS. STANIEWICZ shuts the door of the cupboard again, still glaring at SZCZUKA.

Mrs. Staniewicz : *Yes, what is it?*

Camera on Szczuka, who looks very serious.

Szczuka : *You know I only came back from abroad a month ago.*

Camera on Mrs. Staniewicz, very ill at ease.

Mrs. Staniewicz : *I know, I got your letter.*

Szczuka : *I wrote three.*

Mrs. Staniewicz : *I'd nothing new to tell you. I still haven't.*

Throughout this exchange, Mrs. Staniewicz's guests go on talking off, though presumably they are out of Szczuka's hearing.

Puciatycki : *The Western powers'll strike quick as lightning, you'll see. In a year at the most, Rose, we shall be able to return the hospitality to Catherine and the Colonel in our Chwaliboga . . . I hadn't the slightest idea his name was Mroczek. Well, our Mroczek comes loaded with goodies and says, "Good morning, count." "What count?" I replied. "Are you mad? Don't you realise we have democracy now?"*

There is general laughter among the guests.

Kotowicz : *And what did he say?*

Puciatycki : *Who, Mroczek? You won't believe it, but he said, "But I don't like democracy, count!" Isn't he wonderful?*

There is more laughter.

Camera on Szczuka; his cordiality has been frozen out by Mrs. Staniewicz's attitude.

Szczuka gravely : *Listen, Catherine, towards the end of 1941 news of Maria's death reached me through friends. I also learned that Marek was staying with you.*

Mrs. Staniewicz : *Do you think I should have sent him to an orphanage, then?*

Szczuka : *I wrote then that I didn't want you . . .*

Camera on Mrs. Staniewicz, hard-faced; Szczuka has his back to us.

Szczuka : *. . . to bring up my son.*

Camera on Szczuka.

Szczuka : *I gave you the names of people, friends of mine, who could take care of Marek until I got back. Did you ever get that letter?*

Mrs. Staniewicz : *No, I never did. But even if I had, I can tell you that Marek would have remained with us. You seem to forget that Maria was my sister, after all.*

The cupboard door swings open noisily again and MRS. STANIEWICZ pushes it back impatiently.

SZCZUKA : *Where is he now?*

MRS. STANIEWICZ : *I don't know. He hasn't been here since October, immediately after the Rising.*

SZCZUKA : *And since then, you've had no news of him?*

MRS. STANIEWICZ : *No.*

SZCZUKA : *And is that all you can tell me about my son? Listen Catherine, he's only just seventeen.*

MRS. STANIEWICZ : *I know. Nowadays, boys of seventeen are grown men.*

SZCZUKA : *Who is he now? What kind of man have you made of him?*

MRS. STANIEWICZ : *A good Pole, I can assure you.*

SZCZUKA : *I can imagine, with your patriotism. I can easily guess what sort of man you could bring my son up to be.*

Camera on SZCZUKA.

SZCZUKA : *But he is only seventeen. If he is alive, I can tell you, sooner or later my son is going to be mine.*

SZCZUKA opens the door behind him and goes out. MRS. STANIEWICZ turns round thoughtfully. A door in the hall opens and WAGA appears.

WAGA : *Who was it?*

MRS. STANIEWICZ : *Nothing. Nothing important.*

WAGA nods towards ANDRZEJ in the room behind him; ANDRZEJ comes out, pulling his coat collar up.

WAGA : *Wait a moment, this apartment is not very safe.*

ANDRZEJ pulls his coat tightly around him.

The bar of the Hotel Monopol is now filling up with customers. PIENIAZEK is still at the counter, as is MACIEK, who is talking to the very busy KRYSTYNA. She is moving around, constantly leaving him to serve other customers, then coming back. Dance music can be heard coming from an adjoining room. MACIEK glances at his watch.

KRYSTYNA : *Are you in a hurry?*

MACIEK : *Why, no. I'm waiting for somebody.*

KRYSTYNA : *A girl?*

MACIEK : *Displeased?*
KRYSTYNA off : *Who?*
MACIEK : *You.*
　　She re-appears and approaches MACIEK.
KRYSTYNA : *Me? What do I care about your dates?*
MACIEK : *Not at all?*
KRYSTYNA : *I certainly hope not.*
　　She moves away from him again and camera follows her,
　　leaving MACIEK.
MACIEK : *What if I don't believe it?*
KRYSTYNA : *Please yourself.*
MACIEK : *In that case, I don't. What time do you finish?*
KRYSTYNA : *Closing time.*
MACIEK : *Really? And you don't have any help all that time?*
　　She passes MACIEK on her way to the other end of the counter.
KRYSTYNA : *For the time being. A friend comes at ten to help out.*
MACIEK off : *You see?*
　　Over the preceding conversation random off-screen voices are
　　heard.

189

VOICES: *The coffee is marvellous. I expect you don't know my brother-in-law was a commissioned officer before the war? — But that's most interesting; I seem to remember that he was a man of the left. Am I right, darling? I hoped you were going to support me. For myself, I've always respected strong personalities, people with ideas, no matter if I agree with them or not. I believe this is the right attitude for a civilized man to adopt. I hope you agree, don't you? — What about the Nazis? Do you respect them too? — I'm sorry, but I'm not sure what you mean. — Well, some of them have pretty strong personalities. And they have strong ideas. — My dear friends, have mercy. Do you absolutely have to talk about Nazis? And what about the Jews? I don't want to hear about all that any more. Why do you men always have to talk either about war or women? It's awfully boring. — I'm sorry, forgive me. — More coffee? — Please ...*

KRYSTYNA is back with MACIEK again.

KRYSTYNA: *No, I don't see. When the place is crowded we can both hardly manage. There she is, the girl you've dated!*

MACIEK turns round to look.

MACIEK: *That's right, you've remembered him.*

KRYSTYNA: *Of course, he's good looking.*

ANDRZEJ is walking towards them through the crowded room. MACIEK goes to meet him.

ANDRZEJ stops as MACIEK comes up to him.

ANDRZEJ: *Let's go to the other room. It's quiet there.*

MACIEK: *What's wrong with you? This is the quietest spot on earth. Don't be so fussy!*

An empty table in a corner of the bar; MACIEK and ANDRZEJ enter and walk towards the table.

MACIEK: *Don't you like it here? I think it's great.*

They sit down; MACIEK takes up a position opposite KRYSTYNA'S counter. Throughout the scene his attention is divided between ANDRZEJ and watching KRYSTYNA.

MACIEK: *Not bad, is it?*

Rapid shot of KRYSTYNA.

ANDRZEJ: *Could be worse. Are you going away?*

MACIEK: *Where?*

ANDRZEJ: *I thought you were going to Warsaw.*

MACIEK: *What's happened? Did Florian call it off?*

ANDRZEJ : *On the contrary.*

MACIEK : *Then what do you take me for? Have I ever run away from work? Guess who's staying in the famous Monopol at number seventeen, next to you-know-who?*

ANDRZEJ smiling and slapping MACIEK lightly on the back : *All right. You're O.K. Maciek.*

Rapid shot of KRYSTYNA serving customers at the bar.

MACIEK places his finger on the tip of his nose, flattening it slightly, and looks at ANDRZEJ who continues gazing moodily in front of him.

KOTOWICZ comes into the room and stops and leans on the bar, obstructing KRYSTYNA from view.

MACIEK'S cheerful mood at once changes to irritability.

MACIEK : *Jesus, who is that idiot?*

ANDRZEJ : *Which one?*

KOTOWICZ, seen only from the back so far, turns round and looks at MACIEK as if the comment has reached his ears.

MACIEK : *The one with the stupid back.*

ANDRZEJ : *Face too.*

KOTOWICZ facing KRYSTYNA behind the counter.

VOICE off : *Thank you very much.*

KOTOWICZ : *Good evening, Miss Krystyna.*

KRYSTYNA : *Good evening. The usual? Vodka and vermouth?*

KOTOWICZ raising his finger waggishly : *A cognac today, for a change.*

KRYSTYNA laughingly : *You must have done some good business.*

KOTOWICZ : *Artistic business.*

KRYSTYNA : *What about the show?*

KOTOWICZ : *First class, Everything is ready for tonight.*

SLOMKA is showing MR. and MRS. PUCIATYCKI and MRS. STANIEWICZ to a table.

SLOMKA : *At your service, count.*

They all sit down and SLOMKA departs to call a waiter. There are sounds of a small orchestra tuning up off.

KOTOWICZ off : *Ladies and gentlemen! And now for our artistic soirée!*

KOTOWICZ is standing on a low platform; the audience is visible on either side below him, facing the platform.

KOTOWICZ : *To celebrate this solemn day, the day which has brought war to an end, who better than Miss Hanka Lewicka, that brilliant and unique singer.*

He leads the singer, who is wearing a low-cut evening gown, to the front of the platform, before stepping down to loud applause.

KOTOWICZ is standing in the front line of the audience; he grins and raises both thumbs in a good-luck sign.

HANKA LEWICKA is on the platform singing "The Red Poppies of Monte Cassino". There is a reverent hush in the room during the singing.

MACIEK and ANDRZEJ are in the bar, which is quickly emptying. In the background, the backs of the audience listening to HANKA LEWICKA can be seen. A waiter places a tray on which there are a number of full glasses on a counter at the rear of the bar and then disappears. MACIEK and ANDRZEJ get up. MACIEK goes up to the tray on the counter, sniffs the vodka and looks up excitedly.

MACIEK : *Remember?*

ANDRZEJ seems somehow reluctant to respond; he continues leaning against a pillar, with MACIEK in the background.

ANDRZEJ : *What?*

MACIEK : *The stuff we drank at Ginger's.*

ANDRZEJ : *No.*

MACIEK picks up two full glasses and walks over to ANDRZEJ and makes him sniff one.

MACIEK : *Don't you remember? You must do!*

He walks irritably back to the tray and places the glasses back on the counter.

ANDRZEJ : *No, I don't remember!*

MACIEK starts sliding the glasses bar-room fashion down the polished counter to where ANDRZEJ is standing. MACIEK himself walks up to ANDRZEJ, who has remained very calm and detached.

MACIEK : *No?*

MACIEK strikes a match and lights the spirit in the glasses. ANDRZEJ relaxes and, as each of the glasses catches fire, he recites a name.

192

ANDRZEJ : *Haneczka, Wilga, Kossobudzki, Ginger, Kajtek . . .*

But as MACIEK tries to light the last two glasses, ANDRZEJ blows the match out and raises one of the glasses and offers it to MACIEK.

ANDRZEJ : *We are still alive.*

MACIEK, leaning on his elbows, his back against the counter, throws his head back and laughs loudly, almost hysterically.

MACIEK : *Those were the days!*

ANDRZEJ : *You think so?*

MACIEK : *Sure. When did you have so many real pals? Girls or fellahs?*

ANDRZEJ : *So what? They're all dead.*

MACIEK : *Yes, but the life was better.*

ANDRZEJ : *Because we were different.*

MACIEK : *Younger . . .*

ANDRZEJ : *Not only that. We knew what we wanted.*

MACIEK : *Perhaps . . .*

ANDRZEJ : *And what was expected of us.*

HANKA LEWICKA can still be heard singing in the next room.

MACIEK: *You've got it now! What they wanted from us was our lives. That's clear enough! And they still want the same thing. It's all right, though. We can afford that.*

ANDRZEJ in the foreground, holding his glass. MACIEK seems very emotional and excited. The Monte Cassino song in the next room continues, coming up to the last verse.

ANDRZEJ: *Stop acting. It's easy to die.*

MACIEK: *Depends how.*

ANDRZEJ: *It's all we're good for.*

MACIEK: *Isn't it enough?*

ANDRZEJ: *It's very little.*

MACIEK: *You're exaggerating.* He goes up close to ANDRZEJ. *You shouldn't take it so seriously. The main thing is to get out of this mess and stay out of trouble. Try to have a good time. What else is there?*

ANDRZEJ: *Perhaps you're right.*

They both tilt their glasses back and drain them. In the next room, HANKA LEWICKA is coming to the end of her song; the crowd listens attentively.

ANDRZEJ and MACIEK have remained at the counter on which the glasses are still burning. We are looking along the counter — MACIEK is in the foreground, still leaning with his back against the woodwork. ANDRZEJ is in the background facing the counter. As the song in the next room ends, there is an outbreak of applause.

ANDRZEJ: *Listen Maciek, I've got to talk to you seriously.*

There is more applause and noise from the next room. Additional lights come up in the bar and people begin to come in from the next room; ANDRZEJ and MACIEK move away from them, towards the bar window.

ANDRZEJ: *Noisy brutes!*

MACIEK looks in the direction of the mirror on the wall and, not finding the reflection he had hoped for, turns to look towards the counter.

Close shot of MACIEK and ANDRZEJ with the now crowded bar in the background.

ANDRZEJ: *How will you manage this man?*

MACIEK: *Don't worry, I'll manage.*

ANDRZEJ : *Listen, Maciek. I'm responsible to Florian for this busi-ness.*

MACIEK : *All right, and I'm responsible to you. Everybody has to be responsible to somebody.*

ANDRZEJ : *There's just one other thing . . .*

MACIEK : *The order will be carried out. Anything else?*

ANDRZEJ : *First, Florian doesn't want me to be directly involved in this job. And then . . .*

MACIEK : *What else?*

ANDRZEJ : *I've got to leave here at dawn.*

MACIEK : *That's news!*

ANDRZEJ : *Quite. I'm going to take Wilk's place.*

MACIEK : *Take Wilk's place? What's the matter with him?*

ANDRZEJ : *I'm taking over.*

MACIEK : *So that's it . . .*

MACIEK seems to think for a moment, then looks round.

KRYSTYNA is busy in the crowded bar. She glances towards the window.

ANDRZEJ and MACIEK by the window.

MACIEK : *Listen, Andrzej. You said that no one was waiting for me. That's quite true. Will you take me with you?*

ANDRZEJ is clearly cheered up by MACIEK'S proposal.

ANDRZEJ : *Is that serious, Maciek?*

MACIEK : *Serious? In this country nothing is serious. But if you'll take me, I'll come. I fancy that. In the morning, then?*

ANDRZEJ : *We have to leave at four-thirty. So you see, you haven't much time to settle this man.*

MACIEK : *Wait a minute. The banquet for this crowd starts at ten? It should take them three hours. He'll have to come back to sleep.*

ANDRZEJ : *I'll see you later, Maciek. Take care of yourself.*

ANDRZEJ leaves the table. MACIEK remains alone under the window, looking very thoughtful.

All the stools at the bar counter are occupied. MACIEK appears and stops at a corner of the counter. KRYSTYNA notices him and looks at him mockingly as she draws a glass of beer. He reaches out his hand to snatch a small glass of violets from the bar counter, but KRYSTYNA is too quick for him and snatches up the glass as she goes by.

KRYSTYNA is at the coffee-machine, drawing a cup of coffee,

while there is a loud hiss of escaping steam from the machine. MACIEK drinks from his battered mess mug, then looks around and pushes his dark glasses up and rubs his eyes.

Close shot of KRYSTYNA.

KRYSTYNA: *Alone, are you?*

Camera on MACIEK again, pushing his spectacles back into place.

MACIEK: *Unfortunately.*

KRYSTYNA is wiping a glass. She glances into it to make sure that it is clean.

MACIEK looks on, mock-anxious.

MACIEK: *When is your friend coming? At ten?*

KRYSTYNA remains unforthcoming, but nevertheless seems rather amused.

KRYSTYNA: *Yes.*

Close shot of MACIEK.

MACIEK: *In that case, you can be free, say, about . . .*

KRYSTYNA watches him ironically.

MACIEK off: *. . . ten-thirty. Right?*

Close shot of MACIEK.

MACIEK: *You can say you're not feeling well, or you've got a headache . . .*

Close shot of KRYSTYNA.

MACIEK off: *. . . or something . . .?*

FIRST VOICE off: *Miss Krystyna!*

Camera on MACIEK.

MACIEK: *Let 'em wait.*

KRYSTYNA looks at him coolly, then walks quickly away.

ANOTHER VOICE off: *The bill, please . . .*

Camera on MACIEK, looking irritable.

MACIEK: *Don't go. They can wait.*

Camera on KRYSTYNA; she adjusts a knob on the coffee machine.

MACIEK off: *Will you be able to get away?*

KRYSTYNA shrugging her shoulders: *Suppose I will?*

Close shot of MACIEK.

MACIEK: *I'm staying at this hotel.*

Close shot of KRYSTYNA.

KRYSTYNA: *Really? How nice for you.*

MACIEK off : *First floor, number seventeen.*

KRYSTYNA : *Are you sure?*

MACIEK : *It can be checked easily enough.*

KRYSTYNA : *I'm afraid I only check my accounts.*

MACIEK : *Only that?*

KRYSTYNA : *And that's more than enough. They never tally.*

Close shot of MACIEK.

MACIEK : *Is it true you only check accounts? Anyway, you can try checking something else this once.*

KRYSTYNA looks up at him.

MACIEK looks back questionably and hopefully.

MACIEK : *At least this will tally, I can tell you. Well?*

Camera on KRYSTYNA.

KRYSTYNA : *Well?*

MACIEK picks up the violets again and sniffs them.

MACIEK : *I swear those violets smell even nicer.*

KRYSTYNA smiles mockingly.

MACIEK continuing off : *Room seventeen, ten-thirty.*

KRYSTYNA shakes her head.

Camera on MACIEK.

MACIEK : *I shall be expecting you.* He raises his hand in a scout salute. *Word of honour.*

By way of reply, KRYSTYNA turns to the coffee machine and opens the tap; the steam escapes with a loud swishing sound.

MACIEK retreats before the jet of steam.

KRYSTYNA stands looking in the direction of MACIEK, all her nonchalance gone.

PIENIAZEK off : *Miss Krystyna!*

KRYSTYNA disappears.

MACIEK is walking across the dance floor, between the dancing couples, his fingers still raised in a scout salute.

Close shot of KRYSTYNA drawing a glass of beer.

MACIEK is seen disappearing among the crowd.

KRYSTYNA sticks her tongue out in the direction of MACIEK.

MACIEK gives a final wave, grins and turns to leave the room.

KRYSTYNA, behind the counter, approaches PIENIAZEK.

KRYSTYNA : *Mr. Pieniazek!*

PIENIAZEK : *Yes?*

KRYSTYNA : *Here's your bill, please.*

197

PIENIAZEK : *Oh yes, the bill. A moment, Miss Krystyna.*

Clearly reluctant to pay, he looks about him, desperate for rescue.

VOICE off : *Miss Krystyna!*

PIENIAZEK : *One moment, one moment.*

DREWNOWSKI is moving through the dancing couples.

PIENIAZEK spots DREWNOWSKI and starts to move away from the bar counter, his arms raised in welcome.

PIENIAZEK : *And who do I see here? The Mayor's secretary in person! Are you enjoying yourself?*

PIENIAZEK and DREWNOWSKI together.

DREWNOWSKI stiffly : *Excuse me, I'm on duty.*

PIENIAZEK : *I see the illustrious Town Council is displeased with the press.*

DREWNOWSKI : *I wasn't aware of it.*

PIENIAZEK : *Not able to spare an invitation to the banquet, were you?*

DREWNOWSKI : *Editor Pawlicki was invited.*

PIENIAZEK : *Pawlicki! And I suppose reporter Pieniazek doesn't count.*

DREWNOWSKI : *I'm sorry, but the list was made up by the Mayor himself.*

PIENIAZEK grabbing hold of DREWNOWSKI'S jacket : *Ah yes, that's it. My old friend Swiecki.*

DREWNOWSKI tries to walk round PIENIAZEK, but the journalist's drunken stare visibly disturbs him.

DREWNOWSKI : *What? Why are you staring at me like that?*

PIENIAZEK scratching himself : *Nothing. Though, come to think of it, something did just occur to me which could be of passing interest to you.*

DREWNOWSKI, making as though to leave, turns back at PIENIAZEK'S words.

DREWNOWSKI : *What's that?*

PIENIAZEK : *Just a little problem. When my friend Swiecki . . .*

KRYSTYNA reappears on the other side of the counter.

KRYSTYNA : *Mr. Pieniazek . . .*

Camera on DREWNOWSKI and PIENIAZEK together; DREWNOWSKI has already caught the bait.

DREWNOWSKI : *Yes? Yes?*

All of DREWNOWSKI's reserve has disappeared.

PIENIAZEK : . . . *or, if you prefer, my former friend Swiecki, goes to Warsaw, is he, or isn't he, going to take his present secretary with him?*

PIENIAZEK starts to walk away. DREWNOWSKI tries to hold him back, then starts to follow him.

DREWNOWSKI : *Me? Do you know anything?*

PIENIAZEK laughing : *Pieniazek knows everything.*

He walks away.

KRYSTYNA is standing behind the bar counter. PIENIAZEK appears, DREWNOWSKI following.

PIENIAZEK : *Miss Krystyna, two double vodkas please.*

KRYSTYNA appears with a bottle and pours the vodka out.

PIENIAZEK turns to DREWNOWSKI.

PIENIAZEK : *Have a drink?*

DREWNOWSKI : *You must excuse me. I'm on duty.*

PIENIAZEK : *So much the better. It's your duty to drink the Minister's health.*

DREWNOWSKI gives in and sits down on a stool beside PIENIAZEK.

DREWNOWSKI : *Is it true?*

PIENIAZEK : *Well!*

DREWNOWSKI : *Which ministry?*

PIENIAZEK whispers something into DREWNOWSKI's ear and raises his glass.

PIENIAZEK : *Health!*

They both down their vodkas and PIENIAZEK immediately gives KRYSTYNA a sign to refill the glasses.

DREWNOWSKI : *Not bad, but I'd prefer the Foreign Office.*

PIENIAZEK : *He would, too. Here's to the Foreign Office!*

They drink up again; DREWNOWSKI, already beginning to feel the effects of the drink, sinks into a dreamy mood.

DREWNOWSKI : *Do you think he will take me with him?*

PIENIAZEK : *He will! He will! Scum always comes to the top.*

DREWNOWSKI only laughs happily at this remark.

DREWNOWSKI : *Just wait! You'll see, in five years . . .*

PIENIAZEK : *Of course I shall! To the five year plan!*

SLOMKA is waiting in the hall of the hotel, straightening his tie. In the background, a number of waiters can be seen in the banqueting room.

SWIECKI comes through the door into the hotel accompanied by two other men. The Mayor greets SLOMKA cordially.

SWIECKI : *How are you, Mr. Slomka?*

SLOMKA : *I'm always well, Mr. Mayor.*

SWIECKI turns laughingly to his companions.

SWIECKI : *There, gentlemen, at last a citizen who isn't complaining.*

The men walk on towards the banqueting room. SLOMKA is walking at SWIECKI's side.

SLOMKA confidentially to SWIECKI : *Excuse me, Mr. Mayor, I have the honour to be acquainted with Mr. Deputy Mayor, but who is this other gentleman?*

SWIECKI : *Kalicki?*

SLOMKA : *That's it. I'm afraid I don't know what position . . .*

SWIECKI : *If you really attach so much importance to positions, as from today, you may call me . . .*

He pauses.

SLOMKA inquiring anxiously : *What? What? Mr. Mayor?*

SWIECKI : *Mr. Minister, I'm afraid, my dear Mr. Slomka.*

SLOMKA seems so startled by this information, that he stumbles over the carpet.

SWIECKI : *Careful, Mr. Slomka.*

They stop at the entrance to the banqueting room, SLOMKA showing the way. SWIECKI glances round.

SLOMKA : *Gentlemen . . .*

We see the two of them from behind, with the banquet table and the attendant waiters in the background.

SWIECKI : *Splendid! Well done, Mr. Slomka. And where is Mr. Drewnowski? Has he been here?*

SLOMKA : *Yes, Mr. Mayor . . . I beg your pardon, Mr. Minister. Mr. Drewnowski has been here to see to everything personally and, if I may say so, approved and praised the arrangements.*

SWIECKI : *Where has he got to? He ought to be here now.*

PIENIAZEK and DREWNOWSKI at the bar; both are now quite drunk. PIENIAZEK is trying to stick a fork into some small pickled mushrooms, which keep eluding his thrusts.

DREWNOWSKI has a dreamy expression on his face, as though

making plans for the future.

PIENIAZEK : *Do you want something to eat?*

DREWNOWSKI shakes his head negatively.

PIENIAZEK : *Tell me, what do you want?*

DREWNOWSKI : *Everything. Lot's of money.*

PIENIAZEK in a drunken stammer : *More . . . money! And you shall have it!*

DREWNOWSKI : *Sure. I'm fed up with being poor.*

DREWNOWSKI : *Miss! Same again, please!*[1]

MACIEK is in his room cleaning his pistol. There is the sound of a gentle tapping on the door. When MACIEK hears the tapping, he screws his eyes up and looks up, then he hurriedly begins to wrap the pistol and a number of other things on the table, including his dark glasses, in a cloth. In his hurry, he drops a cartridge on the floor. He crouches down to look for it, moving backwards all the time towards the door.

He stands up against the door as the gentle knocking is heard again.

MACIEK : *Yes? Who's there?*

KRYSTYNA off : *It's me.*

MACIEK claps his hand to his forehead, as though he had forgotten his invitation to KRYSTYNA. He grins and turns to open the door. KRYSTYNA slips quickly into the room and stands against the wall while MACIEK locks the door again.

KRYSTYNA : *Were you sure I'd come?*

MACIEK : *Yes, quite sure.*

KRYSTYNA : *Do you know why I came? No? It's quite easy. Because I could never fall in love with you.* She is looking in the opposite direction to MACIEK. There is a pause. *Hallo?*

MACIEK : *You don't want to fall in love?*

KRYSTYNA : *With you?*

MACIEK : *In general.*

KRYSTYNA smiling : *Not if I can help it.*

MACIEK : *Is that a principle?*

KRYSTYNA : *Why complicate life?*

---

[1] Another sequence concerning the arrival of KRYSTYNA's helper LILI at the bar, was scripted at this point in the final scenario.

MACIEK impatiently : *It complicates itself.*

KRYSTYNA : *Then why make it worse?*

> MACIEK keeps on circling round, looking surreptitiously for the lost cartridge, making conversation to gain time.

MACIEK : *Tell me about yourself.*

KRYSTYNA : *What for?*

> KRYSTYNA moves away and disappears.
>
> Camera pans round the room, picking up first KRYSTYNA, then MACIEK, who is still searching for the lost cartridge, trying to keep out of her field of view.

KRYSTYNA : *I lived in the country, on my parents' estate.*

MACIEK : *Before the war?*

KRYSTYNA : *Yes. Near Poznan.*

MACIEK : *And later?*

KRYSTYNA : *We moved to Warsaw.*

> KRYSTYNA sits down on the bed.

MACIEK : *We?*

KRYSTYNA : *My mother and I. Father was arrested by the Germans immediately.*

MACIEK : *Did you lose him?*

KRYSTYNA : *Yes . . . in Dachau. What else is there? I suppose that's about all.*

MACIEK : *Mother alive?*

KRYSTYNA : *No. She was killed in the Rising.*

> MACIEK crouches to look under the table. Then he crawls out from underneath the table and kneels in front of KRYSTYNA.

MACIEK : *Mine too. Any brothers or sisters?*

KRYSTYNA : *Luckily not.*

MACIEK : *Luckily?*

KRYSTYNA : *Cuts my losses.*

> MACIEK finds the missing cartridge and, much relieved, straightens up, free at last to give himself to his guest.

MACIEK : *That's true. I had a brother. He was killed in action, in forty-three. Father's in England. I expect he'll stay there.*

KRYSTYNA : *No family?*

> She caresses MACIEK's hair.

MACIEK : *None. Are you going to stay here?*

KRYSTYNA : *I don't know. For the time being.*

MACIEK : *And then what?*

KRYSTYNA: *I'm not thinking that far ahead.*
MACIEK: *Really, I wasn't at all certain you'd come. Do you believe me? I'm a complete stranger to you.*

KRYSTYNA smiles down at him at this confession.
KRYSTYNA: *And I to you.*

At the bar counter; DREWNOWSKI is trying to feed the pickled mushrooms to PIENIAZEK. PIENIAZEK finally gets off his stool and starts trying to drag DREWNOWSKI away.
PIENIAZEK: *Come on! You've invited me, so come on. Are you the Minister's secretary, or aren't you?*
DREWNOWSKI: *I have invited you, but that's not the way.*
PIENIAZEK: *All ways are good.*
DREWNOWSKI: *For me, as from today, there's only one.*
PIENIAZEK: *Rubbish! You can go this way or that. And if one way isn't all right, then the other is.*

SWIECKI and PAWLICKI are standing at the entrance to the banqueting room to greet the incoming guests.
PAWLICKI: *Are you taking Drewnowski with you?*
SWIECKI: *Certainly.* He shakes hands with one of the guests. *He's a smart boy. Working class. I'll make a man of him. Good evening, comrade.*

More guests walk through the door and are greeted politely by SWIECKI.

DREWNOWSKI and PIENIAZEK in the bar.
DREWNOWSKI: *I'm going to be the director.*
PIENIAZEK: *You will, you will.*
DREWNOWSKI: *Sure?*
PIENIAZEK: *Qu-i-i-i-te sure!*
DREWNOWSKI: *Anyway . . . I'll be the director.*

PIENIAZEK at last succeeds in dragging DREWNOWSKI away from the bar.
PIENIAZEK: *The fierce eye . . . the foul cloth. Come on.*[1]
DREWNOWSKI: *Not this way.*
PIENIAZEK: *Both ways are lost.*

We are looking down a corridor; PIENIAZEK is dragging DREWNOWSKI along.

---

[1] A quotation from a poem by Mickiewicz, describing a rogue.

203

PIENIAZEK : *And where are the directors going? They are going to the banquet.*

SWIECKI and PAWLICKI are still at the door, welcoming guests. They are especially effusive with a young lady in uniform.

PAWLICKI : *Good to see you, come in.*

SWIECKI : *Good evening. This way, please.*

DREWNOWSKI and PIENIAZEK are at the entrance to the lavatory. MRS. JURGELUSZKA is sitting outside, knitting. PIENIAZEK puts a loving arm round her.

PIENIAZEK : *Mrs. Jurgeluszka, Poland has arrived.*

DREWNOWSKI : *Arrived.*

PIENIAZEK kisses JURGELUSZKA and takes DREWNOWSKI by the jacket.

PIENIAZEK : *Come on, let me lead you into a bright future. To the banquet!*

Rapid shot of SWIECKI and his companions greeting more guests at the door.

PIENIAZEK leads DREWNOWSKI by the tie down the corridor towards the door of the banqueting room. They stop there,

204

look at one another and heave together; the door swings suddenly open under the pressure. Inside are a crowd of people; some of them are in uniform, but most of them are civilians. SWIECKI and PAWLICKI are nearest the door. All the people turn to stare in the direction of the intruders.

SWIECKI notices DREWNOWSKI and approaches him, before realising what state his secretary is in.

SWIECKI : *What is the meaning of this, Mr. Drewnowski? Where have you been?* He lowers his voice. *What's this scoundrel doing here?*

DREWNOWSKI's drunken assurance disappears completely.

DREWNOWSKI : *Quite. It just happened . . . I've been thinking, Mr. Mayor . . . I beg your pardon . . . Mr. Minister . . . that the press . . . generally . . .*

SWIECKI : *Stop talking nonsense. What's the matter with you?*

PIENIAZEK crowds in on SWIECKI, whose features register distaste.

PIENIAZEK : *Congratulations, sir. On behalf of the democratic press, my heartiest congratulations. Hip, hip, hurrah!*

PAWLICKI comes to call SWIECKI away.

SWIECKI as he leaves : *It's an outrage, Drewnowski.*

SWIECKI goes to the door again to greet two officers in uniform; SWIECKI shakes hands with one of them, a Soviet Major.

SOVIET MAJOR in Russian : *A happy day indeed. Congratulations.*

SWIECKI : *Thank you very much, major.*

As the major, with the other officer, disappears, SZCZUKA enters with PODGORSKI and WRONA, the chief of security. A hush falls on the gathering, signalling the entrance of the principal guests. SWIECKI approaches SZCZUKA respectfully. PODGORSKI makes the introductions.

PODGORSKI : *Let me introduce comrade Szczuka; comrade Wrona, head of security.*

Hurriedly getting through the ritual greeting, SZCZUKA and WRONA immediately resume what is clearly an absorbing conversation.

WRONA : *After the events of this morning, I'm ashamed to look you in the face. I hardly expected victory to look like that, back in the forest.*

SZCZUKA : *We're out of the forest now.*

205

They move away, still talking. SWIECKI glances after them. PAWLICKI presses forward and forces PIENIAZEK to retreat until the short, angular reporter is pushed right against the wall.

PAWLICKI : *Get out of here.*

PIENIAZEK : *Me! You get out! Is this a democracy, or isn't it . . .?* The officers and civilians begin to take their places at the banqueting table.

PAWLICKI is still grasping hold of PIENIAZEK and trying to push him into a corner.

PAWLICKI menacingly : *You won't?*

PIENIAZEK : *Are you thre . . . threatening me? And who was grovelling when the Pilsudski[1] regime was in power?*

PAWLICKI : *Shut your foul mouth.*

PIENIAZEK : *You were, weren't you?*

PAWLICKI : *And what about you?*

PIENIAZEK proudly : *I? Certainly. I was grovelling.*

PAWLICKI : *Then shut up.*

PIENIAZEK : *Temper! Temper! But you were grovelling.*

There is an empty seat at the table; DREWNOWSKI appears and climbs into it clumsily. He takes a card out of his pocket with his name printed on it and places it in front of him on the table; he looks round in drunken pride. His neighbour shakes a fist at him.

SWIECKI looks angrily up and down the table.

PIENIAZEK approaches DREWNOWSKI from behind and leans drunkenly over his shoulder.

PIENIAZEK : *Poland's arrived!*

DREWNOWSKI looking up drunkenly : *Am I going to be a big shot?* He gets up to follow PIENIAZEK on his tour round the table.

WRONA and SZCZUKA are seated next to each other.

WRONA : *There aren't enough of us.*

SZCZUKA : *Yes, we ought to be winning the people over; we've got to integrate . . .*

WRONA : *What do you mean?*

SZCZUKA : *The nation . . .*

---

[1] The actual term used in the script is *sanacja* (sanitation); this was the popular term for the pre-war regime, which self-avowedly struggled to "restore the republic to health".

PIENIAZEK enters and leans drunkenly against WRONA, who supports him good-humouredly.

WRONA : *You seem to be rather drunk.*

PIENIAZEK : *Sure. And you ought to be drinking as well. Sshhh . . . Ssshhhh . . .*

He passes behind WRONA, finds a free place on the other side of him and sits down, ignoring KALICKI's attempts to stop him. WRONA speaks to him confidingly.

WRONA : *I hate these affairs. They're good for the bourgeoisie.*

PIENIAZEK : *You hate them? You'll get to like them, you'll see.*

He stretches across the table and picks up a carafe. Everyone is now seated round the table. PIENIAZEK stands up and strikes the carafe with a knife; the sound reverberates loudly through the room.

PIENIAZEK momentarily seeming sober : *Silence, please, for Mr. Minister Swiecki.*

SWIECKI places his glass on the table and slowly rises to his feet, glaring resentfully across the table.

SWIECKI : *Comrades and citizens! Today, the eighth of May, 1945, is a great victory day for liberated Poland. Our sacrifices in the struggle against the Nazis have not been in vain.*

In the corridor, SLOMKA approaches MRS. JURGELUSZKA, who is still knitting.

SLOMKA : *How are things, Mrs. Jurgeluszka?*

The old woman rises from her stool.

MRS. JURGELUSZKA : *The speeches . . .*

SLOMKA straightening his bow-tie : *Yes? Oh, the Minister himself is speaking.*

The mention of the title makes no impression on MRS. JURGELUSZKA.

SLOMKA : *Anyone been sick yet?*

MRS. JURGELUSZKA : *Course not. Too early yet. Everything at the proper time. First, speeches; then they come running.*

SLOMKA : *You're going to make a packet tonight.*

MRS. JURGELUSZKA : *I think so, but you never know. It's God's will. He takes one, let's off another.*

SLOMKA walks away.

He stops at the entrance to the banqueting room and listens attentively.

MRS. JURGELUSZKA: *Still at it?*

SWIECKI's voice is heard coming from the banqueting room. SWIECKI off: *The historic victory of the Soviet Union has cleared the way for our march towards a glorious future. Another page of our history has turned over. For the first time in centuries, power belongs to the Polish people. There will be no more exploitation. In this solemn hour, let us drink to our Fatherland, the People's Poland!*

The speech is followed by loud shouts of, *And long may it live!*

SLOMKA: *Long live who?*

MRS. JURGELUSZKA: *May be somebody's birthday.*

SLOMKA: *What birthday? There's no birthday.*

MRS. JURGELUSZKA: *Or anniversary.*

SLOMKA: *Rubbish. It's all because of Poland.*

Camera moves slowly up KRYSTYNA's face as she lies in bed. The light has been switched off and only a pale reflection from the window and the glow of MACIEK's cigarette lights her face. Her eyes are half-closed.

MACIEK : *Do you know what I'm thinking? We only met a few hours ago, and yet it feels as if I've known you for ages.*

MACIEK's face appears.

KRYSTYNA : *Tell me . . .*

MACIEK : *What?*

KRYSTYNA : *What are you really like?*

MACIEK : *What do you mean?*

KRYSTYNA : *Quite different now . . . than before.*

MACIEK : *Is that bad?*

KRYSTYNA : *Jesus! . . . I don't think it matters.*

MACIEK : *Are you sure it doesn't?*

KRYSTYNA : *I don't know . . . Come closer.*

This image dissolves quickly to another close shot of KRYSTYNA cuddling closely to MACIEK and resting her head on his arm. Camera pans slowly to show her hand gently caressing MACIEK's head.

MACIEK : *Are you cold?*

KRYSTYNA : *A little bit.*

MACIEK : *Is it better now?*

KRYSTYNA : *A bit better.*

KRYSTYNA passes her hand up to caress MACIEK's *face.*

KRYSTYNA : *Why do you always wear those dark glasses?*

MACIEK : *A souvenir of unrequited love for my country. No, it's really because, during the Rising, I stayed too long in the sewers.*

Dissolve to KRYSTYNA's face nestling against MACIEK's shoulder.

KRYSTYNA : *No! No!*

MACIEK : *No what?*

KRYSTYNA : *I don't want to. It's stupid. I don't want to.*

MACIEK : *Why?*

KRYSTYNA : *Can't you understand? You're going to leave. I don't want any goodbyes or memories. Nothing to get over.*

Camera moves over to MACIEK's face against the pillow.

MACIEK : *Not even pleasant memories?*

KRYSTYNA : *Not if that's all they'll ever be. When are you leaving?*

MACIEK : *Probably tomorrow. But perhaps I could still change things.*

KRYSTYNA : *What things?*

MACIEK : *Various things.*

KRYSTYNA : *Could you?*

MACIEK : *Perhaps.*

KRYSTYNA : *But what for?*

There is the sound of heavy footsteps in the corridor and of the door being opened in the next room. SZCZUKA has come back from the party. The sounds have an immediate effect on MACIEK; he tenses up, listening.

KRYSTYNA : *Listen, I've got my life to live and you've got yours. We met by chance and that's nice. So what else can you ask for?* She notices MACIEK's tenseness. *What's the matter?*

MACIEK : *Nothing. Nothing. I think our neighbour has come back to his room.*

But he has clearly become nervous and he raises himself on one elbow and looks round. In the next room, there is the sound of a window being opened, and then more pacing.

KRYSTYNA rests her head again on MACIEK's chest.

KRYSTYNA : *You really do hear everything through this wall.*

MACIEK : *Everything. Kiss me.*

KRYSTYNA raises her face to him and rolls over on to him. Camera pans down her naked back. Fade out.

We are looking through the double entrance doors of the hotel lounge, which are narrowly ajar. ANDRZEJ is approaching the doors from the other side; he opens them brusquely and looks around.

The PORTER is dozing, his head resting on the reception desk. ANDRZEJ's hair is wet from the rain, which can be heard streaming down outside. He suddenly moves away from the doors. He approaches the PORTER, who wakes up.

ANDRZEJ : *Have you any cigarettes?*

PORTER : *Certainly, sir. American or Hungarian?*

ANDRZEJ : *Hungarian, please.*

As the PORTER reaches for the cigarettes, ANDRZEJ glances quickly towards the pigeon-holes which contain the room keys. Close shot of the number seventeen pigeon-hole; there are no keys. The PORTER hands ANDRZEJ a packet of cigarettes.

PORTER : *There you are, sir.*

ANDRZEJ : *Thank you.*

ANDRZEJ pays quickly, nervously handing a crumpled note to the PORTER, and walks away.

The PORTER settles down at his desk again and prepares to go to sleep.

ANDRZEJ, in the first-floor corridor, stops at the door of MACIEK's room. He is about to knock when he hears voices on the other side of the door.

MACIEK off : *What are you doing tomorrow?*

KRYSTYNA off : *Today. It's tomorrow already.*

MACIEK off : *Shall we spend the day together? Would you like that?*

KRYSTYNA off : *You know I would.*

ANDRZEJ goes away from the door with a thoughtful, clouded face.

ANDRZEJ jostles his way through the crowd of dancers below. He looks in the direction of the bar.

The bar is very crowded. Another girl, dark-haired and very plain, quite different from KRYSTYNA, is serving the customers. ANDRZEJ removes his wet coat and hangs it on a clothes stand, then moves away through the dancers.

211

Interior of the offices of the Security Police. WRONA enters a corridor through two barred doors. Four young men stand facing the wall, their hands raised. A number of policemen stand around guarding them. WRONA walks along the line of prisoners, addressing each one in turn.

WRONA : *Where were you captured?*

FIRST PRISONER : *In Miedzyborski forest.*

WRONA : *Wilk's gang.*

SECOND PRISONER : *Captain Wilk's detachment.*

WRONA : *Your name?*

THIRD PRISONER : *Krzysztof.*

WRONA : *Is that all?*

THIRD PRISONER : *Krzysztof Zawadzki.*

WRONA : *Your name?*

The fourth prisoner remains silent.

WRONA : *Turn round.*

The prisoner turns round. This is MAREK, a young man, with a defiantly arrogant face.

WRONA : *How old are you?*

MAREK: *A hundred.*

WRONA slaps his face hard.

WRONA: *How old are you?*

MAREK: *A hundred and one.*

SZCZUKA is standing in the hotel lounge, looking absent-mindedly at the dancing couples. He turns round; he is holding an unlit cigarette in his hand and searching his pocket in vain for matches.

KRYSTYNA and MACIEK slowly come down the stairs, seemingly reluctant to part. MACIEK notices SZCZUKA and stops.

MACIEK: *Must you go?*

KRYSTYNA: *I ought to. Lili is going to kill me.*

She slowly moves away. SZCZUKA appears, mounting the stairs; he brushes against MACIEK, stops, looks at the young man with a flicker of recognition.

SZCZUKA pleasantly, tapping MACIEK lightly on the shoulder: *Can you give me a light please?*

MACIEK: *Certainly.*

MACIEK takes out his box of matches, strikes the match for SZCZUKA and lights his cigarette for him.

SZCZUKA: *Thank you.*

He goes on up the stairs. KRYSTYNA climbs up again towards MACIEK, who is bending low over the banisters, almost as though in pain.

MACIEK looks up suddenly, sees KRYSTYNA, goes rapidly towards her and hugs her tightly.

KRYSTYNA: *What happened?*

MACIEK: *Nothing. Let's stay together, for half an hour, anyway. Please!*

KRYSTYNA: *Yes.*

They walk on down the staircase.

MACIEK skips lightly down the final few stairs into the hall, followed more slowly by KRYSTYNA. As she comes down, MACIEK grabs hold of her and swings her round in time to the dance music, before leading her away by the hand.

Outside the hotel: MACIEK and KRYSTYNA appear, coming out of the entrance.

KRYSTYNA: *It's starting to rain.*

213

MACIEK removes his jacket and throws it over KRYSTYNA'S shoulders. He takes her hand and pulls her along with him. A detachment of infantry is marching along the street.

MACIEK and KRYSTYNA walk by on the pavement in the opposite direction.

KRYSTYNA: *A penny for them.*

MACIEK removing his arm from round KRYSTYNA and waving despairingly: *I've been thinking about something I shouldn't think about. I've finished now, so don't look so reproachful.*

KRYSTYNA: *I'm not.*

A car drives along the street and the marching soldiers burst into a Russian song.

MACIEK: *Then what?*

KRYSTYNA: *You still don't know?*

There is a flash of lightning, followed by thunder.

KRYSTYNA: *It's going to throw it down in a minute.*

MACIEK: *Want to go back?*

KRYSTYNA: *No.*

MACIEK hands plunged deeply into his trouser pockets: *God, life could be so beautiful.*

KRYSTYNA: *Touch wood!*

MACIEK: *It's just a wish.*

Another column of infantry marches past.

KRYSTYNA: *Touch wood. You're going to get wet.*

The rain has begun to come down quite heavily.

MACIEK: *Well, life is dangerous.*

He looks around for possible shelter and seems to see something across the street.

MACIEK and KRYSTYNA run into a bombed church, which is now not much more than a shell with a rubble-covered floor. KRYSTYNA hands MACIEK his jacket and they walk slowly round.

MACIEK: *Are you cold?*

KRYSTYNA: *No. Look, there's an old tombstone . . .*

She runs towards the wall, into which the old tombstone has been built, with hardly distinguishable lettering on it.

KRYSTYNA continuing: *. . . and an inscription.* She starts reading: *So often . . .*

MACIEK pulls his jacket tightly round him.

KRYSTYNA continuing off : . . . *are you as a blazing torch* . . .

    KRYSTYNA looks round with a puzzled expression towards MACIEK.

    MACIEK goes on buttoning his jacket around him.

KRYSTYNA continuing off : . . . *With flakes of burning hemp* . . .

    KRYSTYNA traces out the inscription with her finger on the wall.

KRYSTYNA continuing : . . . *falling about you. Flaming, you know not if flames freedom bring, or death, consuming all that you most cherish, if ashes only will be left and want.*

    MACIEK turns and puts a cigarette in his mouth.

KRYSTYNA off : *Chaos and tempest* . . .

    MACIEK strikes a match and lights his cigarette.

    Resume on KRYSTYNA.

KRYSTYNA continuing : . . . *shall engulf* . . .

    She turns towards MACIEK.

KRYSTYNA : *The letters are blurred.*

    MACIEK throws the box of matches towards her.

    KRYSTYNA catches the box.

    MACIEK with his back to camera.

MACIEK : *It's from a poem by Norwid.*

    KRYSTYNA strikes a match to try to make out the rest of the inscription.

    MACIEK, now seen in profile, as he bends slightly under a low archway, recites the ending of the poem from memory.

MACIEK : *Or will the ashes hold* . . .

    KRYSTYNA, her face bright from the light of the match, looks up from the inscription in the direction of MACIEK.

MACIEK continuing off : . . . *the glory of a starlike* . . .

    MACIEK raises his head.

MACIEK continuing : . . . *diamond, the Morning Star of everlasting triumph.*

    KRYSTYNA is clearly very moved by MACIEK's recitation of the final lines.

KRYSTYNA : *It's beautiful. "Or will the ashes hold the glory of a starlike diamond . . ."*

    MACIEK throws his cigarette away.

    KRYSTYNA straightens up from her position near the inscription.

KRYSTYNA : *And what are we?*

MACIEK turns his head towards KRYSTYNA.

MACIEK : *You're certainly a diamond.*

MACIEK starts to walk away from the tombstone. KRYSTYNA appears and they both move away.

MACIEK : *Listen, I want to tell you something.*

KRYSTYNA : *Is it sad?*

A crucifix hangs upside down in the centre of the church; the head of Christ is apparently dripping with rain. MACIEK and KRYSTYNA walk towards it from the background, talking. They stop, one on either side of the figure, separated by Christ's head.

MACIEK *his voice echoing eerily in the church*: *No. I don't know what sadness is really. I'd like to change certain things. Arrange my life differently. I can't tell you everything . . .*

KRYSTYNA : *You don't have to. I can guess.*

MACIEK : *Really?*

KRYSTYNA : *Is it so difficult?*

MACIEK laughs uneasily.

MACIEK : *You see, till now I didn't think about those things. I took*

216

life as it came, just to survive. You follow me?
KRYSTYNA: *Yes.*
MACIEK: *I'd like to live normally, to study. I've passed my entrance exams, so maybe I could study engineering. What about you?*
KRYSTYNA: *You said it wouldn't be anything sad.*
MACIEK: *Is it sad? Should I touch wood?*
> MACIEK moves away from the crucifix, laughing ironically, hands in pockets.
MACIEK: *If only I'd known yesterday what I know now!*
> KRYSTYNA follows some way behind MACIEK.
KRYSTYNA softly: *I wouldn't have come to you . . .*
MACIEK laughing: *Just think. Till now, I'd no idea what love was.*
> As KRYSTYNA walks over the rubble, the heel of her shoe snaps off on the uneven ground. MACIEK runs across to support her. He picks up the damaged shoe.
MACIEK: *Don't worry, I've mended bigger things.*
> Supporting KRYSTYNA, MACIEK looks around for a suitable spot to carry out repairs.
> KRYSTYNA and MACIEK enter a bombed-out chapel in another

part of the church. There is a small altar there on which is a holy effigy and a pair of snuffed-out candles. Below it is a frame of sorts covered with a shroud.

MACIEK finds a small hand bell on the altar and starts to hammer the broken heel back into place with it. The sound of the hammering resounds in the empty building.

KRYSTYNA is looking on, when suddenly an old WATCHMAN enters the chapel, obviously woken up by the noise.

WATCHMAN : *What's going on here? What do you think you're doing? You're not just anywhere, you know.*

MACIEK waves the bell in the direction of the WATCHMAN, then continues hammering on the shoe.

MACIEK : *Keep cool. Can't you see the lady's in trouble? I can't find a cobbler at this time of night.*

The WATCHMAN is utterly outraged, while KRYSTYNA tries to suppress her amusement.

WATCHMAN : *Shame on you!*

MACIEK drops the bell on the floor.

WATCHMAN : *Young people today! Can't even respect the dead.*

MACIEK : *What?*

WATCHMAN : *Acting the fool over the murdered. That's what!*

MACIEK puts the bell back on the altar and turns round towards the shroud.

KRYSTYNA : *Maciek, what's the matter!*

MACIEK bends and suddenly whips the shroud away : the faces of the two shot workers are exposed. MACIEK, transfixed by horror, stares straight ahead. KRYSTYNA's sudden cry of revulsion reverberates momentarily in the empty church.

Inside SZCZUKA's room at the hotel; there is an old cast-iron bed on the right. SZCZUKA himself is standing at the window. He turns round as he hears knocking at the door.

SZCZUKA : *Yes? Come in.*

The door opens slowly and an outlandishly huge gramophone horn appears round it. For a second it appears to be moving into the room by itself. In fact, the newcomer turns out to be PODGORSKI carrying an old-fashioned gramophone and a bottle of wine.

SZCZUKA smiles and walks towards him.

PODGORSKI places the gramophone on the table, winds it up and starts a record; it is an old choral record of a Spanish marching song.

SZCZUKA : *Where did we hear that?*

PODGORSKI : *Don't you remember?*

SZCZUKA : *Yes, I do. I was very drunk then.* He picks the bottle of wine up and looks at the label. *That wine was very treacherous. Alba Seta. Our first days in Spain.*

PODGORSKI : *Grabowski was killed in the forest. Kubacki in France in 1944. This was the beginning of 1936, remember? Good old times. Who is there left now?*

The gramophone record comes to an end. Drunken voices can be heard below.

SZCZUKA : *There'll be good times again.*

SZCZUKA walks towards the window. PODGORSKI makes a despairing gesture, indicating the noise below.

PODGORSKI : *I can't understand all that. I'd like to break their necks.*

SZCZUKA shuts the window and turns round.

SZCZUKA: *That lot down there isn't Poland.*

PODGORSKI pours out some wine.

PODGORSKI: *I know, but it doesn't make me feel any better.*

PODGORSKI passes a glass of wine over the table in the direction of SZCZUKA.

PODGORSKI: *I don't know how to use power.*

He reaches out to stop the still-revolving turntable of the gramophone. As he does so, SZCZUKA becomes visible, standing near the window.

SZCZUKA: *Don't take it like that, Franek. Listen to me. There's too much misery, too much pain, too much suffering in this country.*

He crosses over to where PODGORSKI is sitting at the table.

SZCZUKA: *Try to understand.*

PODGORSKI: *What is there to understand?*

He places a number of empty cartridge cases on the table; SZCZUKA looks at them.

SZCZUKA: *German? Have you got them yet?*

PODGORSKI: *Not yet, but I shall. There are some British. What's the difference, though, if you're on the receiving end?*

They drink and PODGORSKI gets up.

SZCZUKA: *Let's get some sleep. We'll start things moving tomorrow.*

PODGORSKI: *O.K. I hope it'll turn out fine. It's stopped raining. See you tomorrow.*

SZCZUKA warmly: *See you tomorrow.*

PODGORSKI goes out of the room, leaving the gramophone on the table. SZCZUKA sits down at the table and picks up a number of the cartridge cases and arranges them upright.[1]

MACIEK and KRYSTYNA are walking through the courtyard of the hotel. There is some light from the windows, and the sound of music and the crashing of crockery. They stop.

KRYSTYNA: *When are you leaving?*

MACIEK very upset: *Probably tomorrow.*

MACIEK: *Perhaps I could change everything.*

KRYSTYNA: *Change what?*

MACIEK: *Certain things.*

He kisses her gently on the tip of the nose.

---

[1] The scene between SZCZUKA and PODGORSKI does not appear in the original script.

KRYSTYNA : *Could you?*
MACIEK grinning : *Perhaps.*

He takes the bunch of violets from her, then pulls her to him passionately, kissing her violently on her mouth and neck. Suddenly she breaks away from him and runs to the back door of the hotel.

MACIEK remains alone, holding the bunch of violets. A white horse wanders into the yard, as if from nowhere. MACIEK looks at him, tickles his nose with the violets, then walks away.

MACIEK enters the corridor leading to the lounge of the hotel. He seems startled by something he sees.

ANDRZEJ is having his cigarette lit by a waiter.

MACIEK turns quickly and disappears.

ANDRZEJ glances round and notices MACIEK.

MACIEK stops in the corridor just by JURGELUSZKA, who looks up at him. ANDRZEJ appears in the background. MACIEK opens the door leading to the lavatories and enters.

MACIEK runs down the stairs inside the lavatories.

ANDRZEJ appears and catches him up. They are in a dingy lavatory, with closed cubicles on one side and a urinal on the other; it is lit by a single naked bulb.

ANDRZEJ : *Been buying flowers for yourself?*
MACIEK : *Listen, I've got to talk to you seriously.*
ANDRZEJ superciliously : *I thought we had already talked.*

A slight sound distracts ANDRZEJ and he walks over to one of the cubicles and opens the door.

PIENIAZEK is sitting asleep on the lavatory seat, snoring from time to time. ANDRZEJ closes the door and turns back towards MACIEK.

ANDRZEJ : *Well?*

MACIEK leans against a cubicle door.

MACIEK : *You know I'm not a coward.*
ANDRZEJ off : *So?*
MACIEK : *You've got to understand, Andrzej. I don't want to kill any more or keep on hiding. I want to live, that's all. Just try to understand.*
ANDRZEJ off : *I don't have to. Are you confiding in me as a friend, or as a soldier?*
MACIEK : *I don't get you.*

221

ANDRZEJ : *Perhaps you don't want to. Because, as far as I'm concerned, I can only talk to you about this as your superior officer. You asked for it yourself. You agreed to do it.*

> While ANDRZEJ is speaking, MACIEK turns his back on him and walks away. Then he turns round again.

MACIEK : *You're my only friend.*

ANDRZEJ : *Leave those sentiments out of it. You've fallen in love, which is your affair. But if you want your personal affairs to come before our cause, you know the name for it.*

MACIEK in a choked whisper : *Andrzej, I'm not a deserter.*

ANDRZEJ : *You used the word. Didn't you undertake to do the job?*

> MACIEK stands with bowed head, then suddenly looks up.

MACIEK intensely : *It is possible to change, can't you understand? I'm not running away.*

ANDRZEJ : *But you really want to, and you want me to give my blessing because you're in love and you should be able to do what you like. How many times have we been in action together? Did you think of falling in love then? Would you have done it when we were in the Old Town?*

MACIEK : *That was different.*

ANDRZEJ : *No, my friend. You forget that you always have been, and still are, one of us. That's what counts.*

Noises and singing can be heard coming from the banqueting room.

In the banqueting room, the banquet is in its last stages. Many of the guests have left the table and are standing together talking. DREWNOWSKI is wandering drunkenly around. He tries to approach SWIECKI, but the Mayor pushes him irritably away. A fire extinguisher on the wall attracts DREWNOWSKI'S attention. He takes hold of it and starts playing with it, holding it like a gun, muzzle out. He presses the trigger and a jet of foam shoots out. As the guests shout and shriek, DREWNOWSKI, with reckless abandon, climbs on to the long table and walks down it, shooting foam from left to right. In the lavatory, ANDRZEJ and MACIEK look up, listening to the noise.

DREWNOWSKI, still on the table, guns everyone in sight with

foam. He jumps off the end of the table, seizes the table cloth and pulls it off the table bringing all the crockery with it. Pawlicki gets hold of him and they struggle together. Drewnowski tries to hold him off, measuring up to him like a prize-fighter, then he raises his hands above his head and is led away, laughing hysterically, by Pawlicki.

Maciek and Andrzej are still listening to the noise; Drewnowski's hysterical laughter becomes audible from the corridor.

The door at the top of the lavatory stairs opens and Pawlicki pushes Drewnowski down the steps. He slides down, hardly able to control his limbs.

Pawlicki: *You can say goodbye to your career.*

Drewnowski: *Scram!*

Pawlicki: *You'll be singing a different tune tomorrow. The Minister'll see to that.*

Pawlicki goes out and Drewnowski picks himself up with some difficulty. He straightens up and, seeing no one, clumsily starts to climb the stairs.

At the top of the stairs he takes a handful of visiting cards out of his pocket and throws them in the air.

DREWNOWSKI : *I don't care. Everything's collapsed like a house of cards. Let the bastard do for me.*

In the corridor, MRS. JURGELUSZKA is holding a glass of water. DREWNOWSKI brushes against her. Then he goes on his way, giggling and holding more of the cards out.

He opens a door in the corridor and goes out into the courtyard and, laughing hysterically, walks towards the white horse. ANDRZEJ and MACIEK in the lavatory below; ANDRZEJ suddenly throws his cigarette away and holds out his hand. MACIEK takes out his pistol and, holding it by the barrel, offers it to ANDRZEJ. Just as the latter is about to take the gun, MACIEK impulsively withdraws it.

MACIEK : *All right. I'll take care of it.*

ANDRZEJ : *You'd better be careful.*

MACIEK : *Don't worry, I want to live.*

ANDRZEJ : *I'll be waiting for you at four-thirty, remember.*

MACIEK : *No, I'm not going with you.*

ANDRZEJ disappointed : *This is the parting of the ways, then. I doubt whether we shall ever meet again. Only one of us will be proved right. Good-bye.*

He walks away, but MACIEK runs after him shouting, still holding the gun in his hand.

MACIEK shouting : *Andrzej! Tell me, do you think it's right yourself?*

ANDRZEJ : *Me? That's not important.*

ANDRZEJ disappears up the stairs. MACIEK hides the gun in his shirt and remains gazing at the stairs, his hand over his mouth.

ANDRZEJ comes out of the main door of the hotel into the street. He is immediately surrounded by several children selling violets.

A BOY : *Please take it, mister. Zoska, you go home.*

To get rid of them, ANDRZEJ gives the boy some money and takes the bunch of violets almost mechanically. He walks on, then stops suddenly and appears to hesitate. Only now does he seem to realize that he is holding a bunch of flowers and he irritably throws them on to a rubbish heap. He then walks on.

225

MACIEK is alone in the empty lavatory, almost as if waiting for ANDRZEJ to return. He mounts the stairs and disappears, just as the voice of KOTOWICZ becomes audible.

KOTOWICZ off : *How goes it, Mrs. Jurgeluszka?*

MRS. JURGELUSZKA off : *It's quiet, gov.*

He opens the door of the lavatory and comes down the steps.

KOTOWICZ : *It's good when it's quiet.*

He goes towards one of the cubicles.

SZCZUKA is asleep in his bed in his room at the hotel. He is awakened by a loud knocking on the door. He sits up. We see him through the decorative ironwork at the head of the bed.

SZCZUKA : *Come in.*

We hear the door open as someone comes into the room.

OFFICER off : *Excuse me, comrade Szczuka. Forgive me for troubling you, but the matter is of the utmost importance.*

SZCZUKA : *Yes?*

OFFICER : *I've been sent by Major Wrona.*

SZCZUKA : *Yes.*

The OFFICER walks round the end of the bed and halts beside it, as SZCZUKA sits on the edge of it.

OFFICER: *Do you have a son, comrade?*

SZCZUKA: *Yes. Marek. He's seventeen.*

OFFICER: *It's an awkward business.*

SZCZUKA: *What happened to him?*

OFFICER: *He was a member of Wilk's gang. He was captured and is now in custody. Could you wait here, please? The Major is sending a car to pick you up. I'll ask the porter to let you know when it comes.*

SZCZUKA: *All right, I'll wait. Thank you.*

The OFFICER salutes and leaves the room.

SZCZUKA looks gravely at the door, then grips the bed-rail tightly.

MAREK is sitting with a spotlight on his face; WRONA is in the background.

WRONA: *Is the name Wilk familiar to you?*

MAREK: *No.*

WRONA: *What did you do during the Rising?*

MAREK: *I shot Germans.*

WRONA: *And now you shoot Poles.*

MAREK: *And you — sparrows?*

SZCZUKA gets up from his bed. He is already wearing his trousers and shirt. He struggles to put on his raincoat.

MACIEK is coming out of the restaurant into the lounge, just as the young OFFICER we have seen with SZCZUKA is descending the stairs.

OFFICER: *Porter!*

MACIEK watches and listens.

PORTER: *Yes, sir?*

OFFICER: *A car is coming to fetch Mr. Szczuka. Will you let him know at once when it arrives?*

PORTER: *Certainly. Mr. Szczuka, room eighteen.*

MACIEK walks towards the staircase.

He stands in the alcove beneath the staircase.

A little later; MACIEK is still waiting in the same place. In the background the PORTER is beginning to close up — shutting

227

the doors, putting out the light. The soft light of early dawn is coming through the window. The PORTER moves away.

MACIEK looks up as SZCZUKA's footsteps are heard on the staircase.

SZCZUKA descends the stairs; only his feet are visible. Between the steps, through the vertical iron lattice-work, MACIEK's eyes are visible. We look down on SZCZUKA who is nervously pacing the lounge, looking at his watch. MACIEK is also visible under the stairs.

MACIEK looking through the grating in the staircase. SZCZUKA walks forward, then stops suddenly, a very worried expression on his face.

MAREK's arrogant face is caught in a beam of bright light. In the background, WRONA can be seen opening an office window. A moth is flying round the lamp near MAREK's face. MAREK watches it intently.

SZCZUKA glances down at his watch. He turns and starts pacing again. Suddenly he seems to make up his mind to leave and he walks off determinedly in the direction of the door.

MACIEK appears from his hiding place. The PORTER comes up to meet him with full glasses on a tray.

PORTER : *The war is over. Let's drink to our Warsaw.*

MACIEK, behaving with his usual nonchalance, picks up a glass and gulps it down.

MACIEK : *A beautiful night. Time for a walk before I leave.*

PORTER : *Leaving already?*

MACIEK : *I have a jealous wife, I'm afraid.*

He pushes through the main door and goes out. Outside the hotel, MACIEK paces up and down nervously on the pavement for a few seconds, looking all the time in the same direction. Suddenly he darts away from the hotel along the street.

SZCZUKA is walking along the street as fast as his limp will allow him. It is a narrow, quite deserted street, with the pavement running along a tall fence.

MACIEK is also walking along the pavement very quickly. He has already overtaken SZCZUKA who, deep in thought, does not notice him. MACIEK, keeping up a fast pace, moves ahead by several yards. He reaches inside his shirt and takes out his pistol, removing the safety catch. He stops suddenly, then turns round and walks back towards Szczuka. For a fraction of a second they look at each other and Szczuka's eyes seem to register recognition. A shot rings out and Szczuka staggers. As he does so, Maciek stands, teeth clenched and pistol poised. There is the sound of another shot and Szczuka staggers, clutching his shoulder.

Maciek shoots again, his mouth hanging slightly open as he does so.

Szczuka, receiving another bullet, staggers on towards Maciek.

Maciek, retreating, fires yet another shot.

Szczuka groans.

He still staggers forward along the pavement.

Szczuka, groaning, staggers right into Maciek's arms. The back of his coat is marked with dark patches where the bullets have passed through him.

Maciek clasps the dying Szczuka in his arms. The two figures remain immobile for a few seconds, lit by the light from a cluster of fireworks which shoot up against the dark sky behind them. Then Maciek releases his grip and Szczuka slumps heavily to the ground. The fireworks spread out and explode high in the sky. They fall as a shower of stars, which are reflected in the pool into which Szczuka's body has fallen. Maciek, standing over him, throws his gun away and breaks into a run. More fireworks hurtle into the sky, making a loud screaming noise.

A number of faces are looking out of the windows of the hotel, their features lit by the light of the fireworks; Mrs. Stanie-wicz, Kotowicz and Puciatycki are among them.

Szczuka's body is lying face down in the pool; dying fireworks fall to the ground around it.

Back in his room at the hotel, Maciek is stripped to the waist as he washes. He splashes water vigorously into his face and then blunders round the room myopically in search of a towel. He dries himself hurriedly when he finds one, then goes to the window and lets the blind up. The early morning light streams into the room. He combs his hair hurriedly and collects his things together: soap, towel, toothbrush. He packs them all into the rucksack, then hurriedly pulls his shirt on.

All the guests have left the banqueting room, which now looks like a deserted battlefield. A solitary waiter is clearing up the mess.

In the restaurant, the band is still playing quite vigorously, although there are no guests at the tables. A boy waiter is clearing up, overseen by SLOMKA. The boy drops and breaks a plate; SLOMKA hits the boy and pushes him with cold, silent vindictiveness. Another waiter comes in.

The musicians have now begun to relax on their stand and some of them are preparing to go home. Some are packing up their instruments; the violinist is still sitting, yawning hugely. At the piano, the pianist is playing the notes of a popular Resistance marching song with one finger.

VIOLINIST: *My legs are numb.* To the pianist. *Stop it! I've had*

all my ears can take.

The Pianist laughs and closes the piano, but he starts whistling the same tune. Laughter and the sound of loud voices comes from the bar, where the revelry is apparently still going on. HANKA LEWICKA can be seen through the door, dancing drunkenly on a small platform.

The party in the bar begins to spill over on to the dance floor. The political factions are now intermingled, with SWIECKI, PAWLICKI, KALICKI apparently on the best of terms with MRS. STANIEWICZ, PUCIATYCKI and KOTOWICZ. The latter, drunk but grandly theatrical in his manner, comes forward and stops by the bandstand. The musicians pause and look at him.

KOTOWICZ: *Just a moment, gentlemen!*

HANKA LEWICKA shouting off: *Music! I want to dance!*

KOTOWICZ: *Un moment! Gentlemen! Are you artists, or aren't you?*

TRUMPET PLAYER: *At this time of night, sir?*

He puts his trumpet into its case. KOTOWICZ knits his magnificent brow.

231

KOTOWICZ : *A true artist has no regard for time. I demand your absolute obedience.*

He hums the opening notes of a classical polonaise by Oginski.

TRUMPET PLAYER : *It's no good, sir.*

VIOLINIST : *We've never played it, sir.*

KOTOWICZ gives them an outraged look and continues regardless.

KOTOWICZ : *No excuses, please. Not a word more, young man. A-major!*

The remaining guests are crowding out of the bar.

KOTOWICZ comes back to exhort them.

KOTOWICZ : *Ladies and gentlemen! Ladies and gentlemen! The last dance! A-major, A-major!*

They all go out, leaving KRYSTYNA alone in the bar. She leaves the counter, walks to the window and opens it; the dawn light streams into the room.

MACIEK enters the room.

KRYSTYNA turns round from the window and notices MACIEK.

KRYSTYNA : *What happened?*

MACIEK : *Nothing. I must leave.*

KRYSTYNA : *Now?*

MACIEK : *The train's leaving at four-thirty.*

There is a pause and the noise from the adjoining room can be heard again.

KRYSTYNA : *You couldn't change things.*

MACIEK : *No.*

A cavalcade of revellers has now formed up on the dance floor; the band seems quite resigned to its task.

KOTOWICZ off : *No excuses, gentlemen.*

Meanwhile, in the bar, MACIEK grasps KRYSTYNA's hand as she leans against a pillar. She snatches it away from him and turns away.

KRYSTYNA : *Don't say anything. Just go. It's too late.*

MACIEK turns, head bowed, and walks away, his rucksack over his shoulder. KRYSTYNA remains standing where she is, suffering and powerless.

MACIEK crosses the dance floor quickly and disappears. The party can be seen in the background, with KOTOWICZ in the centre, seen against the light, arms outstretched.

KOTOWICZ : *Marvellous, remarkable! And now a great discovery —
une grande découverte!* He turns towards us. *A brilliant finale,
bidding welcome to a new day.* He turns back again towards the
band, moving with dancing steps. *Ladies and gentlemen, a stroke
of genius: the polonaise! Voilà!*

The revellers look impressed as KOTOWICZ stands with the
band in the foreground.

KOTOWICZ : *Sheer greatness. There's no other word. A gigantic
procession. A national event. Anyone against? No one. I proclaim
universal agreement.*

KOTOWICZ arranges the guests in partners and the couples
start moving in double file. KOTOWICZ goes towards the band
and starts to conduct.

MACIEK is with the PORTER in the hall of the hotel. The
PORTER hands over MACIEK's identity card.

PORTER : *If only we could celebrate an undestroyed Warsaw. Don't
forget, as long as I'm here, you can always have the best room in
the Monopol.*

MACIEK : *That's great. Good-bye.*

He seems impatient to leave, but the PORTER holds him back.

PORTER : *Just a minute! Give my love to Aleje Ujazdowskie!*[1]

MACIEK walks rapidly along the pavement away from the hotel. Then he leaves the pavement and carries on along the cobbled roadway. In the distance, a viaduct crosses the road; a train whistles somewhere in the distance. MACIEK looks about him as he appears, walking down the street towards the viaduct. Then something seems to catch his attention and he stops; he comes back a few steps and peers round a piece of scaffolding. A train passes over the viaduct in the distance.

A truck is parked in an almost deserted square. ANDRZEJ is standing by the truck, glancing impatiently at his watch. Suddenly DREWNOWSKI appears near the truck, carrying a brief case.

DREWNOWSKI : *Cheers! How's it going?*

He runs round to the back of the truck and starts climbing aboard.

ANDRZEJ sharply : *Come here! Give that to me!*

DREWNOWSKI passes the brief-case through the open side window of the truck to the driver.

ANDRZEJ : *So, you've changed your mind!*

He strikes DREWNOWSKI hard, throws him to the ground and starts kicking him violently. DREWNOWSKI lies on the ground, moaning.

MACIEK looks on from behind the scaffolding.

DREWNOWSKI off : *What's the matter? What's this for?*

ANDRZEJ continues kicking hard at DREWNOWSKI.

DREWNOWSKI : *Why? What do you want from me?*

ANDRZEJ : *You still don't know? You've only come because you were thrown out. What are you trying to be now? A hero?*

Delivering a final vicious kick, ANDRZEJ jumps into the truck, which drives off immediately.

DREWNOWSKI picks himself up.

DREWNOWSKI moaning : *Why? Why?*

MACIEK is still looking on.

----

[1] A famous street in Warsaw.

Suddenly DREWNOWSKI notices MACIEK and begins to run hopefully towards him. MACIEK withdraws quickly round the scaffolding and starts to walk swiftly away.

DREWNOWSKI calling: *Hallo, Maciek! Maciek! Wait a moment, Maciek!* His voice is drowned by the rattle of a passing train.

MACIEK walks quickly towards the viaduct, across which a train is now passing. Hearing DREWNOWSKI's voice he breaks into a run. DREWNOWSKI stops.

DREWNOWSKI shouting despairingly: *Maciek, please stop! Please stop!*

On the other side of the arch of the railway viaduct, three soldiers are standing by the wall, chatting casually. MACIEK appears under the arch, running and looking over his shoulder. He turns, but notices the soldiers only at the last moment and cannot stop himself from barging into one of them. On a sudden reflex impulse he grabs for his gun which is not there. Realising this, he runs off in panic.

DREWNOWSKI his voice echoing under the railway arch: *Maciek! Maciek!*

The soldiers grab their rifles and start off in pursuit of MACIEK.

FIRST SOLDIER : *Stop!*

SECOND SOLDIER : *He must be crazy!*

DREWNOWSKI shouting off : *Stop him! Stop him!*

THIRD SOLDIER : *He's got a gun!* Shouting. *Halt! Or we'll fire!*

They fire a number of shots as another train passes noisily over the viaduct.

MACIEK, running very fast, is hit by a bullet and falls. He gets up almost immediately and runs on, staggering, into lines of drying laundry, disappearing from sight. The soldiers follow him, looking among the flapping sheets.

FIRST SOLDIER : *Be careful, he's got a gun!*

SECOND SOLDIER : *Where the hell's he got to?*

The soldiers walk along the lines of drying sheets. As they pass, a stain of blood, quickly spreading, appears on one sheet. MACIEK's hand moves out from behind the sheet and presses the spot where the stain is spreading. MACIEK groans behind the sheet; then his face appears and he sniffs at the hand which has felt the bloodstain. He sinks to the ground, gasping.

The soldiers are still searching vainly among the sheets.

FIRST SOLDIER : *He can't have got far.*

SECOND SOLDIER : *I saw him. He's got to be here somewhere.*

They run away in another direction.

MACIEK attempts to rise and to pick his rucksack up.

KRYSTYNA stands sad and alone in the bar. Couples walking to the rhythm of the polonaise enter in the foreground. A lonely drunkard, walking uncertainly, appears. KOTOWICZ notices him.

KOTOWICZ shouting : *One moment, one moment!*

He runs to KRYSTYNA, grasps her hand and drags her, unresisting, towards the drunkard. They join the polonaise.

MACIEK runs along by a high wall, staggering heavily. He coughs violently — choking, retching coughs.

KRYSTYNA passes with her partner; other couples follow. The movement slows down, becoming stylized, as the music itself